Woodworking Plans & Projects

**35 Woodwork plans
Toy plans, Model plans
Garden furniture plans
& Household item plans**

By A. R. Phillips

Copyright © A. R. Phillips 2011

All rights reserved. No part of this publication may be reproduced, stored in a retrieval system, or transmitted in any form or by any means, electronic, mechanical, photocopying, recording or otherwise, without prior written permission from the copyright owner

Published by
Lulu Press, Inc
3101 Hillsborough St.
Raleigh, NC 27607
EIN 94-3419924

*Cover design, Photographs,
Text, Drawings and Plans
By Andrew R Phillips*

ISBN 978 1 4478 3516 5

Acknowledgements
Kerry Milton (Gwellheans)....Advice funding and support
Carole Prosser...Editing, quality control, encouragement and support
Lizzie Bennet…...Encouragement and support

The Author
Andrew R Phillips is an accomplished woodworker and served his time as a carpenter. He started making toys for his own children and then progressed on to models and designing and drawing woodworking projects for around the home and garden

Introduction

This book will enable you to construct garden furniture, planters, whirligigs, toys, models and household items. The plans are drawn actual size 1 : 1 for the easy projects and on grids and fully dimensioned for the larger projects. The author has designed and drawn traditional projects along with a few designs of his own. It is strongly recommended that you read the plans and instructions, study the photographs and familiarise yourself with the construction of the project before working on it, tips and hints as to how each part was made are explained on the plan pages, as well as a few pages showing handy tips and hints. Fastening and fixings used throughout the book are explained in the fore pages along with a list of basic hand tool requirements. Some of the projects are for outdoors, therefore exterior weather proof wood working adhesive should be used throughout.

Contents

Introduction	*Introduction to plans and projects*
Woodwork projects listing	*List of all the woodwork projects within this book*
Hand tool requirements	*Tool listings and brief explanation*
Sanding and shaping	*List of basic sanding methods*
Measuring and marking	*Measuring and marking tools listing*
Drilling and counter sinking	*List of various drills countersinks and hole saws*
Fastenings and fixings	*List of all fastenings and fixings used to construct projects*
Tips and hints	*Tips and hints relevant to the projects within this book*
Improvised mortise machine	*How to make an improvised mortise machine*
Improvised lathe	*How to make an improvised lathe*
Glossary	*Explanation of words and terms relevant to the projects within this book*

16 Garden Projects

Ornate trough planter	*Decorative trough planter*
Bird whirligig	*Bird whirligig with two sets of rotating wings*
Bee whirligig	*Bee whirligig with 5 wings that rotate around the head and body*
Biplane whirligig	*Biplane with rotating propeller and a pilot that bobs up and down*
Frog on a bike whirligig	*Frog on a penny farthing with rotating legs and front wheel*
Nesting box	*Nest box to suit small birds*
Hanging bird feeder	*Bird feeder with three inner perches*
Hedgehog house	*Small house for small mammals*
Swinging garden bench	*Two person swinging bench of sturdy construction*
8ft x 6ft Pent roof shed	*Garden tool shed with pent roof*
Traditional wheel barrow	*An authentic looking Victorian wheel barrow planter*
Octagonal bird table	*Octagonal bird feeding table*
Square well planter	*Square well planter*
5ft Garden bench	*A 5ft park type bench made using standard size timbers*
Rocking recliner	*3 Positional rocking recliner made using standard size timbers*
Round well planter	*18 Sided well planter making this well practically round*

11 Toy Projects

Clock puzzle	*Learn to count and tell the time clock puzzle*
Mobiles	*Fish theme, dinosaur theme and animal theme mobiles designed to be used with rotating musical movement (see plan page)*
Wheel barrow	*Children's wheel barrow can also be made as a planter*
Pine piano and stool	*Stool and realistic looking pine piano designed to be fitted with a children's battery operated electronic key board*
Tractor and trailer	*A sturdy tractor with tipper trailer and hinged tail gate ideal toy for as a sand pit toy*
Helicopter	*Helicopter with rotating rotor blades (loosely based an the famous Belle huey)*
Small oak chair	*Small oak chair this can be made as a birth chair and a brass plaque with birth details can be inset into the back*
Campervan dolls house	*Sit and ride campervan dolls house with removable top and 75mm (3") diameter wheels*
Tow Truck/ crane	*Sit and ride tow truck/crane with raise, lower and rotating boom and winding hook*

2 Authentic Model Projects

Model Jeep	*Wooden model of a 1942-1945 American army jeep*
Model Packard	*Wooden model of a 1912 Packard Victoria*

5 Household Projects

Pine cabinet	*Pine display cabinet with leaded class*
Pine shelf	*Pine corner shelf with suspended platform*
Corner desk	*Corner computer desk made from one sheet 8ft x 6ft MDF*
Coffee table	*Oak tile topped coffee table*
Bathroom cabinet	*Pine bathroom cabinet with mirror door*

3 Children's Bed Projects

Tank engine bed	*Tank engine bed made from two sheets 8ft x 4ft MDF*
Princess bed	*Princess bed made from one sheet 8ft x 4ft MDF*
Racing car bed	*Racing car bed made from 2 sheets 8ft x 4ft MDF*

Basic hand tool requirements to make the projects listed

Basic wood working requirements

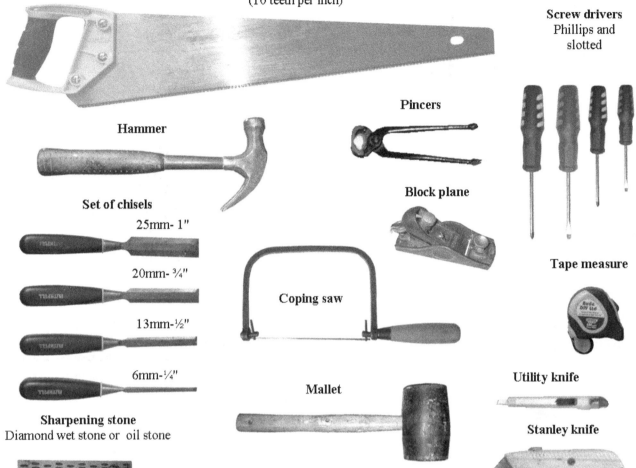

Basic metal working requirements

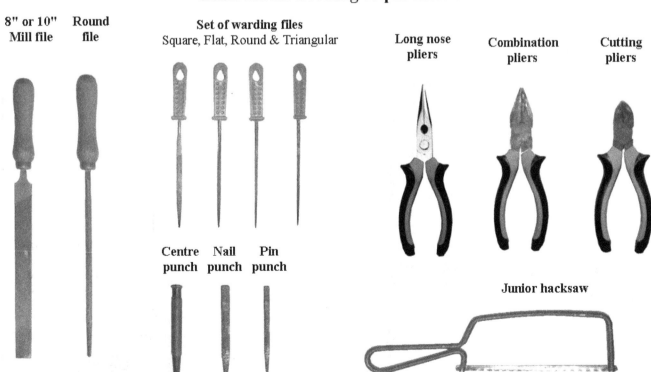

Measuring and marking

Compass/Dividers **Scriber**

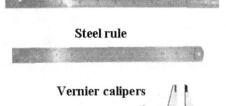

Combination square

Steel rule

Vernier calipers

Sliding bevel

Mortise/marking gauge

Sanding and shaping

Sanding sticks
Make from strip wood or short lengths of dowel with 40 Grit aluminium oxide cloth backed abrasive stuck to its surface with contact adhesive

Emery board
Make from 100mm x 20mm (4" x ¾") timber with 40 Grit aluminium oxide cloth backed abrasive stuck to its surface with contact adhesive

Drum sanders

150mm   50mm   40mm   30mm   20mm

Drilling and counter sinking requirements
(Not all below are required for the easy projects)

Counter sinks   **Set hole saws**   **Spade bits**

50mm 40mm 30mm 25mm

Hole saw arbor

Forstner bits

35mm 30mm 25mm 20mm 15mm

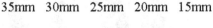

32mm 25mm 20mm 18mm 16mm 13mm 10mm

Centre bits
3mm-10mm

Set of HSS twist drills
1mm-10mm raising in increments of 0.5mm

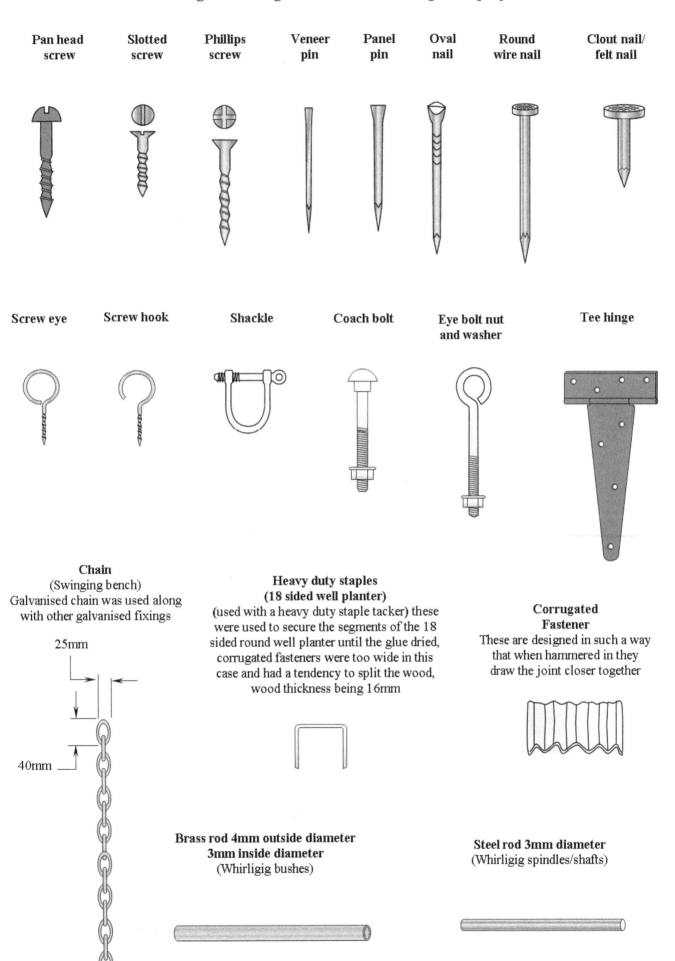

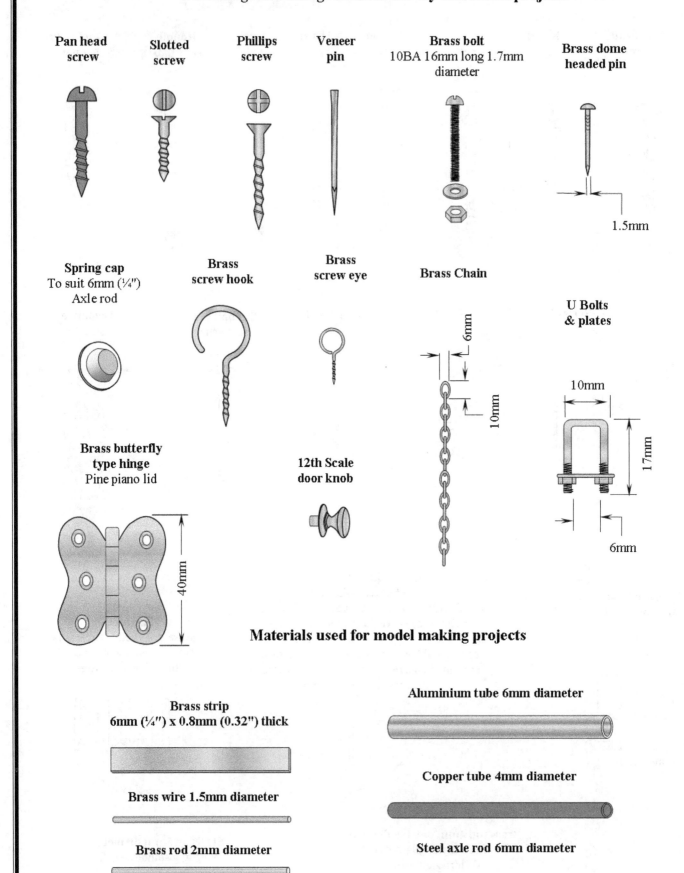

Gluing T & G boards together

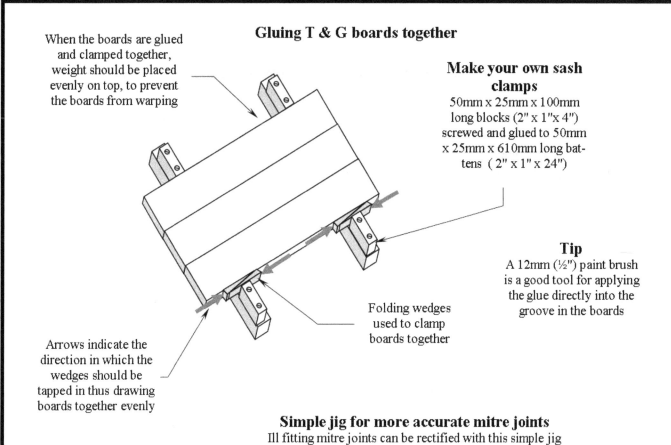

When the boards are glued and clamped together, weight should be placed evenly on top, to prevent the boards from warping

Make your own sash clamps
50mm x 25mm x 100mm long blocks (2" x 1"x 4") screwed and glued to 50mm x 25mm x 610mm long battens (2" x 1" x 24")

Tip
A 12mm (½") paint brush is a good tool for applying the glue directly into the groove in the boards

Folding wedges used to clamp boards together

Arrows indicate the direction in which the wedges should be tapped in thus drawing boards together evenly

Simple jig for more accurate mitre joints
Ill fitting mitre joints can be rectified with this simple jig
(Plan view drawing shown)

Repetitive cutting
Repetitive cutting can be achieved quickly and accurately using a stop pinned into a cutting block as shown below

Secure the frame in the jig with the battens and wedges, then using a tenon saw slowly guide it through each joint in turn when all four are done remove the battens and wedges. The frame should fit together, if not and there are discrepancies then repeat the aforementioned process again

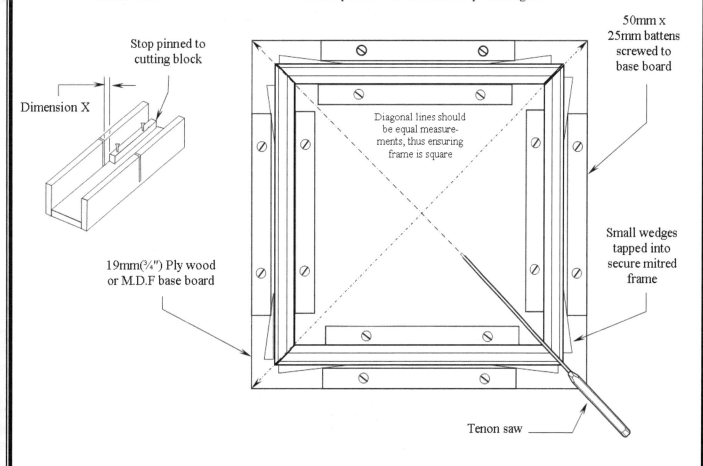

Stop pinned to cutting block

Dimension X

50mm x 25mm battens screwed to base board

Diagonal lines should be equal measurements, thus ensuring frame is square

Small wedges tapped into secure mitred frame

19mm(¾") Ply wood or M.D.F base board

Tenon saw

Table saw set up for forming simple mouldings

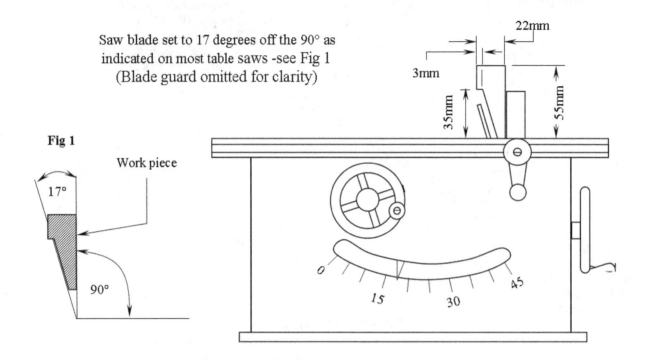

Saw blade set to 17 degrees off the 90° as indicated on most table saws - see Fig 1
(Blade guard omitted for clarity)

Fig 1

Setting an adjustable bevel to a given angle

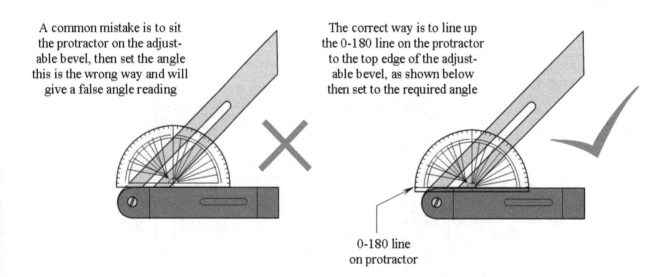

A common mistake is to sit the protractor on the adjustable bevel, then set the angle this is the wrong way and will give a false angle reading

The correct way is to line up the 0-180 line on the protractor to the top edge of the adjustable bevel, as shown below then set to the required angle

0-180 line on protractor

Hole types

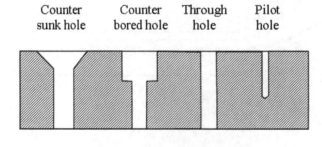

Counter sunk hole | Counter bored hole | Through hole | Pilot hole

Angle jig for repetitive angle cutting
(Saw blade guard omitted for clarity)

This jig is ideal for repetitive angle cutting and proved to be invaluable in the construction of gates, fencing, garden furniture and other projects where the same angle on several pieces needs to be cut. The saw blade should be set so it protrudes **no more than 5mm above the work piece** and a push stick should be used. This should be the case with all table saw blade height settings, The reason for this is that if there is an accident and a hand or finger catches the blade only flesh will be cut and not bone thus saving limbs and finger digits

NB Bade guard omitted for clarity. Never remove blade guards

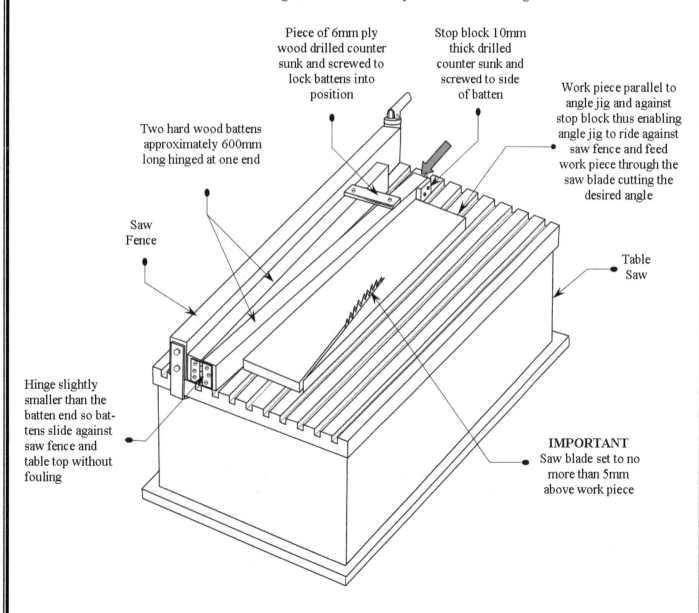

Piece of 6mm ply wood drilled counter sunk and screwed to lock battens into position

Stop block 10mm thick drilled counter sunk and screwed to side of batten

Work piece parallel to angle jig and against stop block thus enabling angle jig to ride against saw fence and feed work piece through the saw blade cutting the desired angle

Two hard wood battens approximately 600mm long hinged at one end

Saw Fence

Table Saw

Hinge slightly smaller than the batten end so battens slide against saw fence and table top without fouling

IMPORTANT
Saw blade set to no more than 5mm above work piece

Improvised mortise machine

A 15mm Forstner bit was used in this set up
(see sketch opposite)
2" x 1" Battens were glued and screwed to 2" x 1½"
This being the rear fence, then the battens were planed down so that they were <u>2mm higher</u> than the drill stand bed, thus allowing the front fence when clamped down to clamp the rear fence also

Rear fence and battens move to and fro thus allowing adjustment of the rear fence

This Forstner bit has side cutting edges as well as its main cutting edges and a centre point this makes it ideal for removing large amounts of timber quickly, and is ideal for the initial cutting of mortises

Sketch of Forstner bit

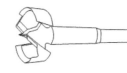

Rear fence set for centre mortise, then 2" x 1½" timber clamped to bench battens and drill stand base allowing for free movement of the work piece between the front and rear fences

Once the bulk of wood has been removed by drilling a series of holes that join each other, the mortise is then ready for squaring the ends and sides

Drill stand and drill set up for improvised lathe

The first improvised lathe I ever made was using an electric drill in some sort of make shift contraption to hold the drill steady in a horizontal position; this proved to vibrate and was difficult to work accurately. So I then decided to use the drill stand with its base turned 180 degrees then laid horizontal and the drill stand base clamped in the work mate jaws. A tool rest was made up of blocks of wood screwed together, this method proved to be good particularly for making model wheels. Electric drills with bearings at the chuck are far superior to cheap drills with brass bushes, this is the heart of the set up and is under considerable stress when initial turning of the work piece begins...

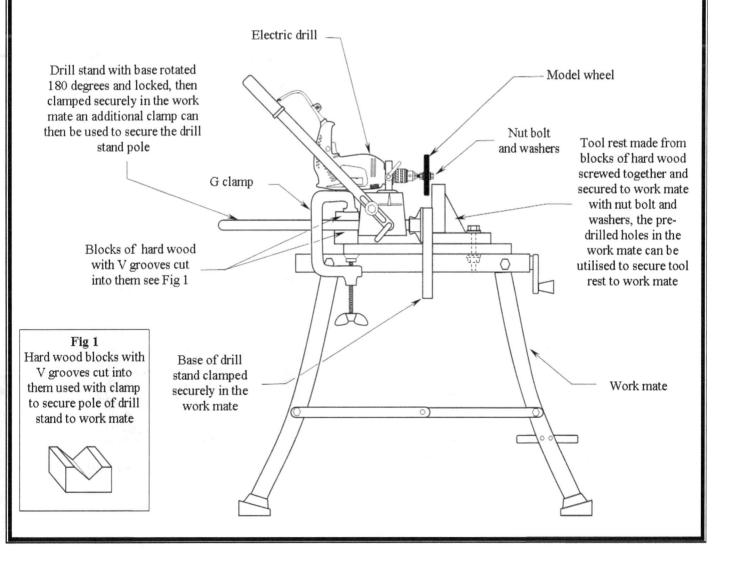

Drill stand with base rotated 180 degrees and locked, then clamped securely in the work mate an additional clamp can then be used to secure the drill stand pole

Electric drill

Model wheel

Nut bolt and washers

Tool rest made from blocks of hard wood screwed together and secured to work mate with nut bolt and washers, the pre-drilled holes in the work mate can be utilised to secure tool rest to work mate

G clamp

Blocks of hard wood with V grooves cut into them see Fig 1

Fig 1
Hard wood blocks with V grooves cut into them used with clamp to secure pole of drill stand to work mate

Base of drill stand clamped securely in the work mate

Work mate

Finishing and painting the toys

Sand smooth all edges and run your finger tips around your finished work to make sure there are no sharp or jagged edges, There are a variety of non toxic lead free oil based paints on the market, and a good range of undercoats, An acrylic under coat was used on the prototypes in this book. Good stationers and hobby shops stock a range of transfers and stickers that can be used to decorate your project

A variety of sand papers are readily available from DIY and hard ware stores

A good quality wood filler is a must in all workshops whether it be the home workshop or professional wood shop

After filling and sanding a selection of brushes can be used to paint your project, before assembling your project some of the small parts can be painted before the final assembly therefore a better finish can be achieved

If your project is to be painted then an all purpose decorators filler can be used to fill end grain and any discrepancies

Garden Furniture Planters & Whirligigs

Ornate trough planter

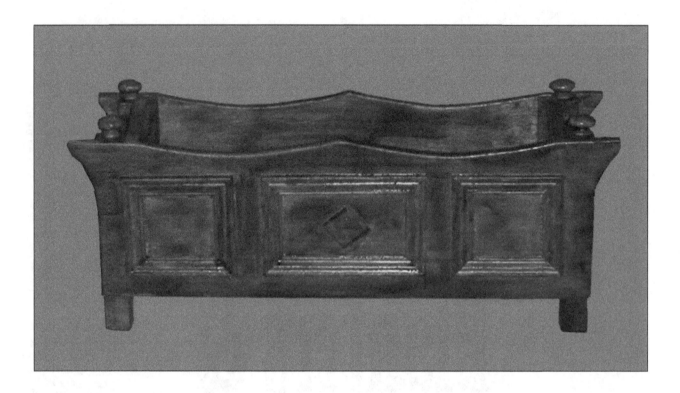

Three pins and a thin piece of strip wood can be used for marking out the gentle curve. Cut the first curve then flip the off cut over so you have a mirror image then mark out and cut the other curve, thus making the front panel symmetrical

This picture shows the rabbet which is formed by cutting away one of the sides that make up the groove in the tongue and groove boards, this is done before any other cutting takes place (see sketch below)

Tongue and groove board
(Not to scale)

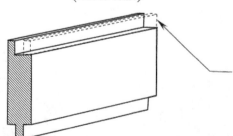

Remove groove wall (Indicate by broken lines) to form rabbet into which the bottom is fitted

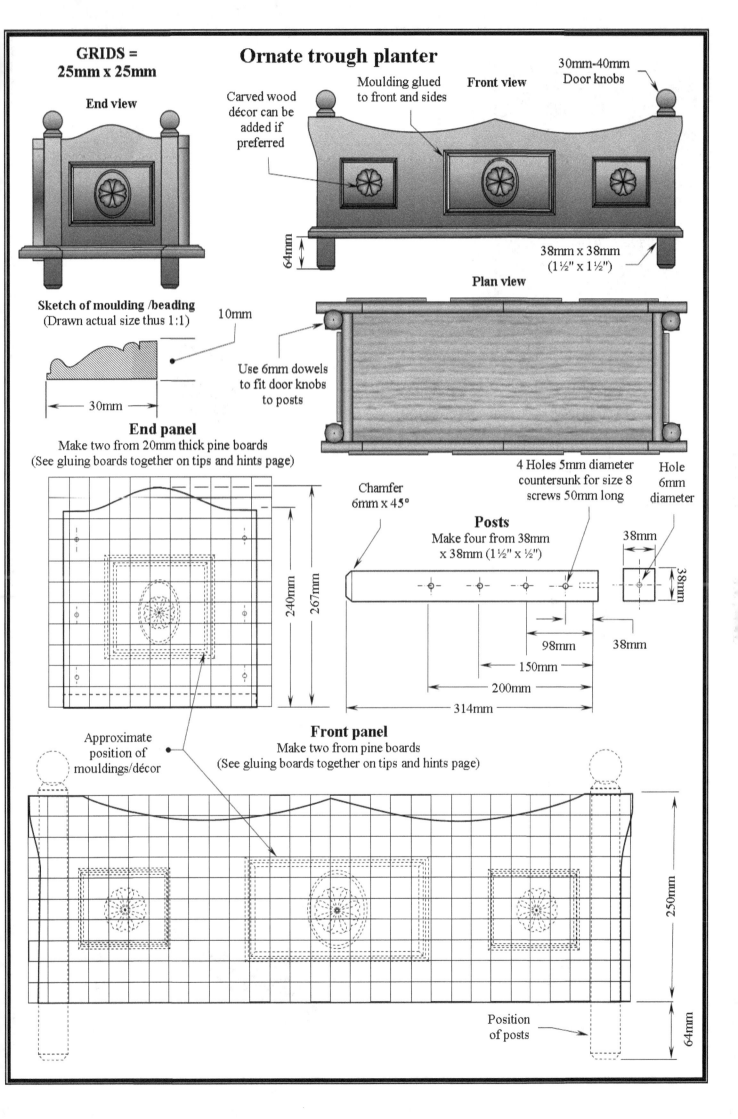

Whirligig Bird

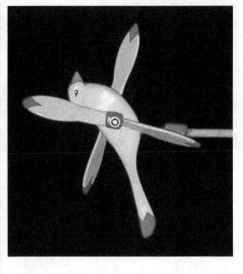

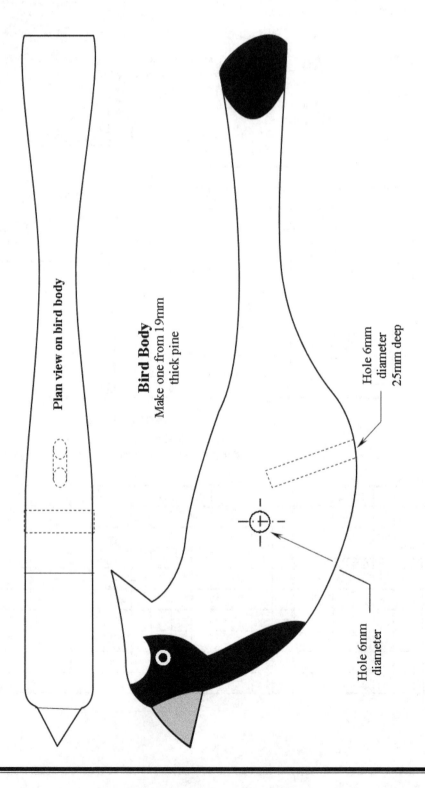

Bird wing
Make four from 3mm thick plywood

Plan view on bird body

Bird Body
Make one from 19mm thick pine

Hole 6mm diameter 25mm deep

Hole 6mm diameter

Also required
One length of (3/16") 5mm diameter rod 72mm long, Two (3/16") 5mm spring caps, One length 6mm diameter hard wood dowel approximately 750mm long

Wing hub
Make two from 20mm x 20mm x 20mm hard wood

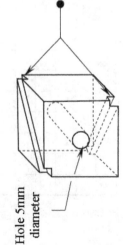

Diagonal slots 3mm wide 5mm deep to fit birds wings to wing hub **Note :** Slots are cut in opposite directions thus giving propeller dynamics

Hole 5mm diameter

Bumble bee whirligig

This bee's wings rotate on an axis between the head and body and when the wind blows gives a realistic flying illusion

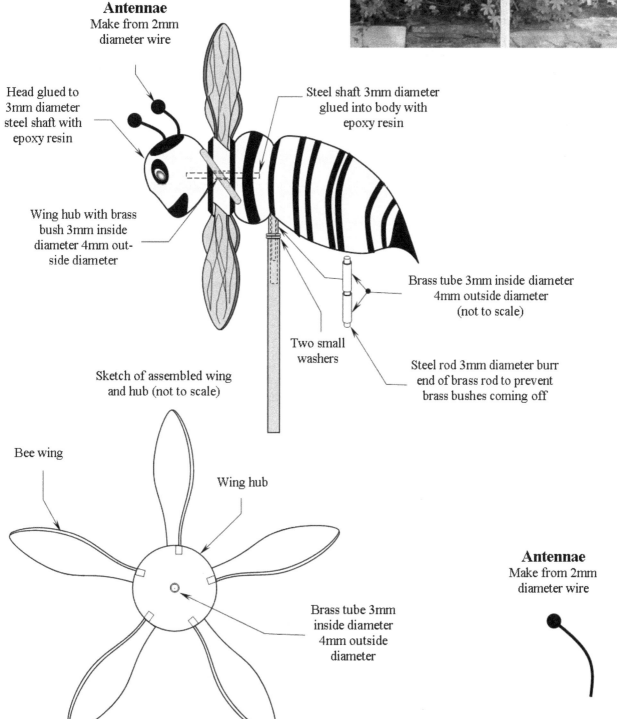

Bee head
Make from 20mm thick pine

Hole 3mm diameter
12mm deep

Bee body
Make from 20mm thick pine

Hole 3mm diameter
12mm deep

Hole 4mm diameter
15mm deep

Bee wings
Make 5 from 3mm thick plywood

Wing hub
Make one from 12mm thick hard wood

Hole 4mm diameter for brass tube

40mm

Wing slots 3mm wide x 4mm deep

12mm

Pattern for the wing slots
To cut the five 3mm wide x 4mm deep slots to house the bees wings the length of the pattern below is equal to that of the circumference of the 40mm diameter wing hub, make a copy of this then glue the pattern to the circumference of the wing hub with a glue stick the type used for sticking paper, the pattern can then be dampened with a cloth then removed after cutting of the slots

Biplane

This biplanes propellers rotate and the pilot bobs up and down in the cockpit
This can also be made as a toy by reducing the propeller size accordingly

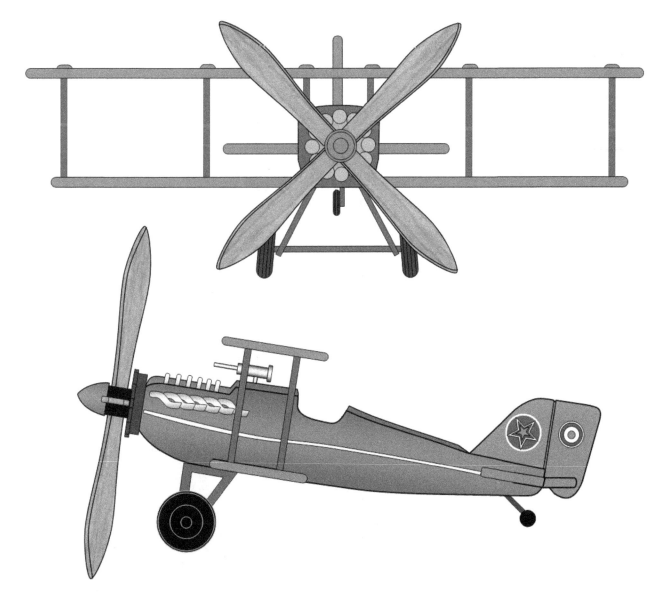

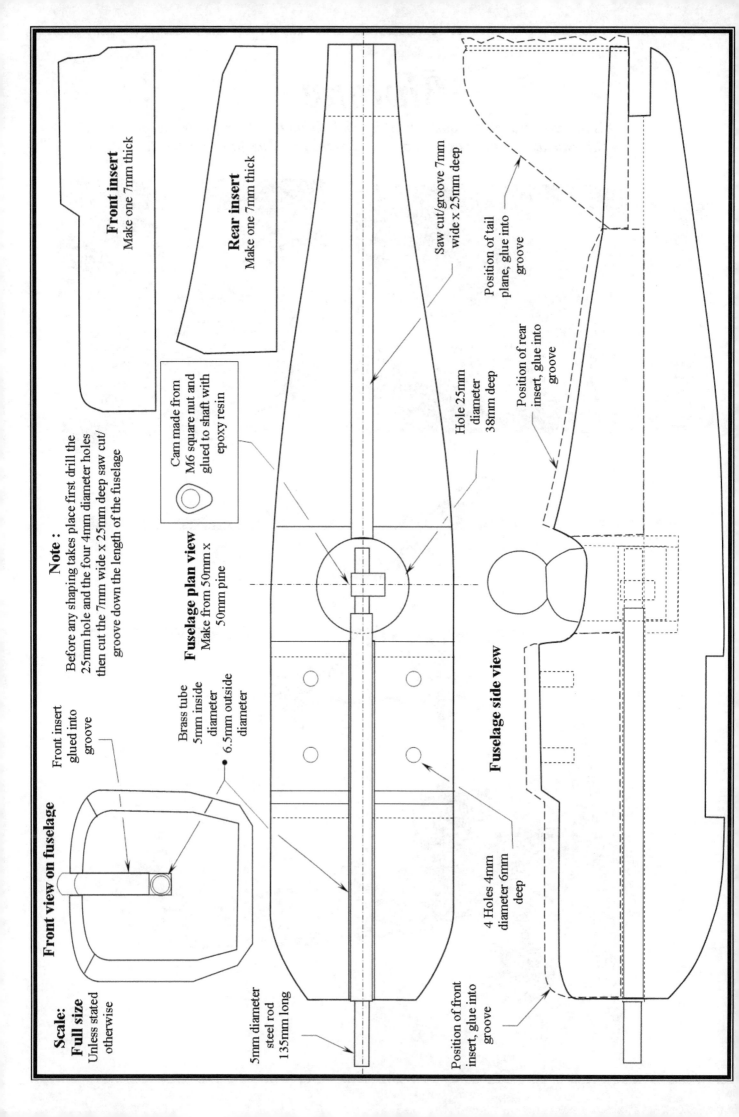

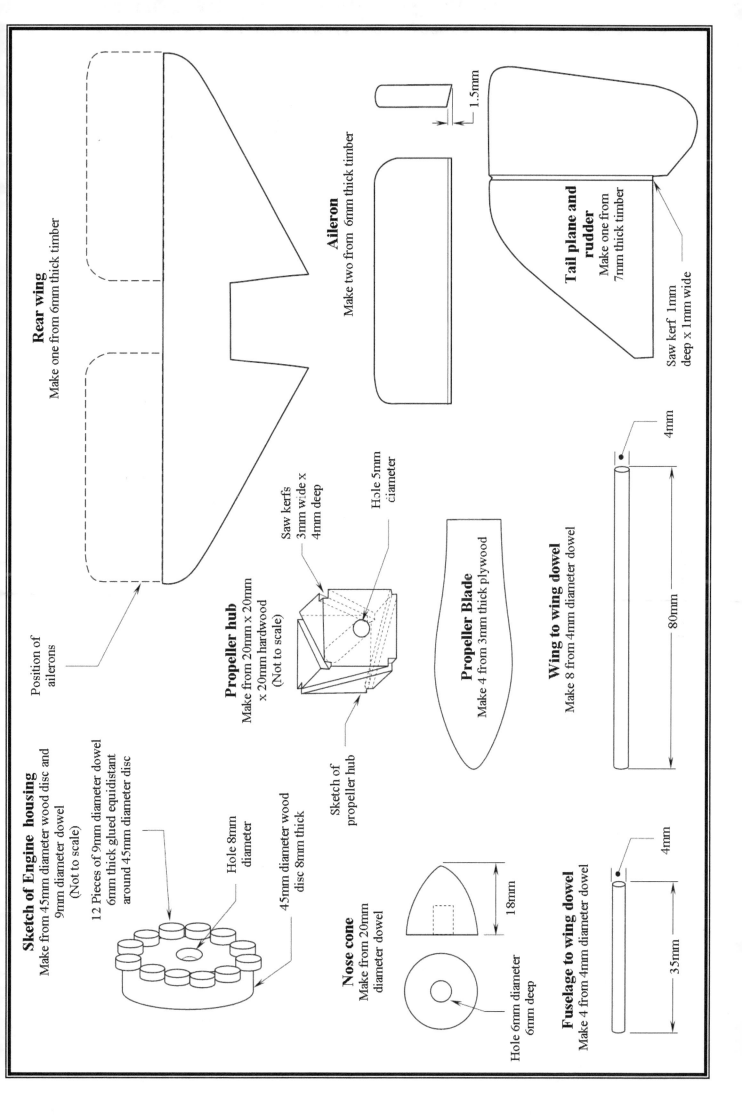

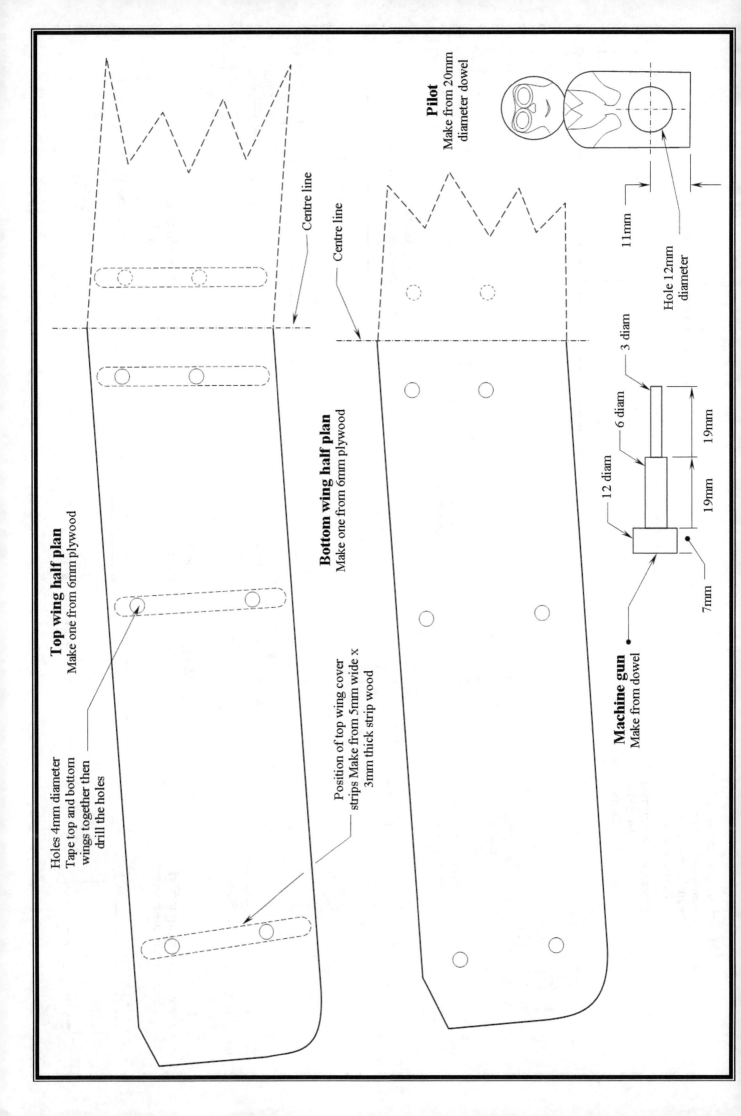

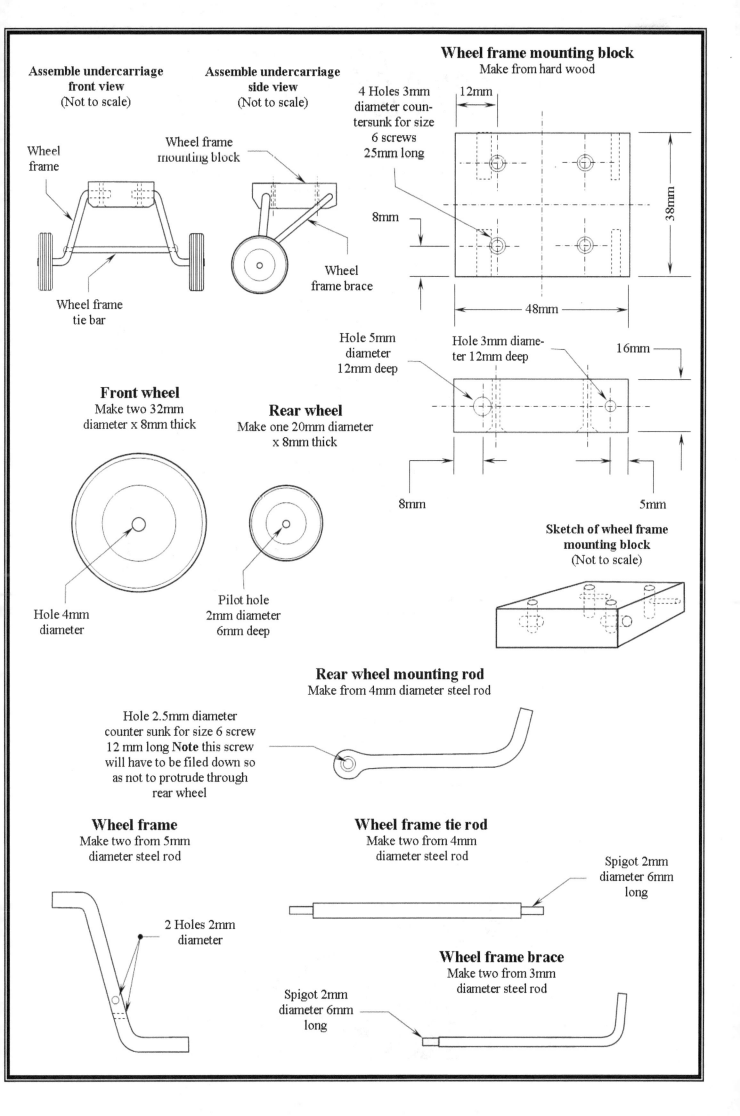

Frog on a bike whirligig

This whirligig was designed to be suspended on a short chain the legs on opposite sides spin in opposite directions and the front wheel rotates, this whirligig is quite amusing and fun to watch in action

Initial design drawing

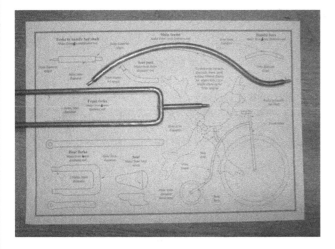

A photocopy of the scale drawing being used to make the penny farthing frame. Note the 3mm diameter x 7mm long spigots on the ends of the main frame and handle bar stem

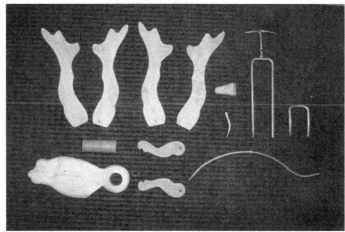

Parts cut out and sanded ready for test fitting

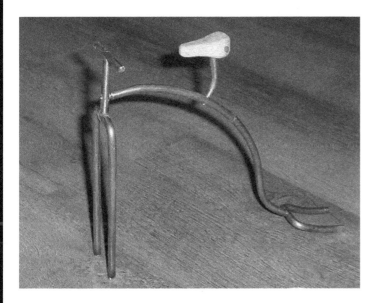

Spigots passed through holes then ends of spigots burred these rivet joins are then reinforced with a build up of epoxy resin and when painted give the appearance of welds

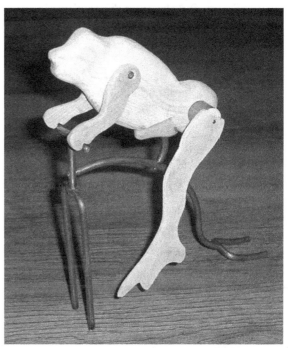

Frog parts temporarily assembled and test fitted on penny farthing frame, any adjustments are made to the frame seat and seat pole so that frog is sitting squarely and the hands are on the handle bars

Wheels made and the corner beading fins being added to the front wheel spokes, these are fitted to the spokes top middle and bottom alternately around the wheel

Finished and painted frog on a bike whirligig suspended from its hanging chain

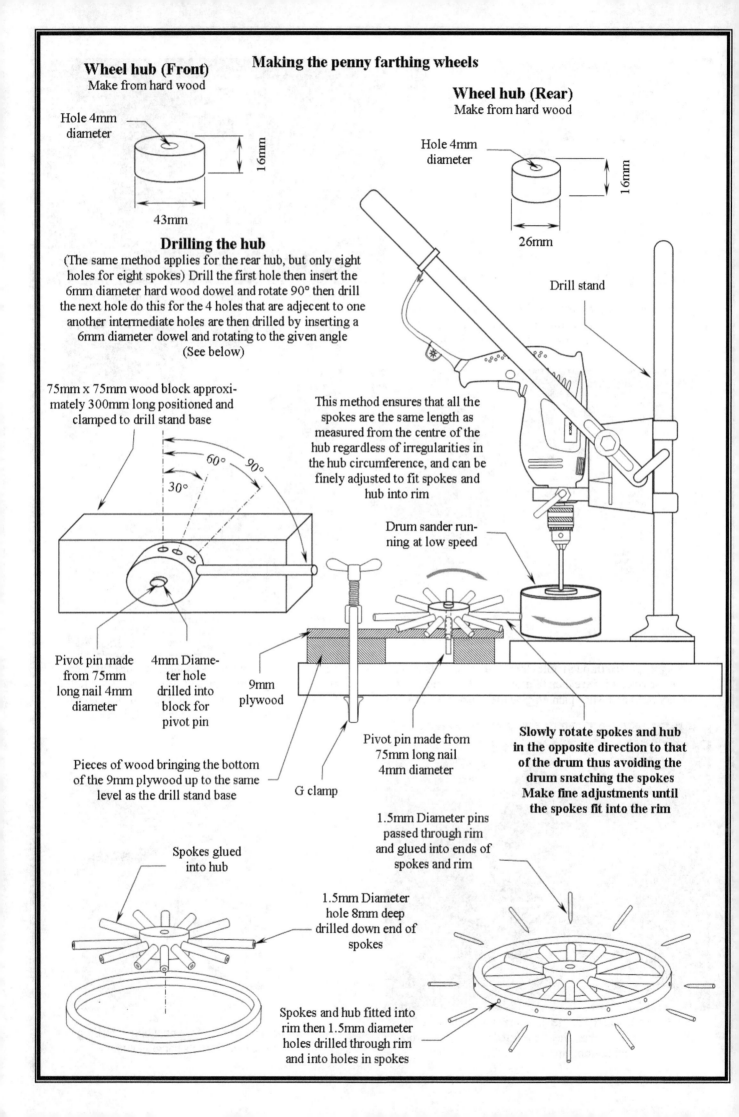

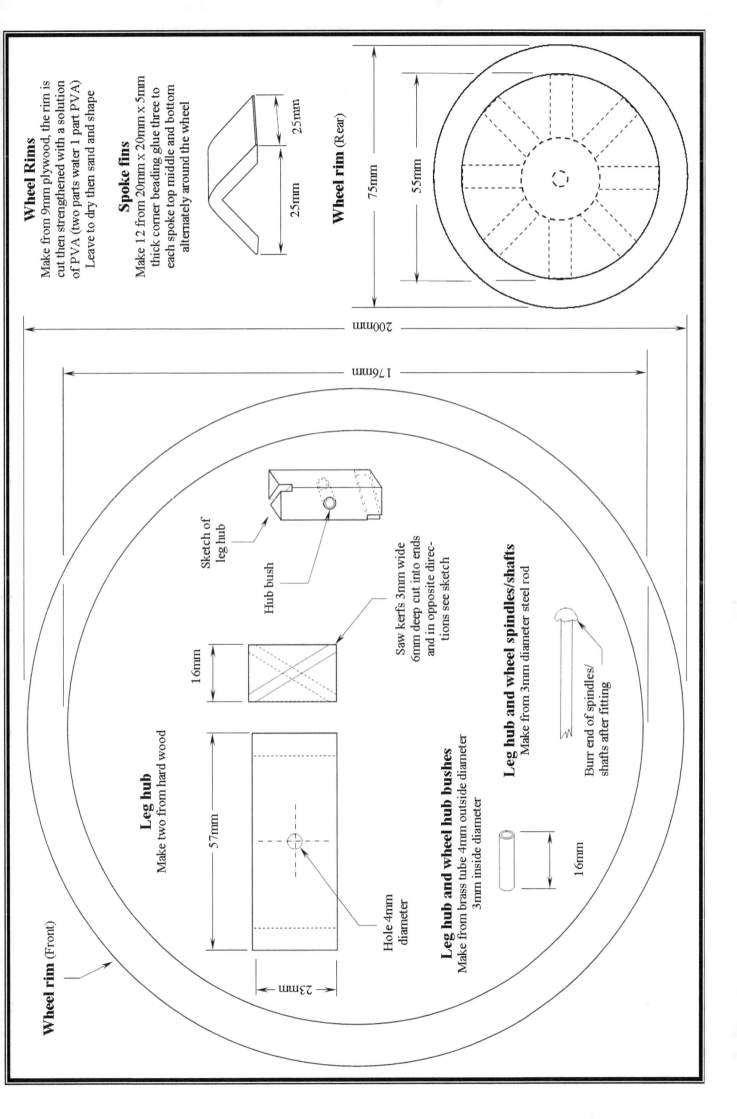

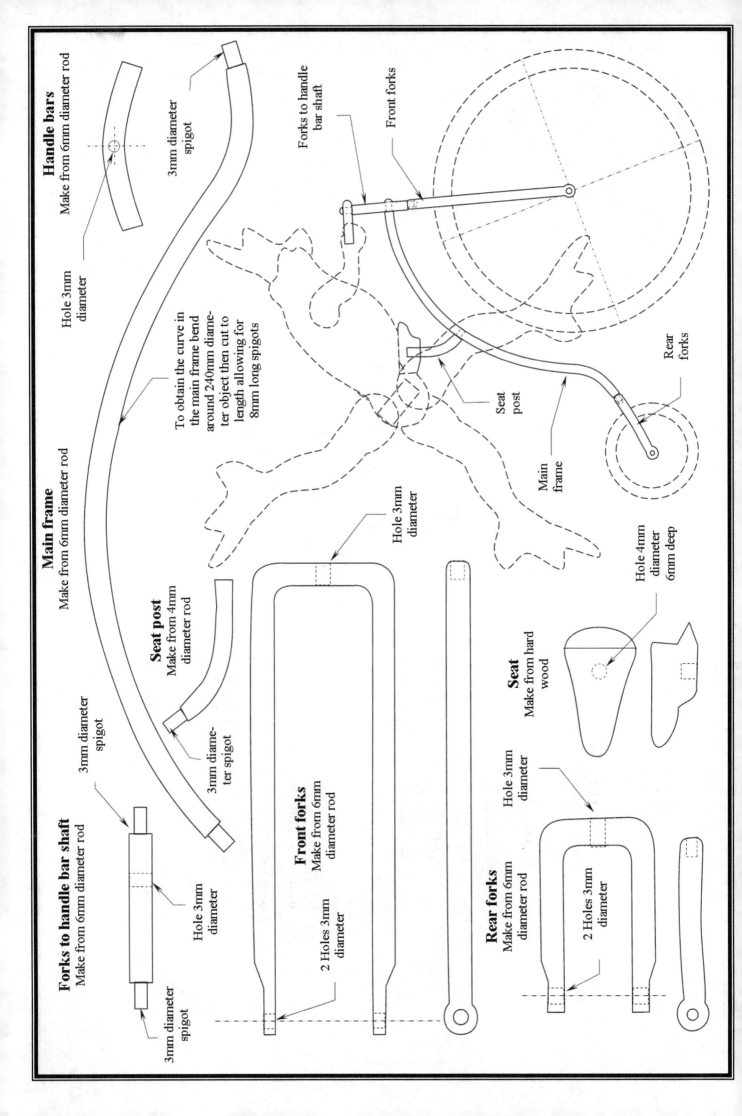

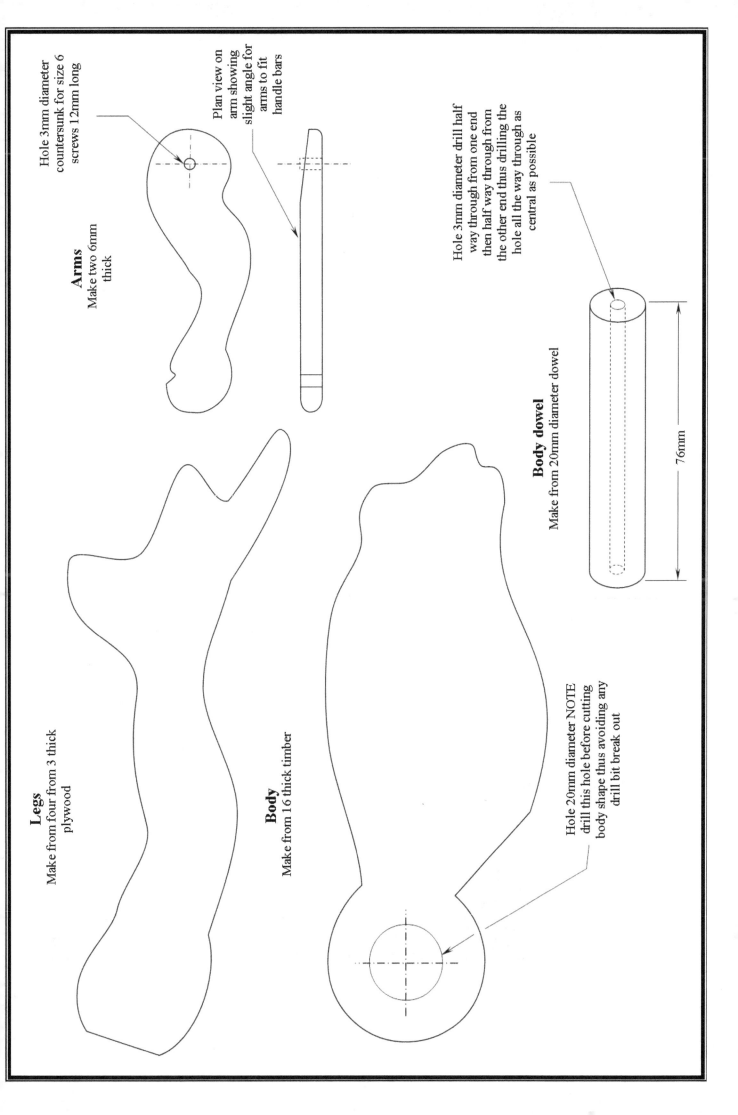

Swinging bench

This swinging bench is of sturdy construction and was designed for two people and will suit most sized gardens

Marking arms for fitting, first the arms were cut to length then the housing for the rear post was cut so as to fit tight

The arm was test fitted then the mortise on the underside was marked out with a pencil from the front post thus ensuring greater accuracy and a closer fitting joint

All parts dry fitted positions marked and ready to be taken apart for the gluing up process, glue is best applied with a small brush

The eye bolt passes through both the arched brace and middle tie beam and is fixed at the top end with threaded bar nuts and washers also there is a dry mortise and tenon (No glue used) thus enabling the frame to be dismantled for storage or carriage, the top of the A frame support was counter bored and fixed to the top beam with 100mm screws

Close up of eye bolt and shackle also showing birds beak cut on arched brace housed neatly on middle tie beam. Threaded bar nuts and washers were used to fix arched brace to top beam. The A frame supports were drilled and counter bored for 100mm size 8 screws to fix A frame supports to top beam

Rear view showing rear braces screwed to rear bottom rail and A frame supports
(A frame bottom tie beams not fitted in this picture)

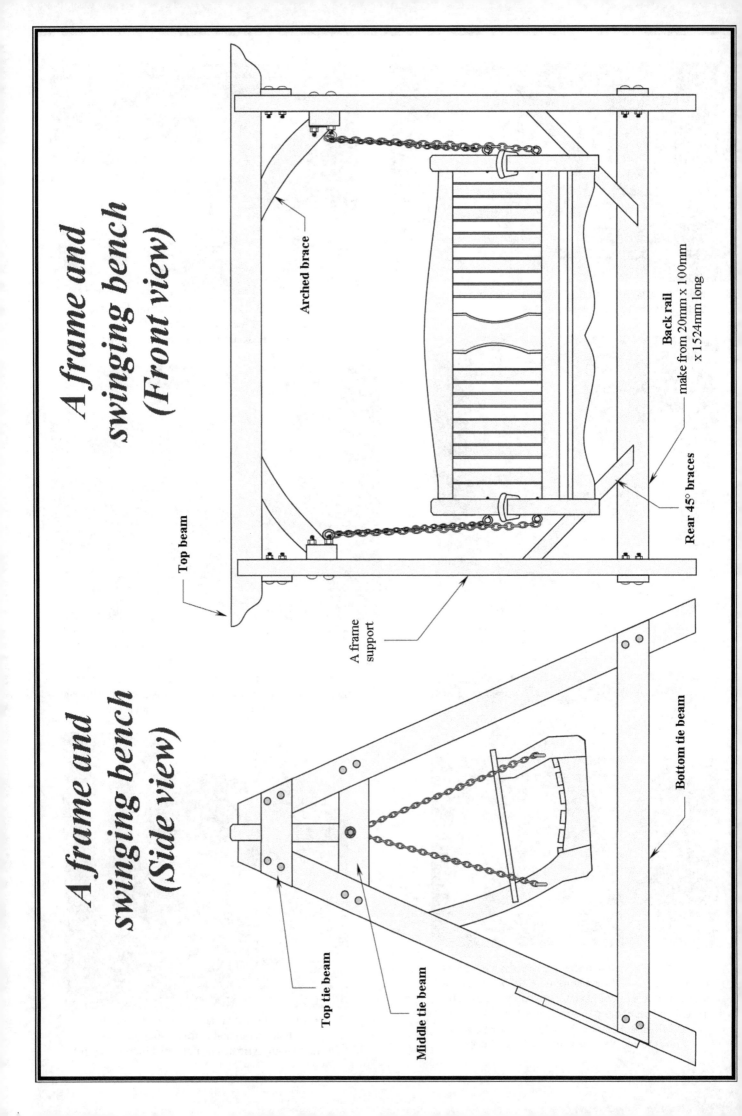

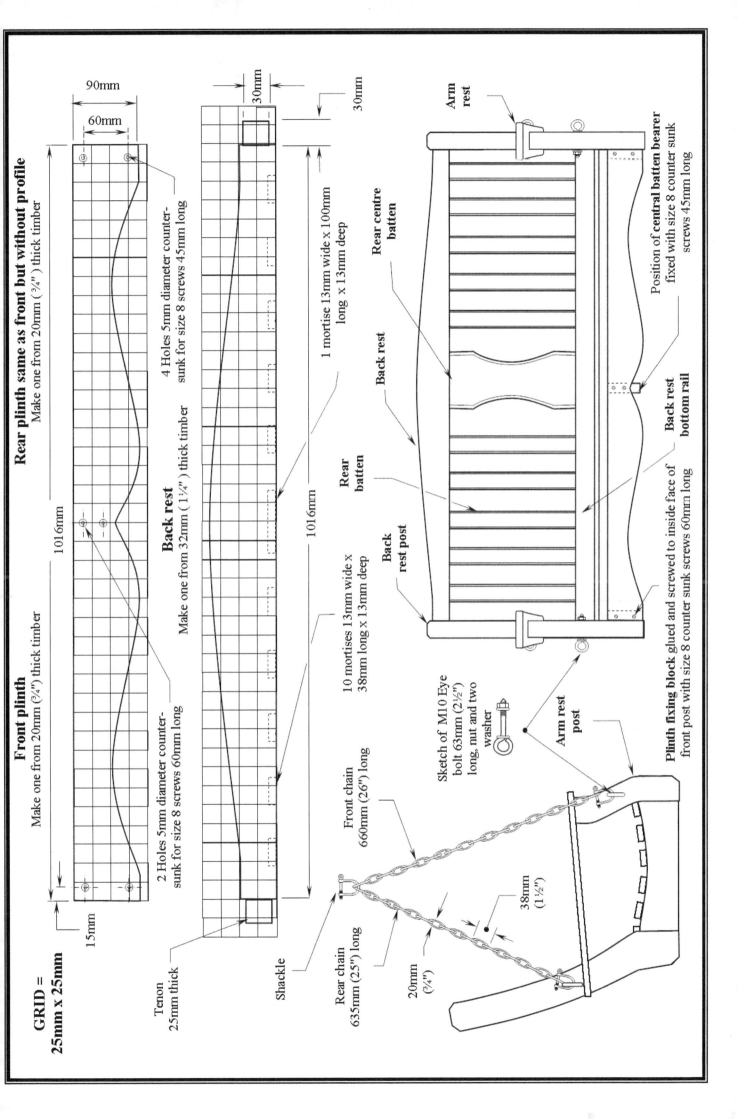

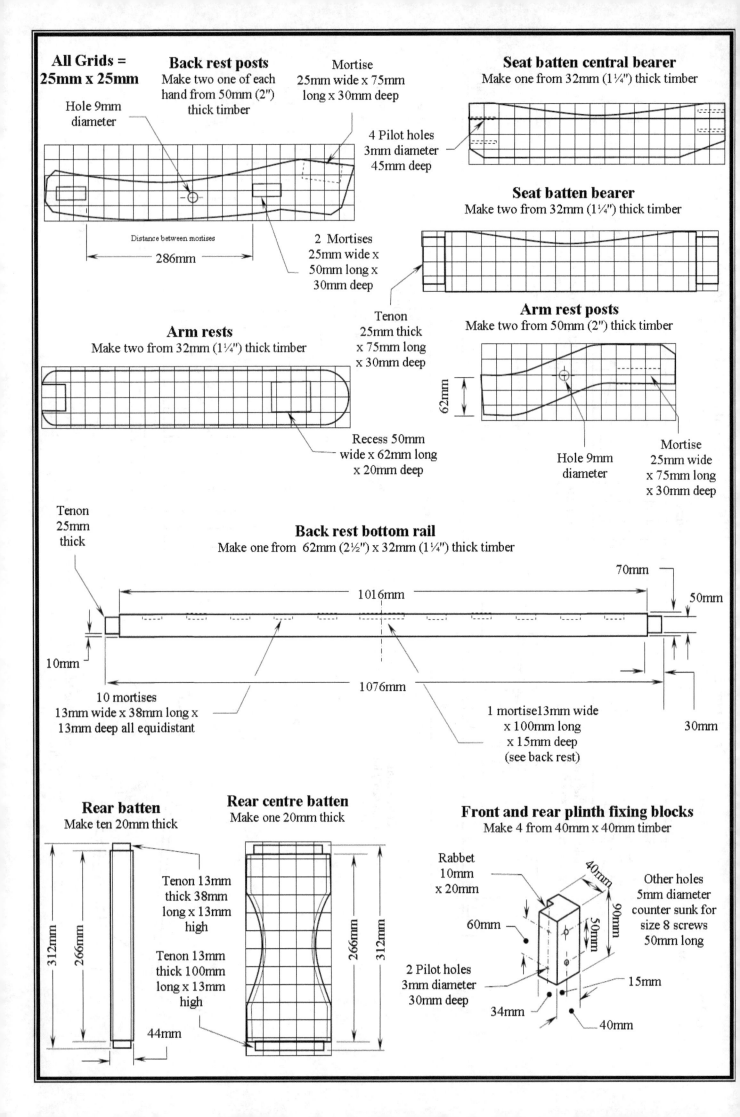

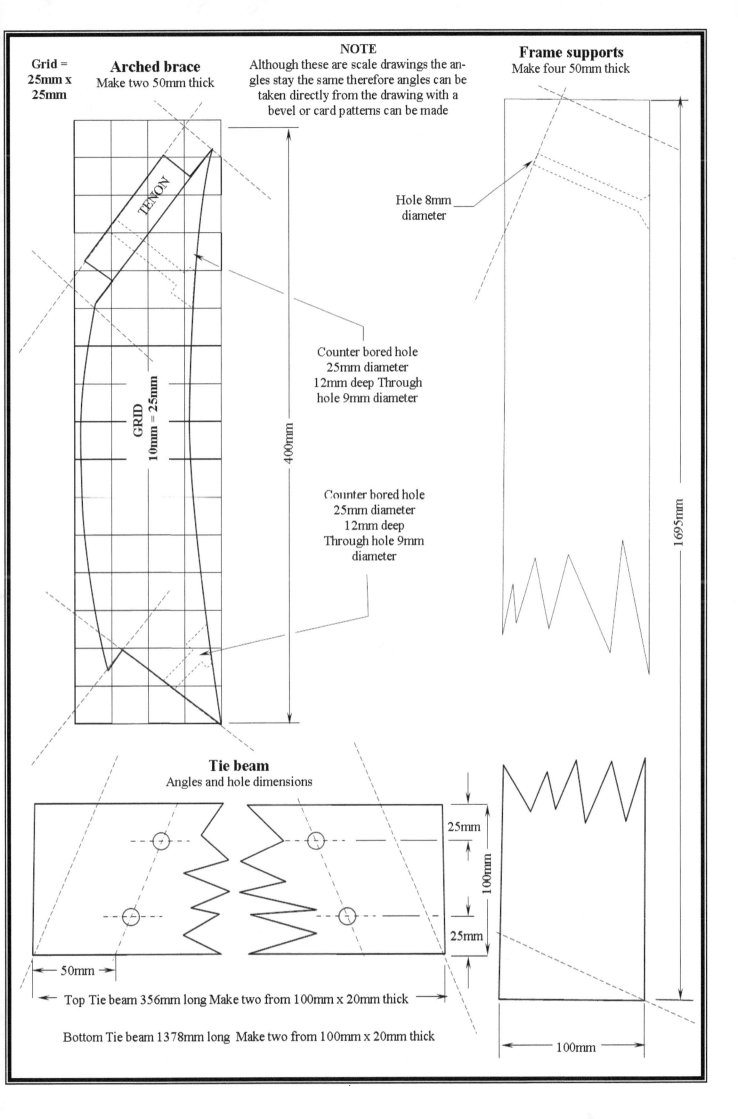

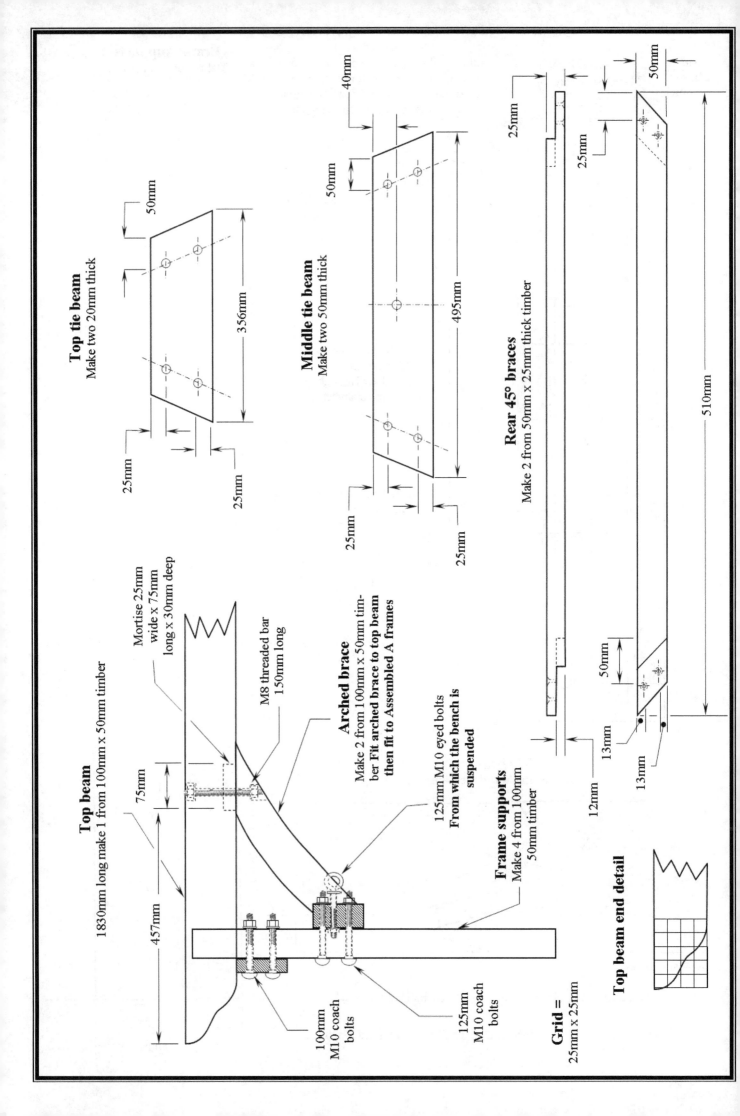

Traditional wheel barrow planter

A traditional Victorian wheel barrow planter approximately the same size as a Victorian ladies garden barrow with added front struts which were used on an 18th century builders barrow, which adds to the aesthetic appearance of this wheel barrow planter. Not only is it a planter but it's also functional

Here are some of the traditional barrows used to get my ideas to work from. These are working barrows and some of the features from these were incorporated into the design of this wheel barrow planter. The handles on all these are shaped for comfort

Note the hopper shape of the inside of this barrow obviously designed for muck spreading

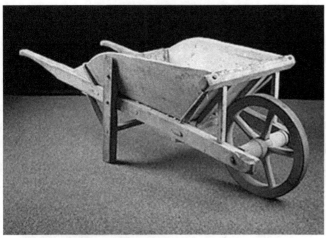

This is a heavy duty builders barrow
Note the front beam and braces, Also the steel threaded bar which passes through the front beam into and through the front cross member tenon bolting the front structure together for strength and durability

This would have been a nice renovation or rebuild project. Note the steel bars through the legs and handles and the leg and rear panel bracing, which I have referred to as braces/décor these pieces are not only functional but are also decorative

This pictures displays the axle block method of holding the axle in position, there must have been a major weakness at this point in the builders barrow, there is no evidence within the picture to suggest that any steel reinforcement was used

This is the end result after a study of each wheel barrow and a few drawings and workings out

My table saw top was used as a guide to squaring up the barrow frame, the grooves in the table saw top were used to find a centre line after the rear cross member was lined up with the square edge of the saw top, also keeping the barrow frame flat on the saw bed insured there was no twisting of the frame whilst the glue was drying

First the main parts were dry fitted (Assembled without glue) using small pins to ensure that these parts fitted satisfactorily. Inset picture clearly show the overall appearance of the barrow was enhanced by the addition of the struts, braces, cross beam, axle block and décor pieces

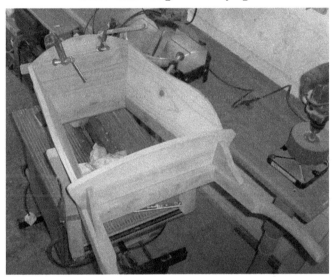

This picture shows that the depth of the barrow was increased by 50mm when measured from the bottom of the handles. 10mm x 10mm strip wood was glued and pinned to these leaving an increased depth of 40mm

The cross beam, outer braces and inner struts were dry fitted prior to gluing

This picture shows the shaping of the handles also showing legs and décor being test fitted prior to gluing

A home made tourniquet clamp made from a piece of rope and a screw driver was used to clamp the rim spokes and hub together whilst the glue dried

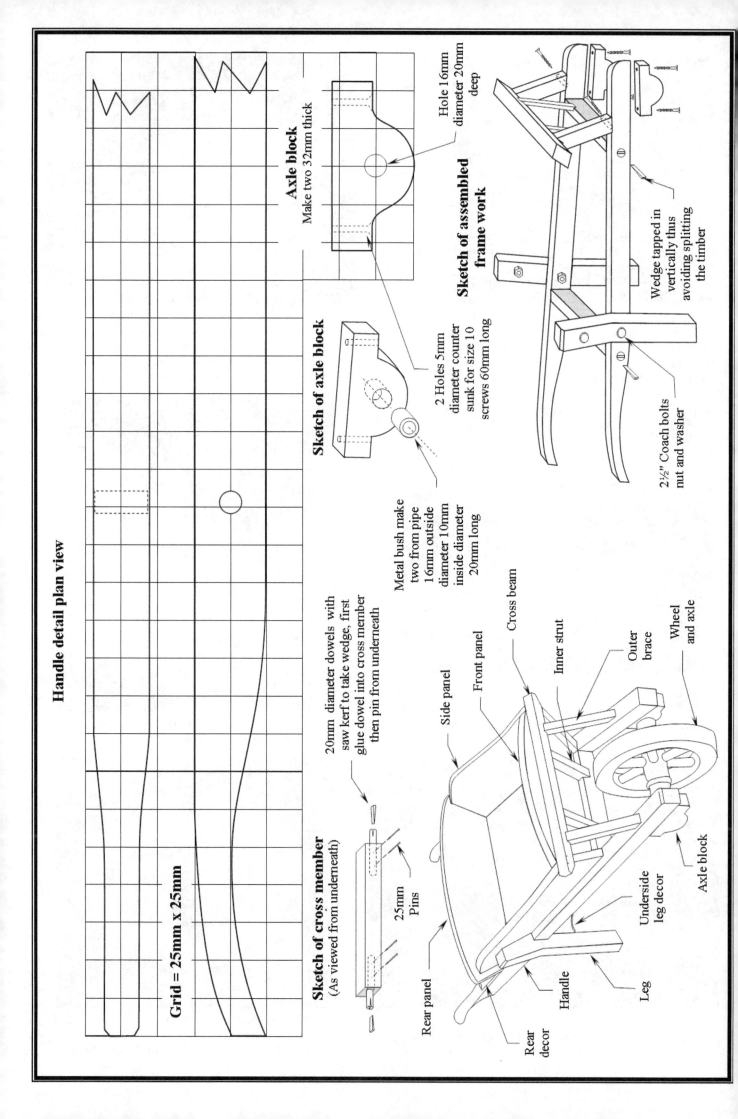

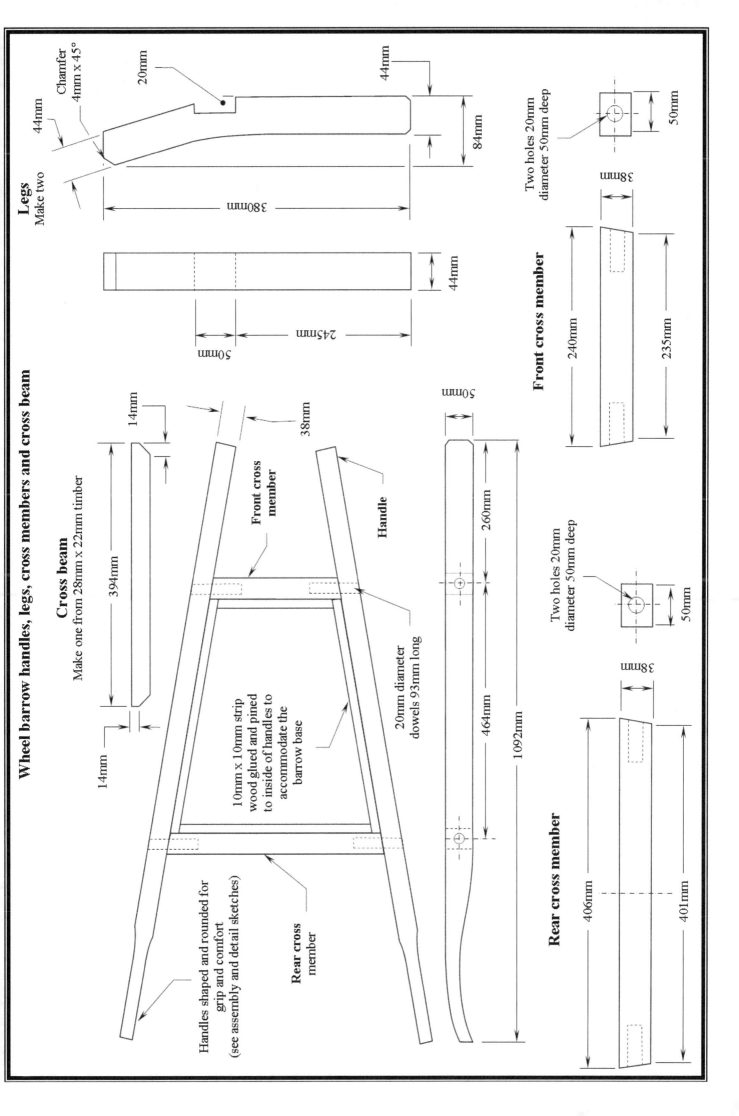

Rear panel and plan view on assembled barrow

Rear panel
Make one 16mm thick

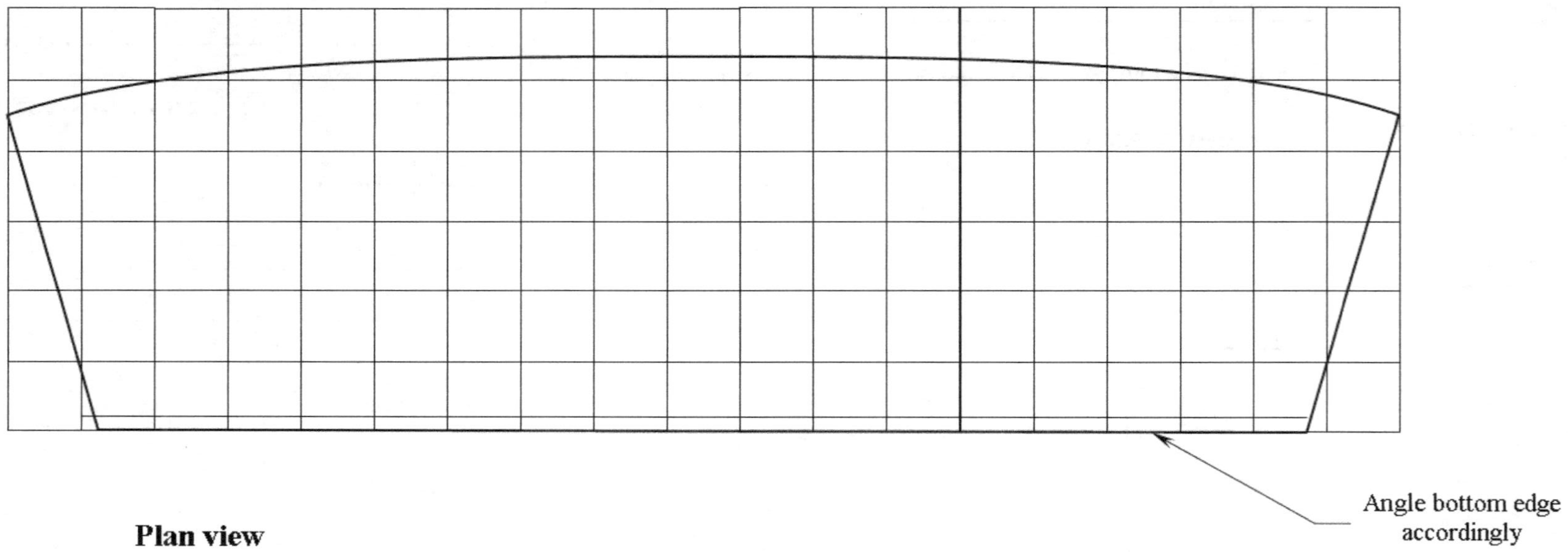

Angle bottom edge accordingly

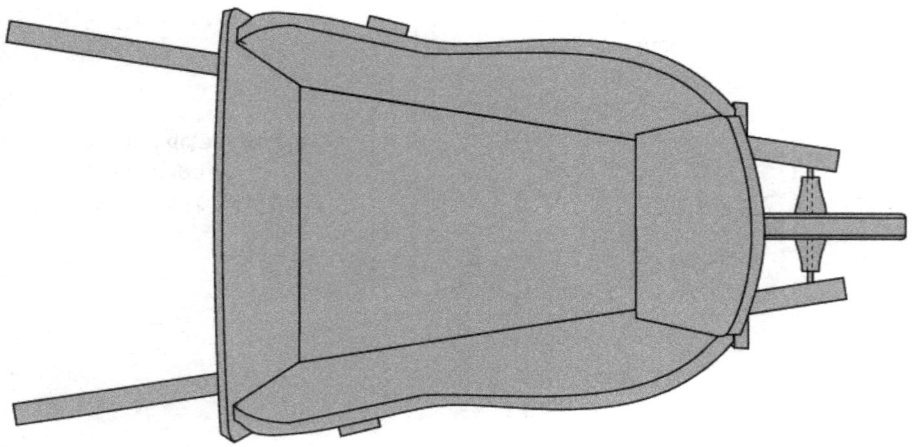

Side view

Plan view

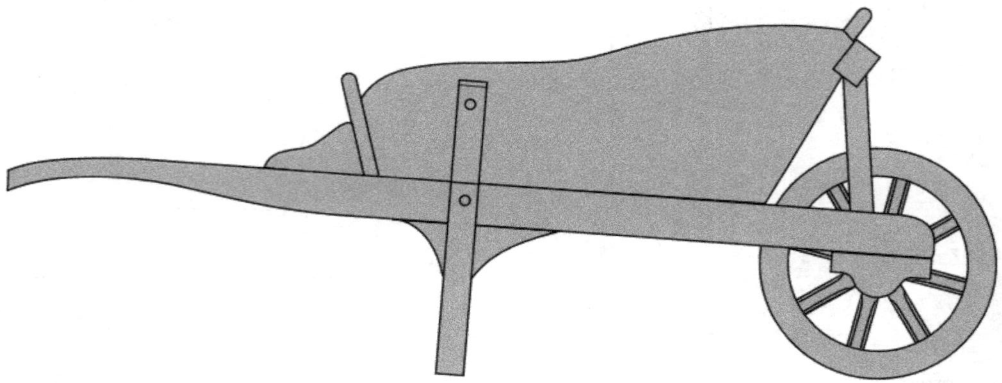

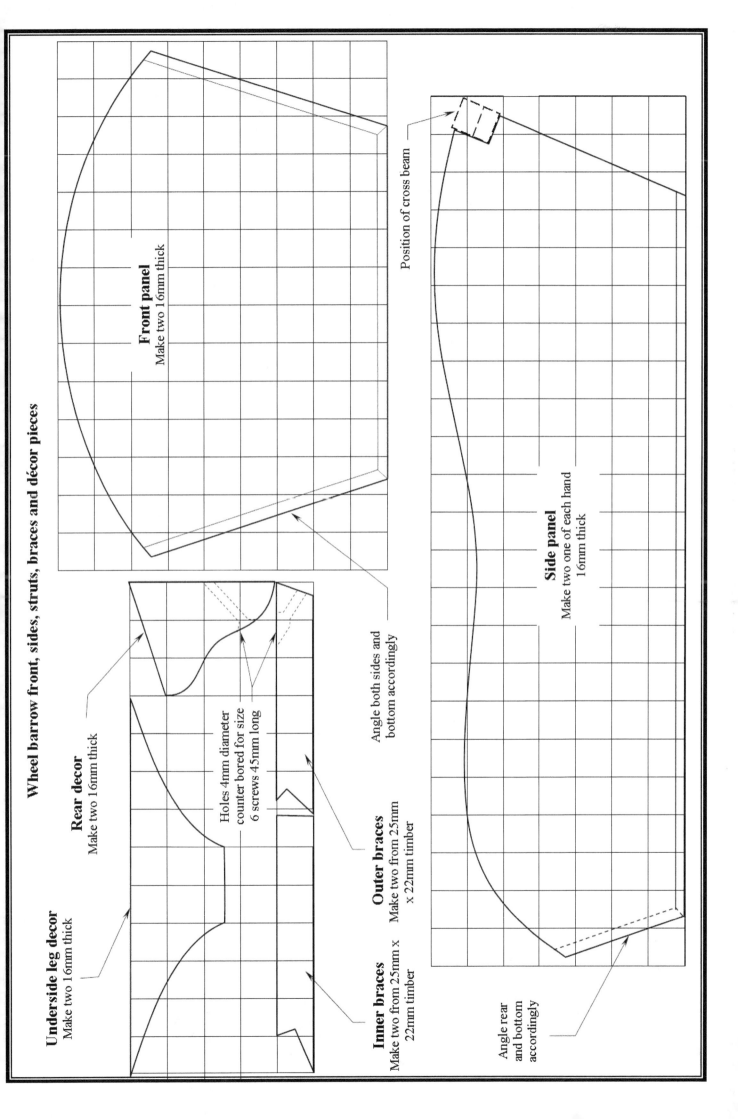

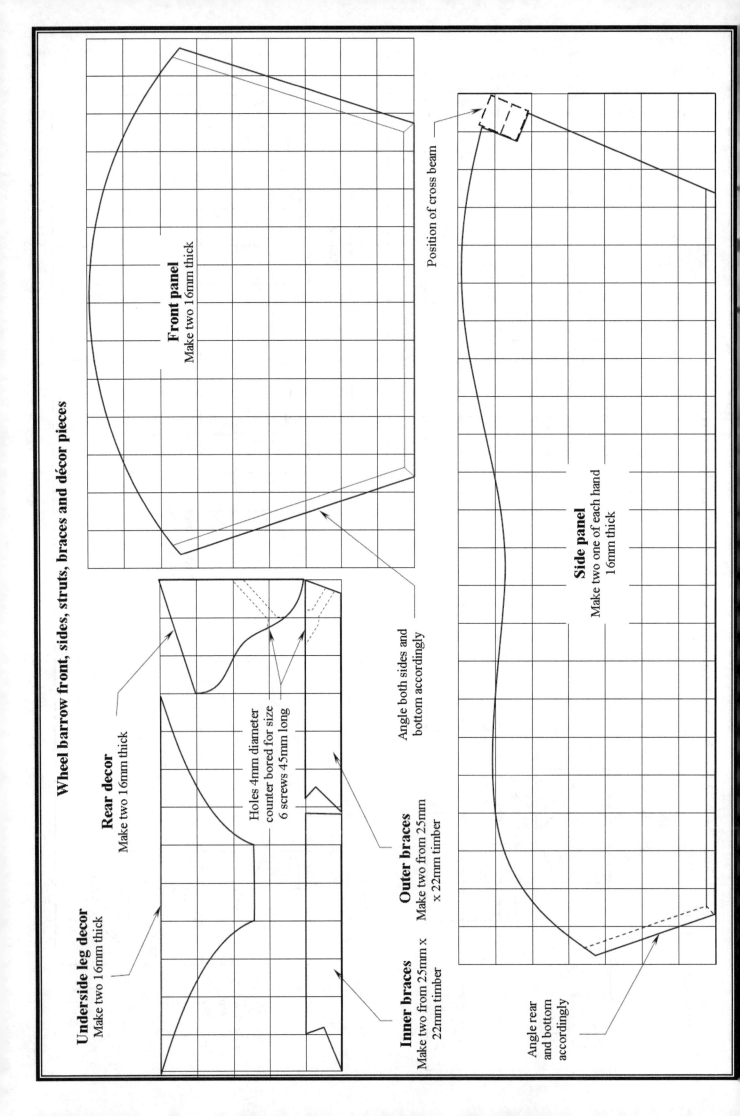

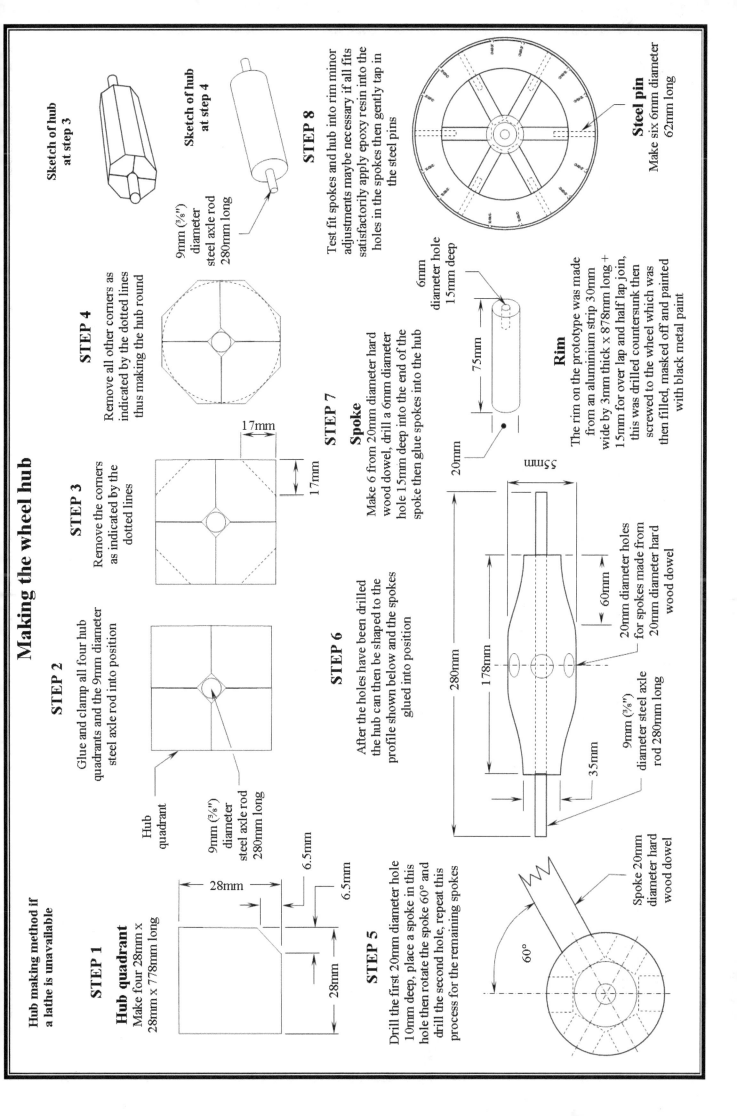

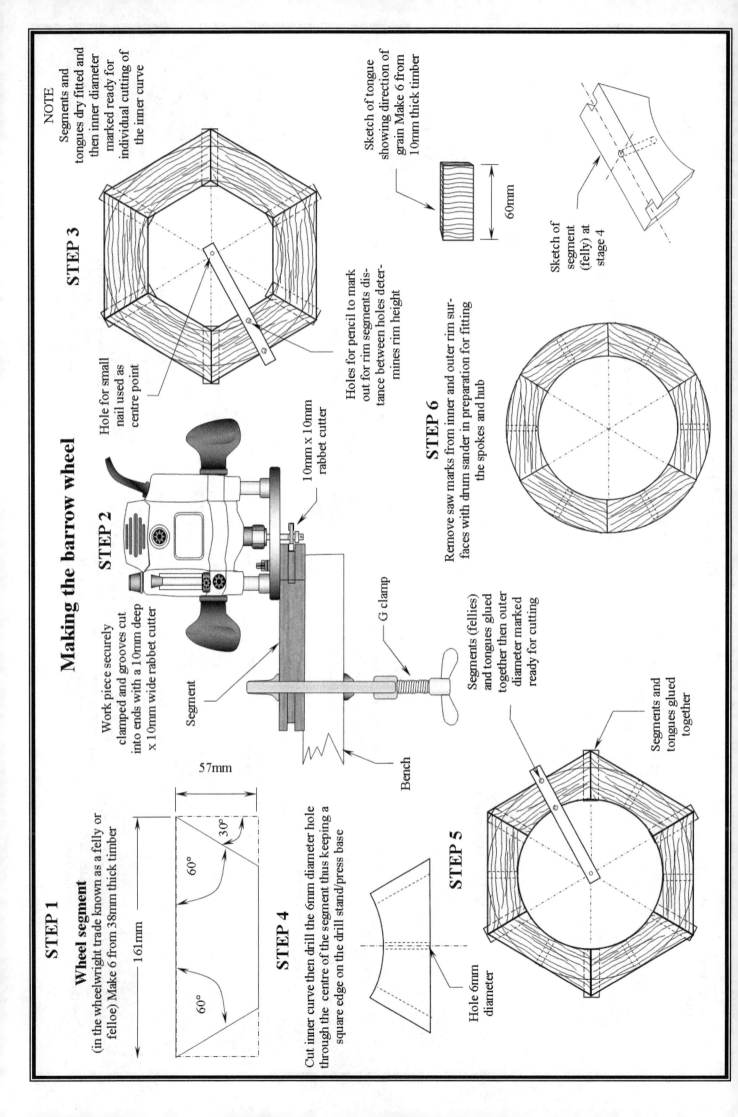

Octagonal bird table

Octagonal bird table with study base that was specifically designed for those more uneven surfaces its symmetric design allows it to be positioned without spoiling the overall appearance

This project is not for reproduction without prior permission from the copyright owner

©A. R. Phillips 2010

Posts glued into recesses cut into the 9mm ply wood base

Posts and ceiling timbers glued and screwed together with size 6 screws 30mm long, also showing 4mm ply wood disc that was used to fix ceiling timbers together

A simple jig was set up using the saw table bed, some blocks and clamps were used to aid gluing of the roof sections

Roof segments glued together and ready for the finial to be made and fitted

The finial being made on the home made lathe

Finial fitted now the roof décor strips can be made and fitted

Roof décor strips cut neatly into finial and glued to roof segments and finial

Roof, finial, finial dowel and wood button glued into position and ready for the arches and parapet to be fitted

Arches, parapets, parapet capping and front decor being fitted

Close up of upper parts. 4mm ply wood disc glued and pinned to ceiling timbers, wood button and dowel passed through these and glued into the hole in the finial. Post to ceiling décor and arches glued and fitted also showing parapet capping which is made from mahogany as were the roof strips and the decorative beading covering the octagonal base plywood end grain

Roof, finial dowel and wood button ready for fitting to main structure glue was applied to top of arches, top of posts hole in finial and base of wood button

Stand detail showing post, out riggers and out rigger braces which when assembled form a square for the post to fit into

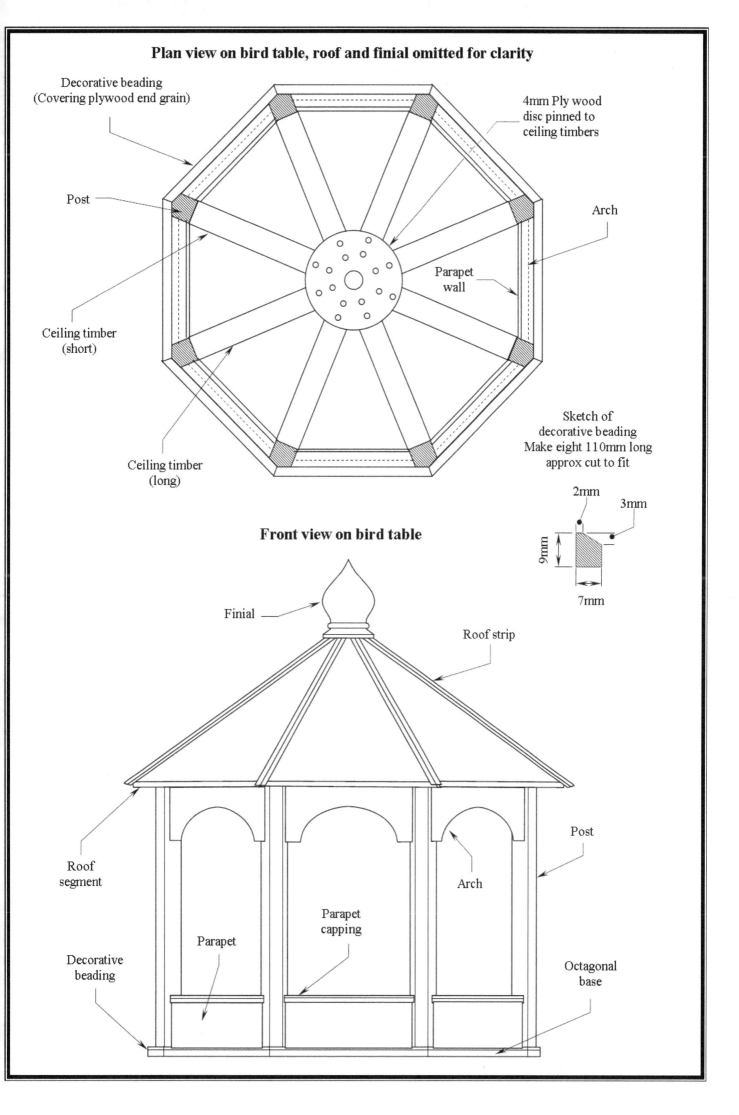

Roof segment
Make 8 from 7mm thick T & G boarding two boards will need to be glued together to obtain the required width

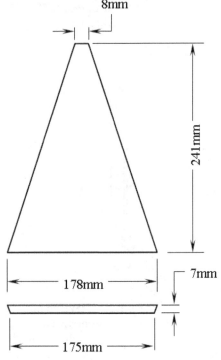

This measurement is nominal assemble segments in pairs then the pairs in pairs creating two halves of the roof these can then be glued together thus allowing for more accuracy when making the roof (see photos)

Post to ceiling décor
Make eight 16mm thick

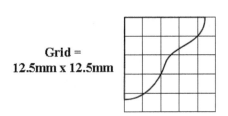

Grid = 12.5mm x 12.5mm

Wood button
16mm thick

Dowel

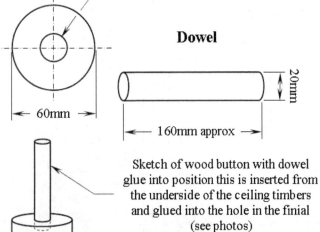

Sketch of wood button with dowel glue into position this is inserted from the underside of the ceiling timbers and glued into the hole in the finial (see photos)

Finial
Make one

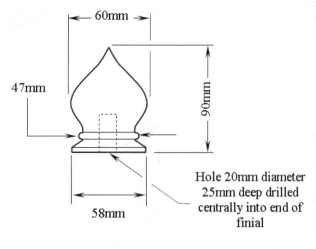

Hole 20mm diameter 25mm deep drilled centrally into end of finial

Roof strips
Make eight 245mm long x 7mm thick these can be made in two halves if preferred

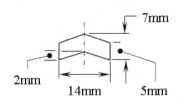

Arches
Make eight 16mm thick

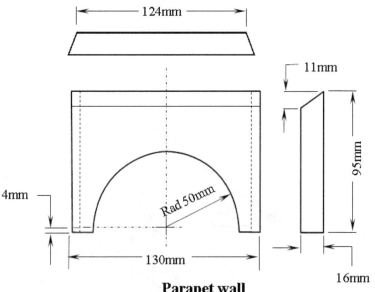

Rad 50mm

Parapet wall
Make eight 16mm thick

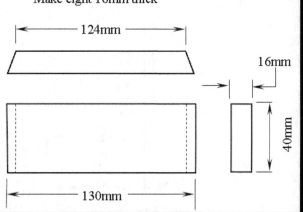

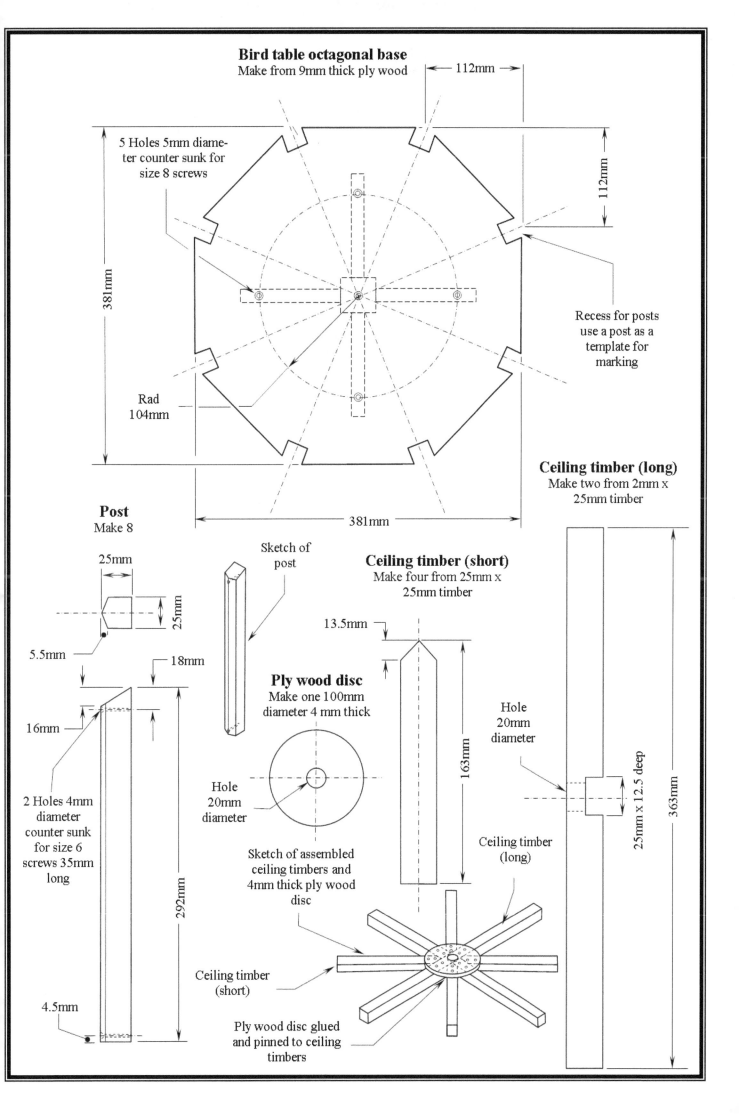

Out rigger braces Type A
Make two from 19mm thick timber

Grids = 12.5mm x 12.5mm

19mm
45mm
4 Holes countersunk for size 8 screws 45mm long
44mm
356m

Out rigger braces Type B
Make two from 19mm thick timber

19mm
45mm
4 Holes countersunk for size 8 screws 45mm long
44mm
356mm

Stand post to table top braces
Make four 19mm thick

Grids = 12.5mm x 12.5mm

Pilot hole 3mm diameter 25mm deep

Hole 4mm diameter counter sunk for size 8 screws 50mm long

Stand post
Make from 50mm x 50mm timber 1475 long

Note
When outrigger braces are assembled they form a square hole that the post fits into (see photo close up of stand base)

Hole 4mm diameter counter sunk for size 8 screws 60mm long

Out rigger
Make four from 50mm x 50mm timber

450mm
350mm
50mm

Nesting box

A quaint little nest box with a 32mm entrance hole suitable for blue tits, house sparrows, fly catchers and other small birds that prefer to build their nest in an enclosed environment

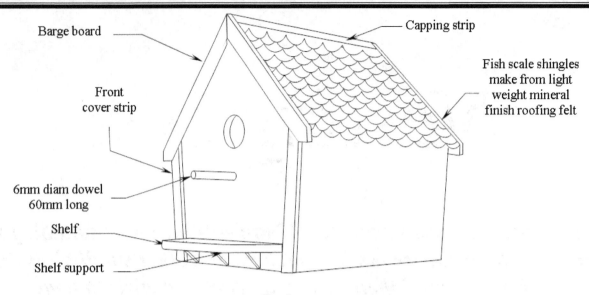

Back
Make one from 9mm thick ply wood

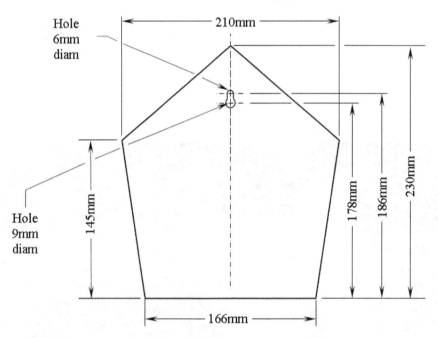

Front
Make one from 9mm thick ply wood

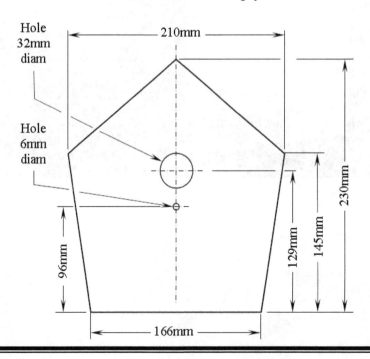

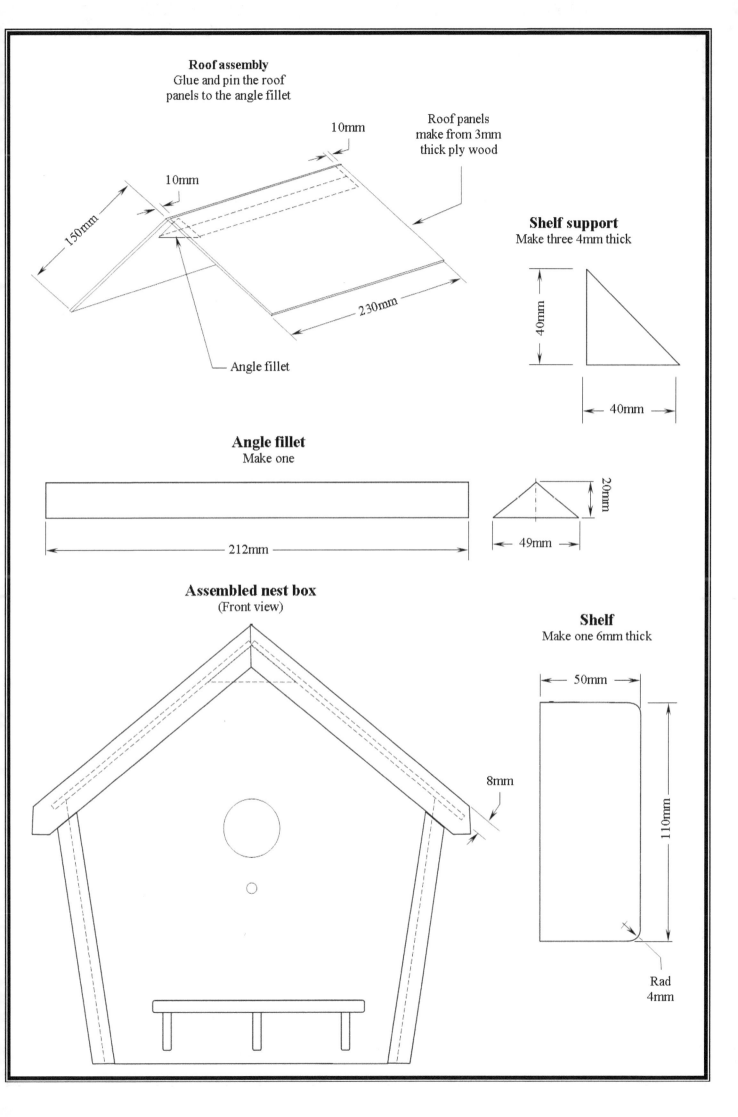

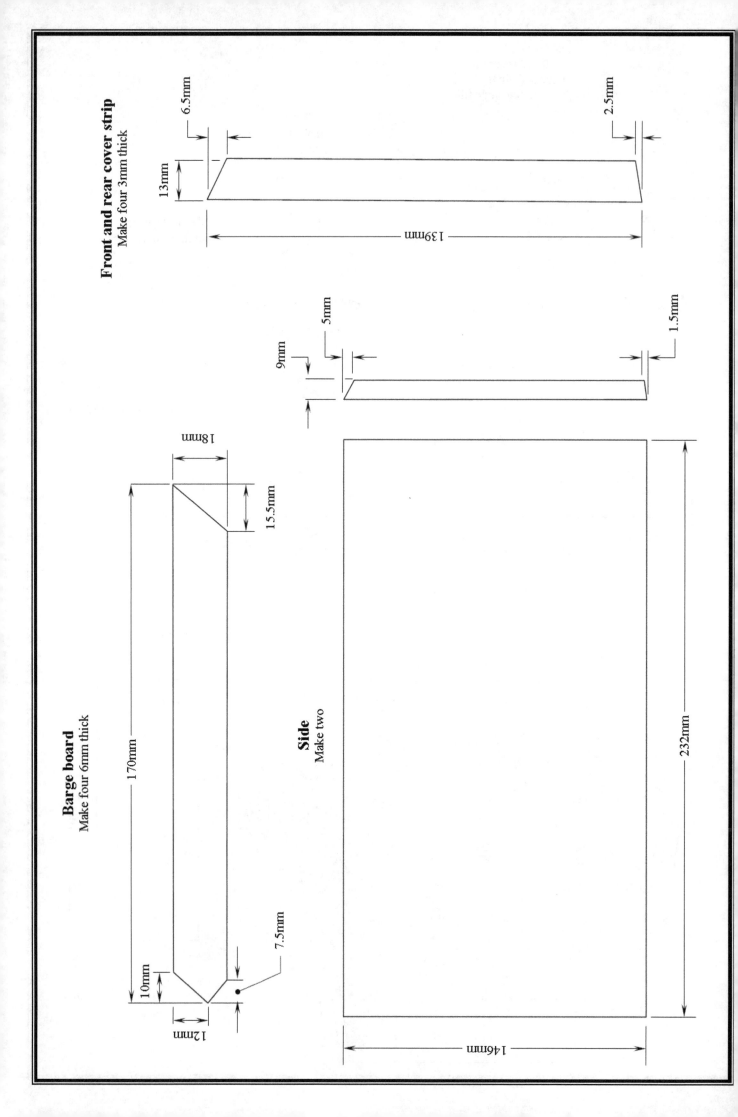

Hanging bird feeder

Bird feeder with three inner perches and two outer perches suitable for all small garden birds this design makes it more difficult for larger scavengers to feed from

Bird feeder assembly diagram

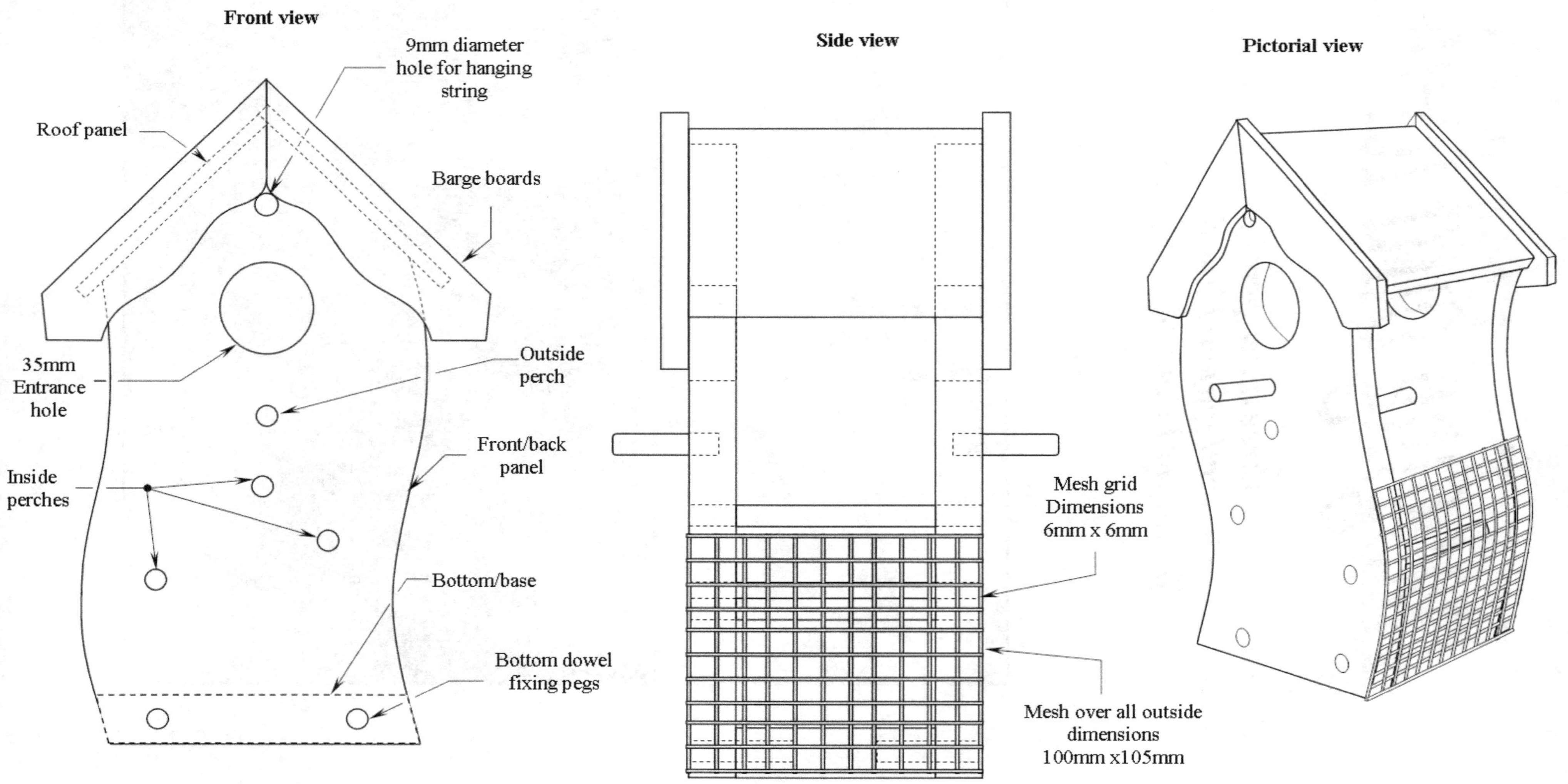

Pictorial view

Side view

Mesh grid Dimensions 6mm x 6mm

Mesh over all outside dimensions 100mm x 105mm

Front view

- 9mm diameter hole for hanging string
- Barge boards
- Outside perch
- Front/back panel
- Bottom/base
- Bottom dowel fixing pegs
- Roof panel
- 35mm Entrance hole
- Inside perches

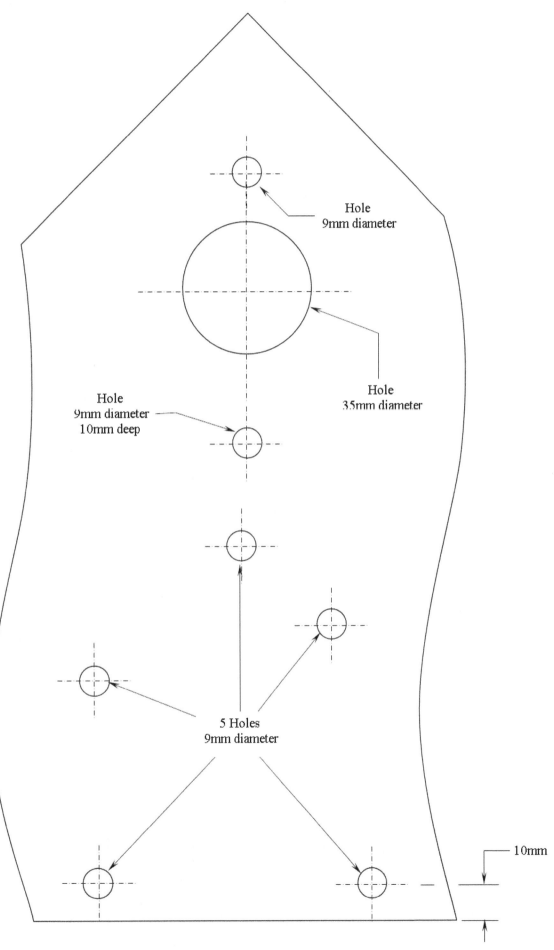

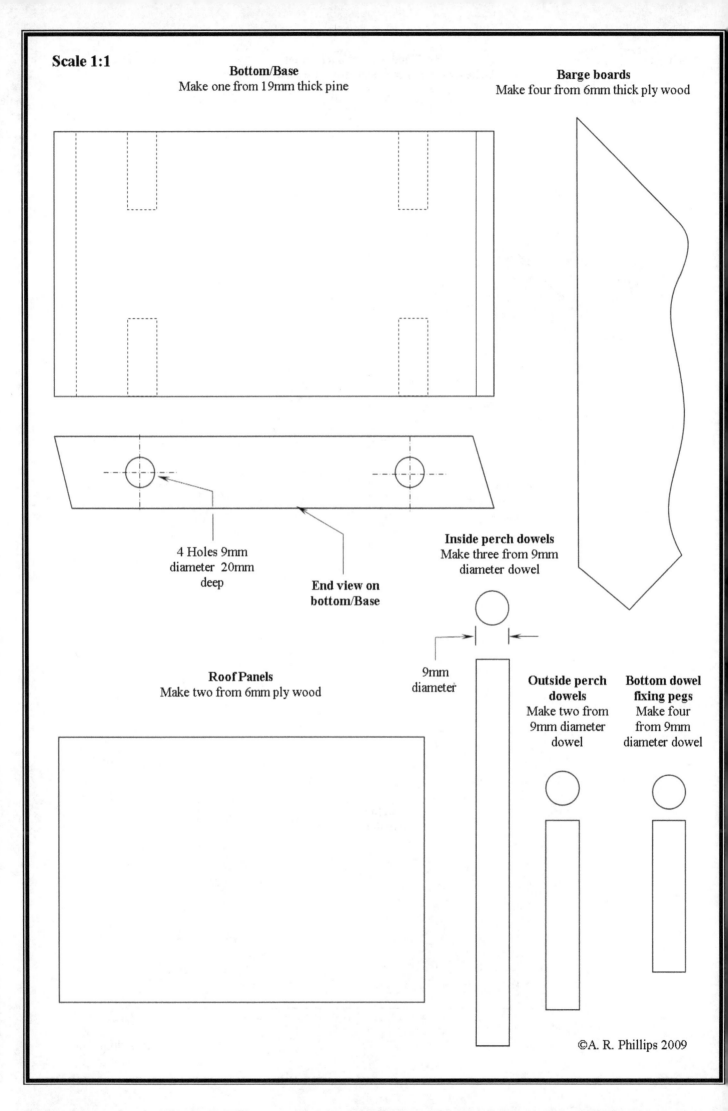

Hedgehog house

This hedgehog house is an ideal winter retreat for hedge hogs and other small mammals that chose to make this its home

Hedgehog house

Hedgehog house floor
Make from 9mm thick ply wood

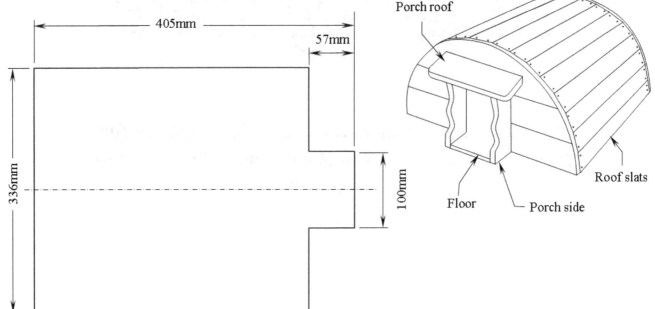

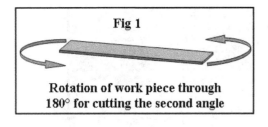

Fig 1
Rotation of work piece through 180° for cutting the second angle

If using a table saw to cut the angles of the Roof slats Tilt the blade of the table saw to 7 degrees then set saw fence to 38mm as measured across the top of the work piece, see diagram below (Table saw set up). Feed the slat through the saw cutting the first angle then turn the slat through 180 degrees (as shown in fig 1.) to cut the second angle NB. The safest method in this case would be to make up the slats in lengths then cut to the requires sizes to fit to roof

Roof Slats (End view)
Make fifteen 368mm long

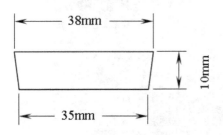

Roof Bottom Slats (End view)
Make two 368mm long

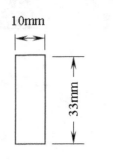

Saw blade set to 7 degrees off the 90° as indicated on most table saws

Table saw set up
For cutting the angles on the roof slats
Saw guard omitted for clarity

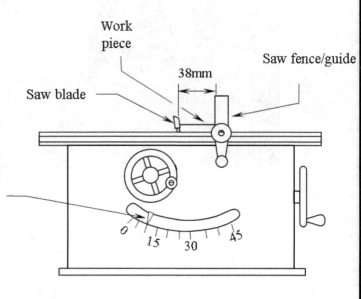

Front/Rear Panels

Make from 150mm x 19mm thick T&G flooring boards cut two pieces 356mm long, glue boards together then follow plan below NB cut out the door way on the front panel only

Recess 10mm wide x 10mm deep cut with a router for cutter details see **Fig 1** below **if a router is unavailable then two pieces of 9mm ply can be used to make this part** cut the first piece to the dimensions shown then cut the other smaller so there is a 10mm deep x 9mm rabbet formed when the two pieces of ply are glued one on top of the other

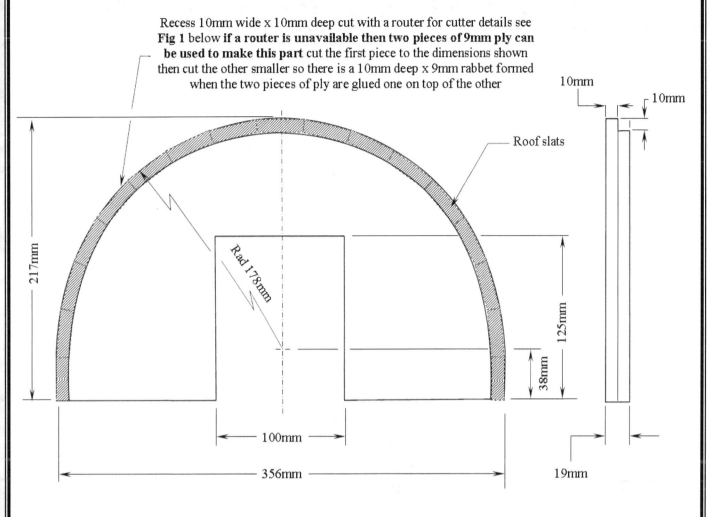

Side of porch
Make two 10mm thick

Porch roof
Make one 10mm thick

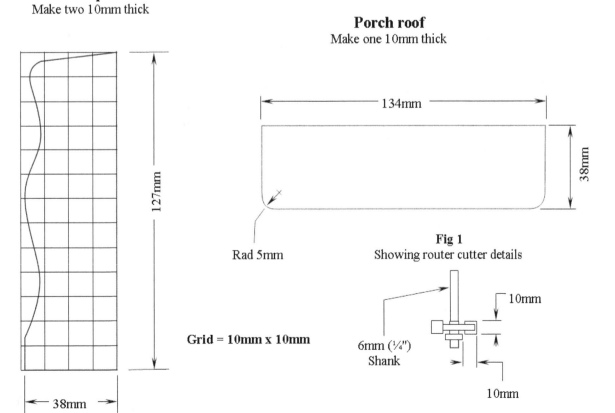

Grid = 10mm x 10mm

Fig 1
Showing router cutter details

6mm (¼") Shank

8ft x 6ft Pent roof shed plan

8ft x 6ft Pent roof garden shed constructed from 50mm x 50mm timber then planked with 150mm feather edged boards the brace and ledge door is of sturdy construction and will house a sturdy pad bolt and lock

© A. R. Phillips 2008

8 x 6 Pent roof shed

Brace and ledge door

1829mm x 762mm (72inches x 30 inches) The door planks are made from 100mm x 16mm tongue and groove boards the braces are from 106mm x 28mm timber (4 1/4" x 1 1/8" door lining) When assembling the door ensure that the door is square by measuring from corner to corner diagonally if the measurements are equal then the door is square if not then adjust accordingly

Roof and floor

Make from 19 mm ply

Three sheets are needed. Cut 635mm off the width of one sheet, this along with a full sheet will do the roof the other full sheet and the remaining off cut will do the floor. Lay out 50mm x 50mm timbers 1829mm long at 400mm centres place the flooring ply on top of these then erect the shed. When making the frame work ensure that the frames are square before nailing the planks on by measuring from corner to corner diagonally, if the measurements are equal then the frames are square if not adjust accordingly. The roof rafters are spaced at 400mm centres then the roof ply is fixed into position. 50mm x 25mm batten is fixed around the top then the roofing felt is nailed to the underside of this. When measuring for the glass allow 4mm less on top and side ways measurements in case of any discrepancies

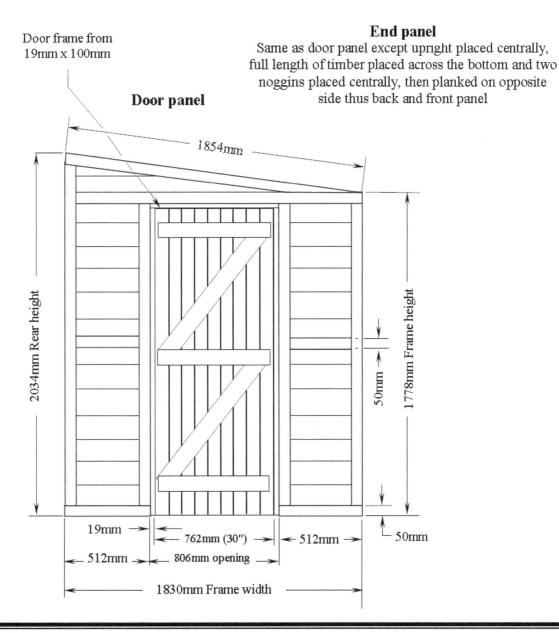

Door frame from 19mm x 100mm

End panel
Same as door panel except upright placed centrally, full length of timber placed across the bottom and two noggins placed centrally, then planked on opposite side thus back and front panel

Door panel

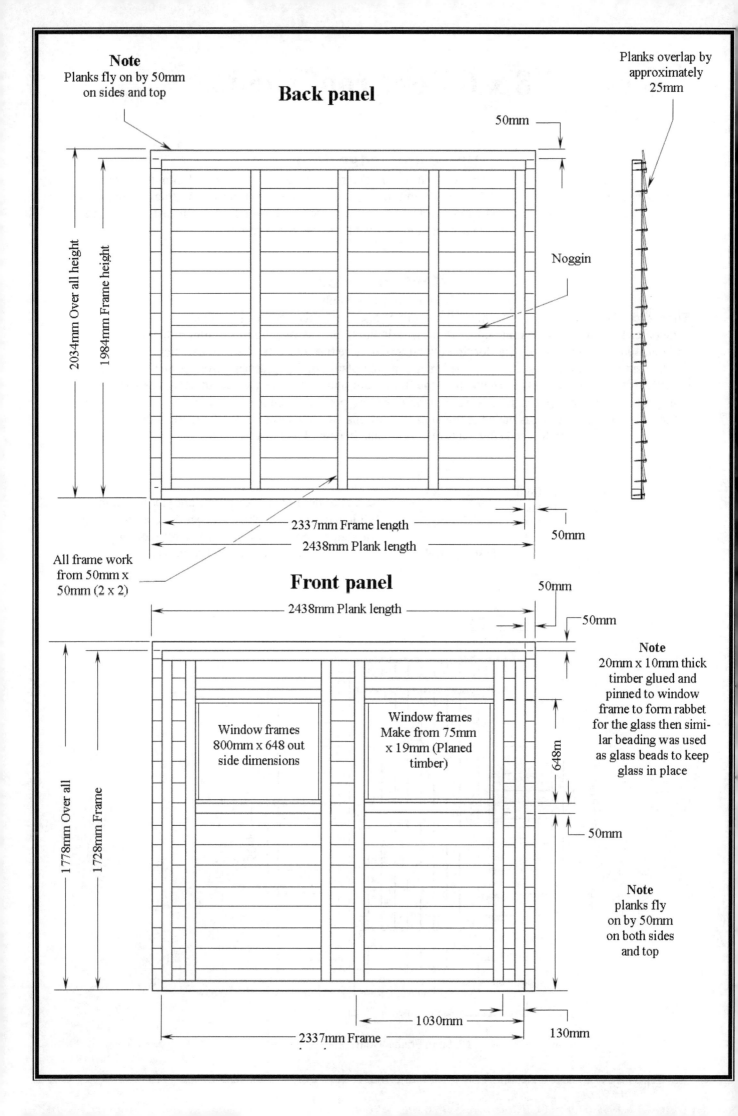

Square well planter

Square well planter this square well planter will enhance the appearance of any garden

Square well planter
10.8cm high x 52.6cm wide (42⅜" x 19 ¾ base width)

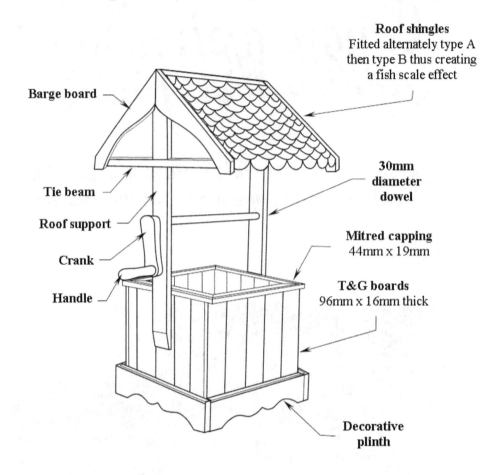

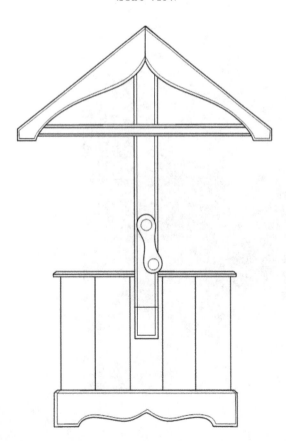

Side view

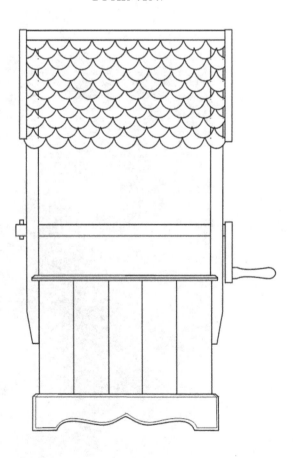

Front view

Well side panel type A
Make two

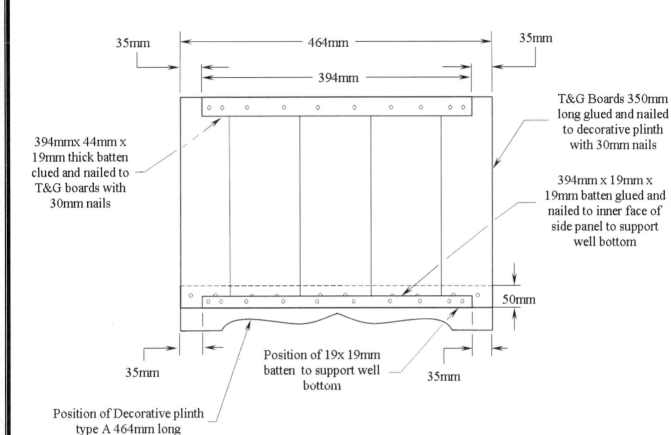

Well side panel type B
Make two

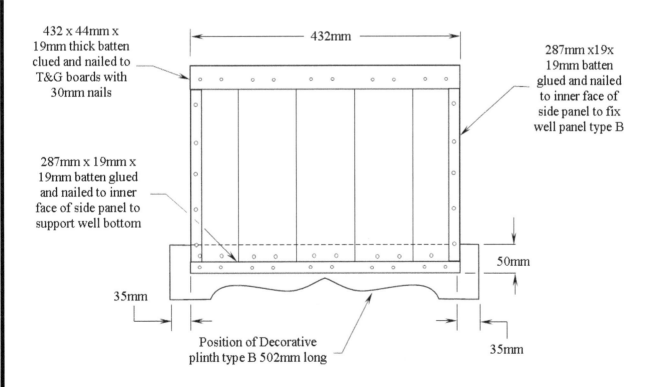

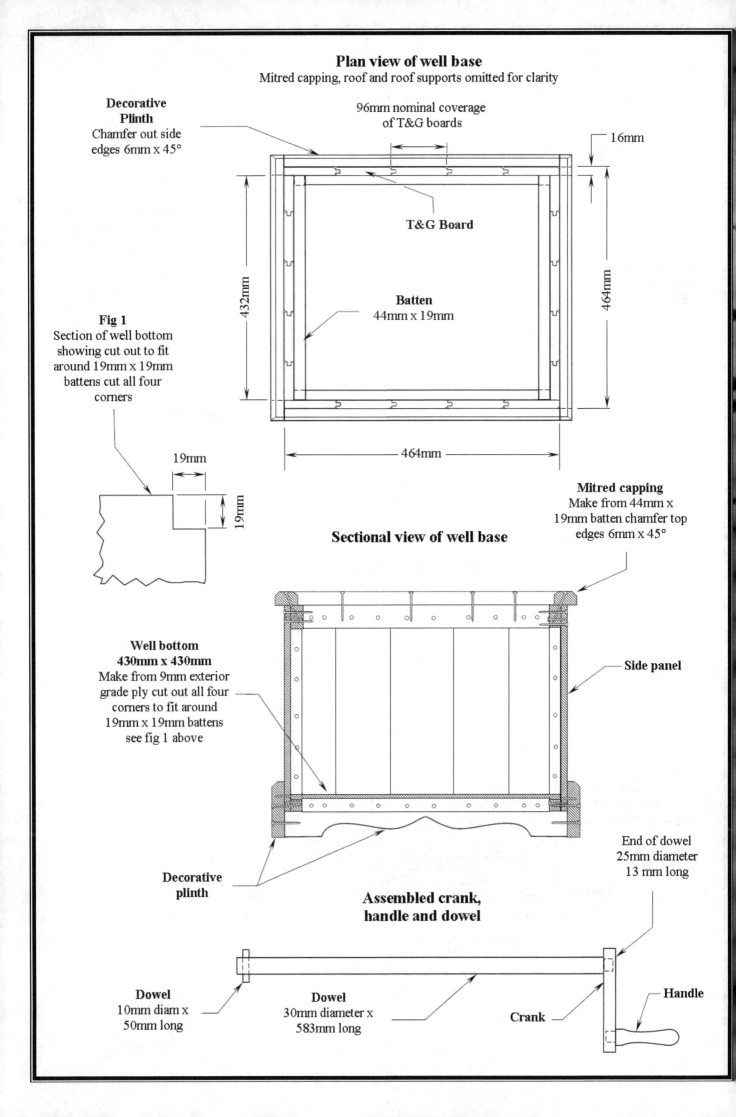

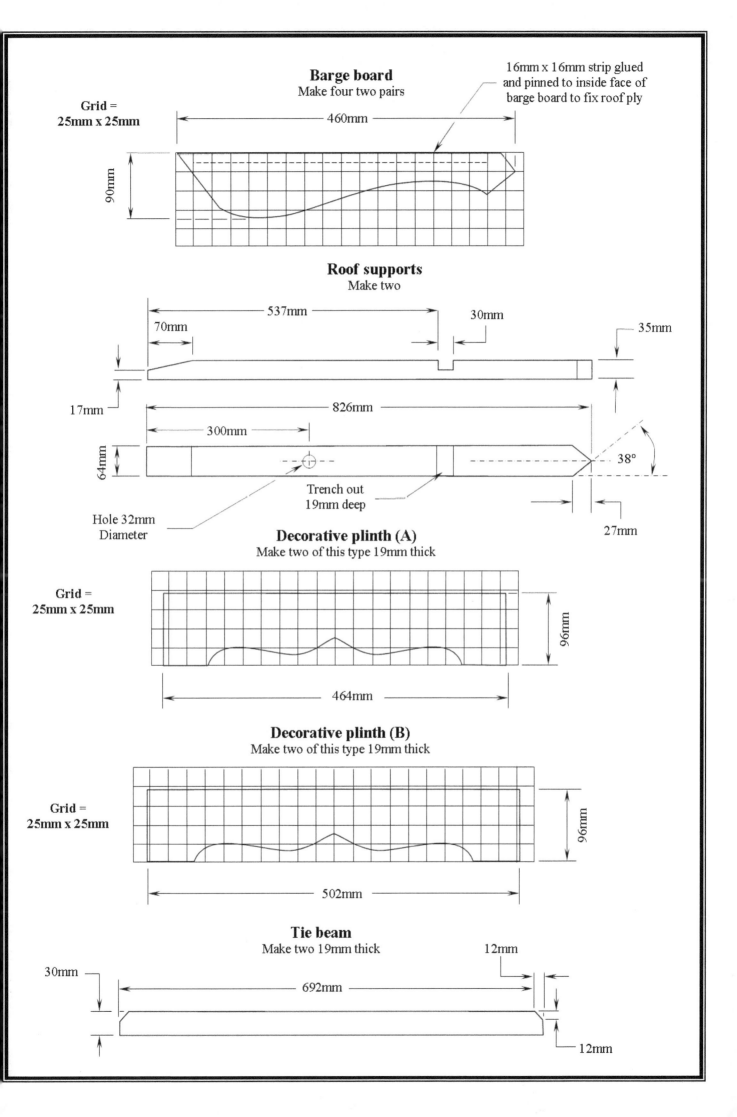

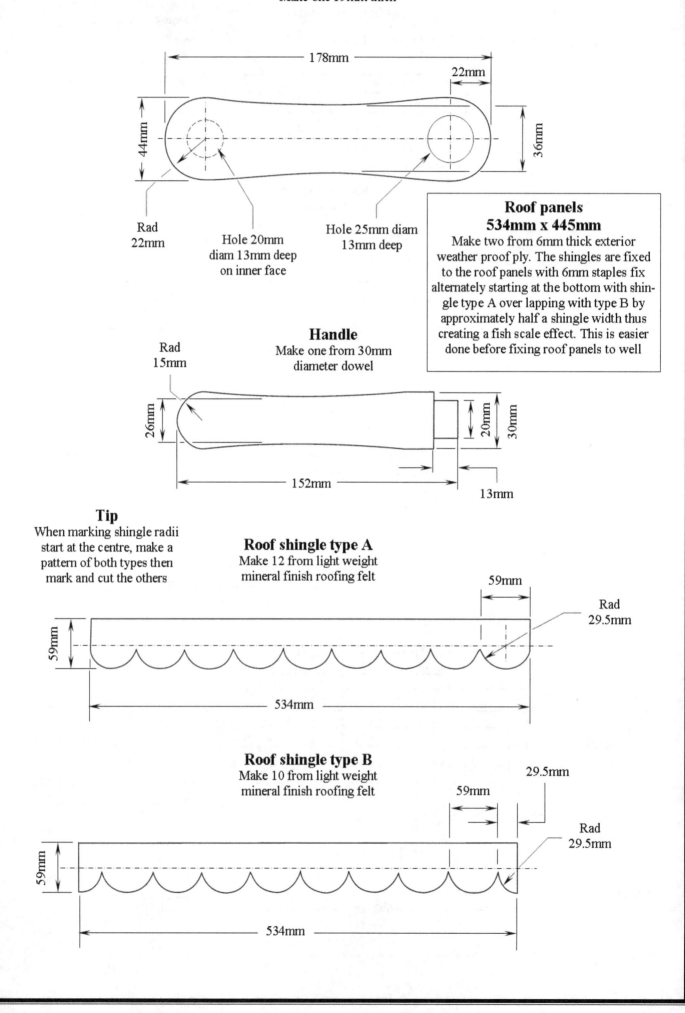

5ft Garden bench

5ft Park type garden bench made using common sized planed timber that can be easily purchased from DIY stores or builders merchants

5ft GARDEN BENCH

Side view of assembled bench

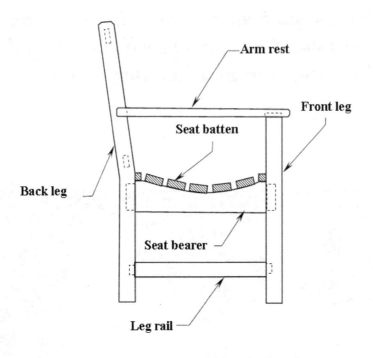

Front view of assembled bench

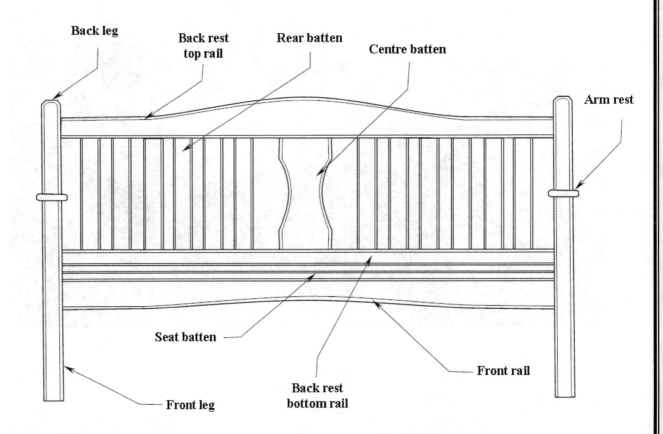

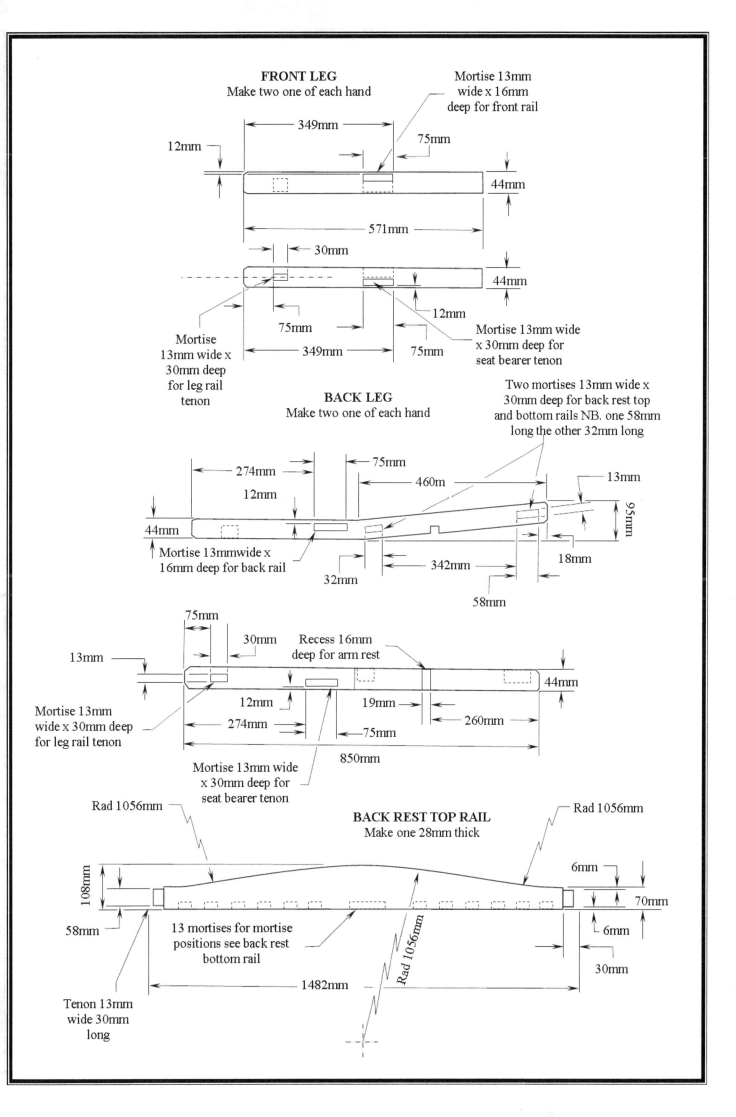

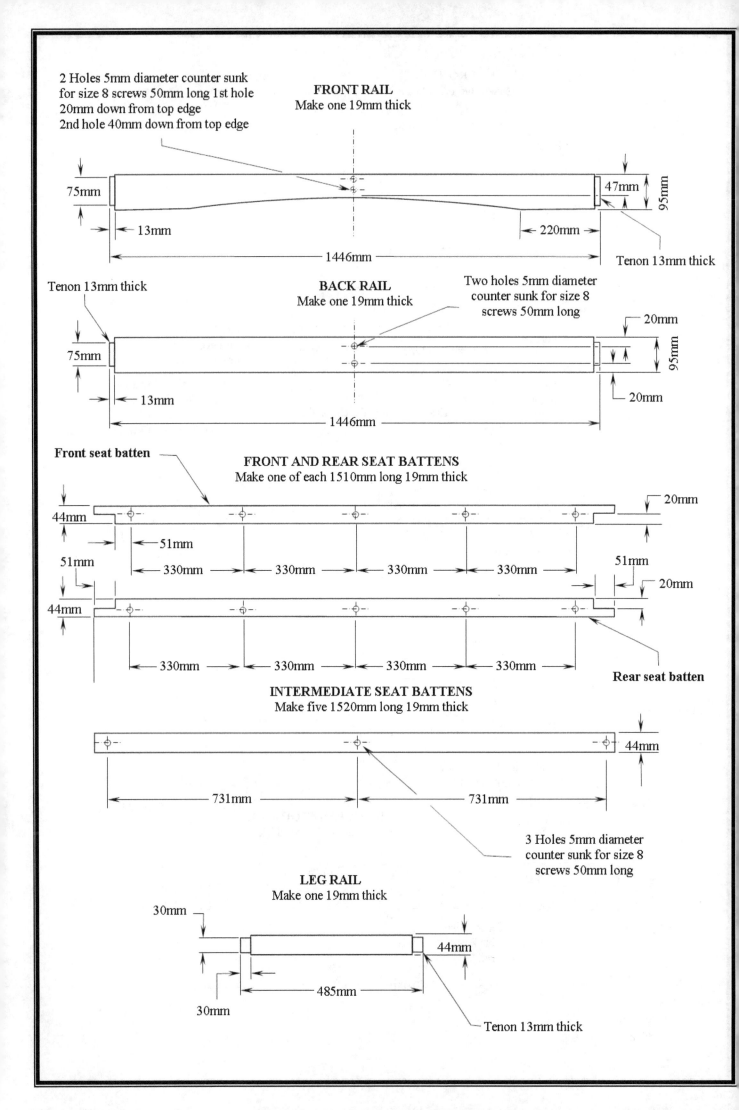

BACK REST BOTTOM RAIL

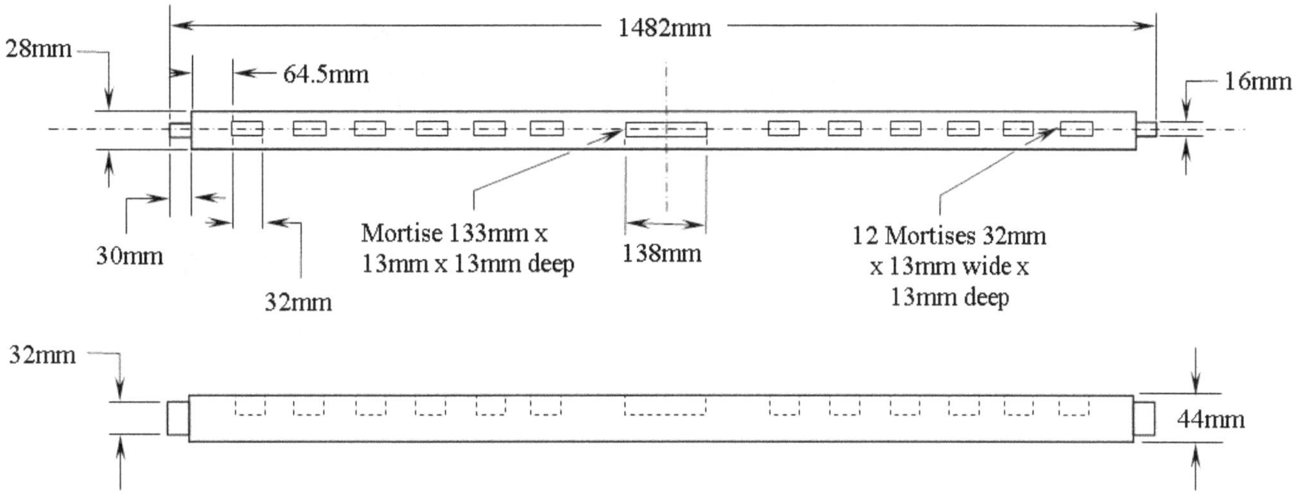

- 28mm
- 1482mm
- 64.5mm
- 16mm
- 30mm
- 32mm
- Mortise 133mm x 13mm x 13mm deep
- 138mm
- 12 Mortises 32mm x 13mm wide x 13mm deep
- 32mm
- 44mm

BACK CENTRE BATTEN

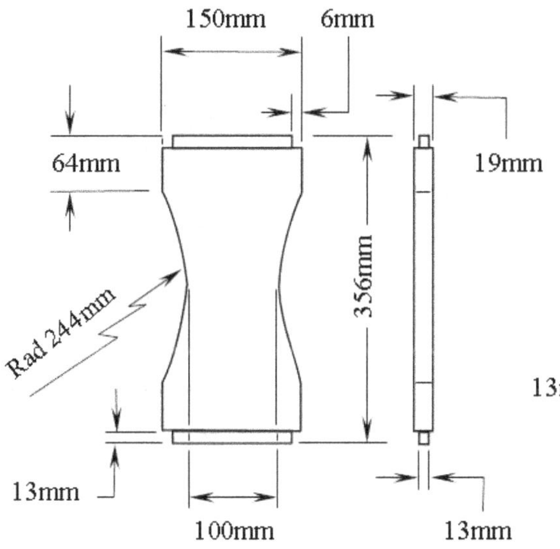

- 150mm
- 6mm
- 64mm
- 19mm
- 356mm
- Rad 244mm
- 13mm
- 100mm
- 13mm

BACK REST BATTEN
Make 12

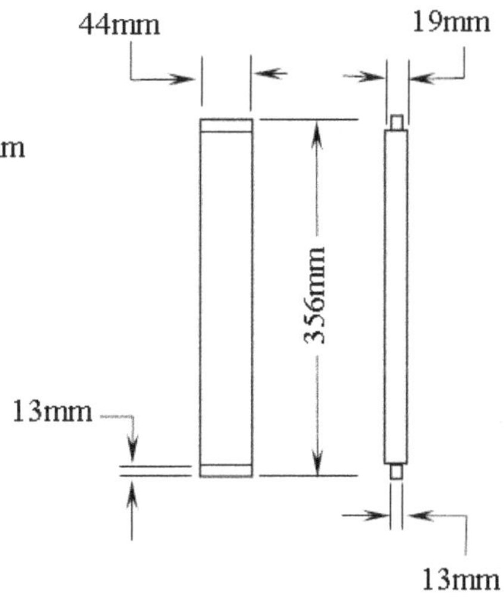

- 44mm
- 19mm
- 356mm
- 13mm
- 13mm

ARM REST
Make two 19mm thick

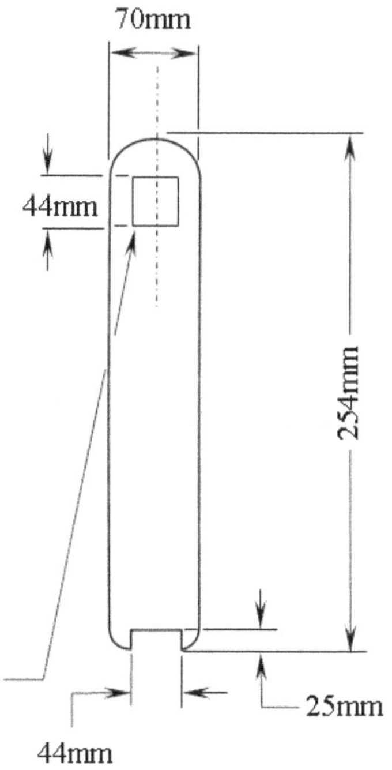

- 70mm
- 44mm
- 254mm
- 44mm x 44mm Recess 6mm deep to fit arm to front leg
- 44mm
- 25mm

SEAT BEARER
Make two 28mm thick

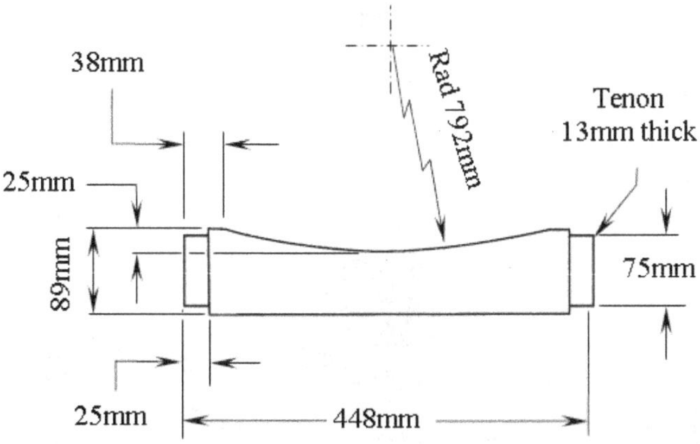

- 38mm
- Rad 792mm
- Tenon 13mm thick
- 25mm
- 89mm
- 75mm
- 25mm
- 448mm

CENTRE SEAT BEARER
Make one 28mm thick

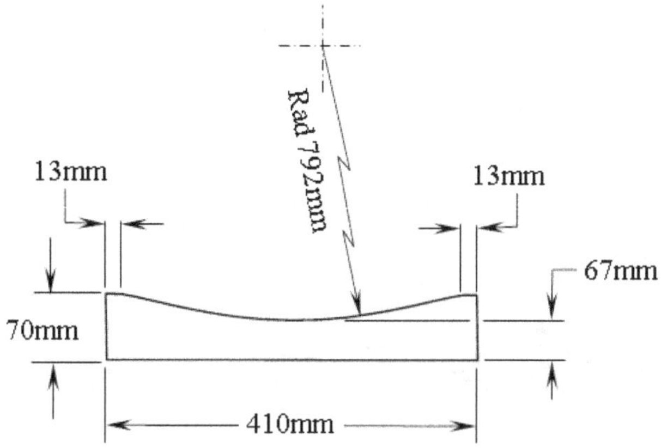

- 13mm
- Rad 792mm
- 13mm
- 67mm
- 70mm
- 410mm

Rocking recliner

Three positional rocking recliner with magazine rack and rear wheels for ease of carriage to a sunny or shaded position

1. Upright position

2. Semi reclined position

3. Fully reclined position

This is the garden seat that inspired the idea for a three positional garden rocking recliner

Rocking recliner in the upright position

Rocking recliner in the semi reclined position

Rocking recliner in the fully reclined position

Close up view of the back rest brace set to the upright position also showing the rear wheels and rear reinforcing pieces

Close up view of the magazine rack

Both side panels with reinforcing pieces glued and screwed. First fit rear cross member and front magazine batten ensuring that the distances between rear cross member and front magazine rack batten are equal then ensure that the diagonal measurements between rear cross member and front magazine rack batten are equal (Squaring up)

The rest of the magazine rack battens and the central cross member fitted

When fitting the seat battens first temporarily fix the front and rear batten there is approximately a 20mm gap between the rear back rest bottom batten and the rear seat batten when the back rest is in the upright position intermediate battens are equidistant

When the back rest in in the fully reclined position the bottom back rest batten and the rear seat batten should be level

Back rest and battens ,the three middle battens are positioned strategically for upright, semi reclined and fully reclined positions when all parts are assemble, and act as stops for the back rest brace, all parts to the back rest are glued and screwed using exterior weather proof wood working adhesive

Metal rubbing strips 35mm wide x 3mm thick drilled counter sunk and ready for fitting after the rocker has been painted.

Back rest brace all parts glued and screwed (Decorative bottom brace not shown in this picture)

Finished rocker shown in the semi reclined position also showing the rear wheels and the magazine rack

Plan view on Rocker, seat battens, back rest and back rest brace omitted for clarity

- Rocker side rear reinforcement piece
- Lateral cross member
- Lateral cross member
- Lateral cross member making up part of the magazine rack
- Magazine rack front batten
- Magazine rack stop glued and screwed to magazine rack front batten make from 44mm x 16mm thick timber
- 150mm diameter wheels fixed with 10mm steel stub axles and spring caps
- Top lateral cross member

Side view on rocking recliner

- Backrest battens
- Three back rest stop battens
- Arm rests
- Seat battens
- Back rest adjustable brace
- Top lateral cross member
- Rocker side bottom reinforcement piece
- Magazine rack and stops

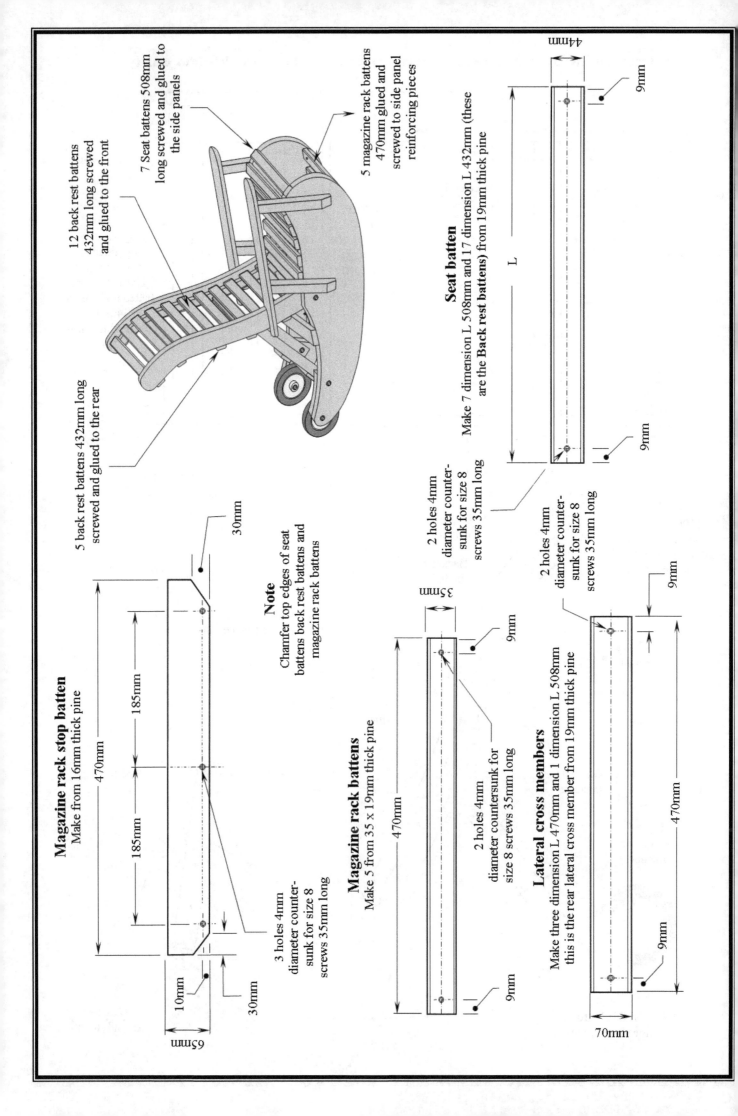

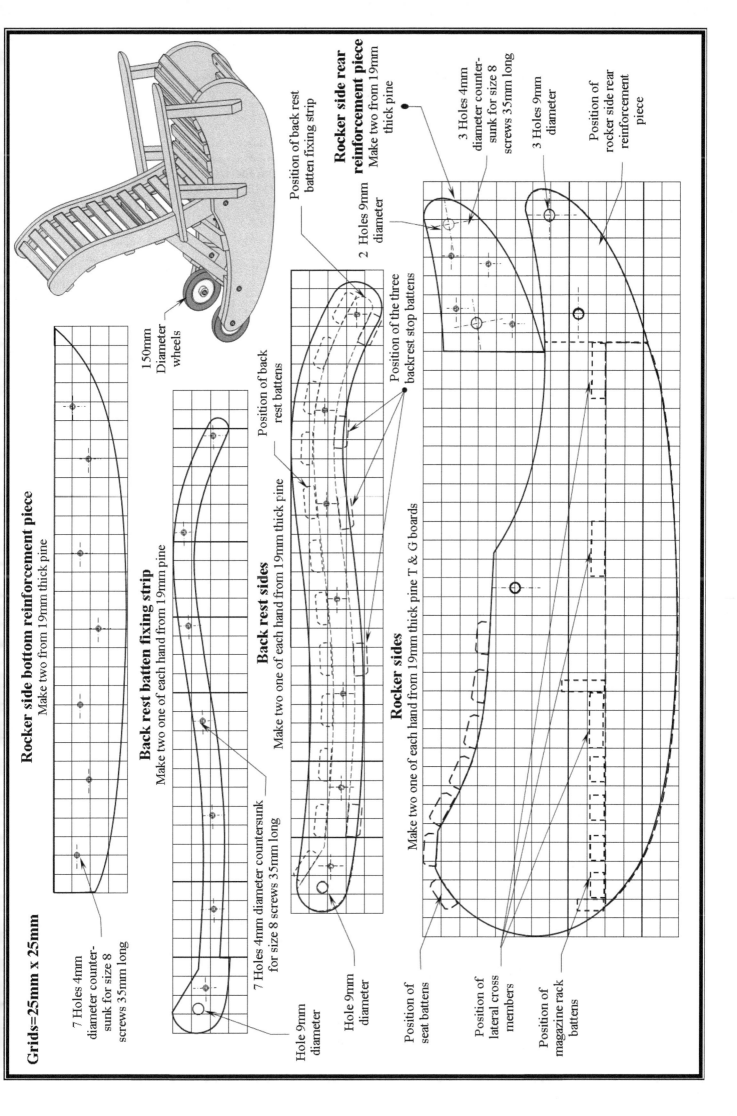

Back Rest Adjustable Brace Construction and Assembly

Post/Strut
Make two from 19mm thick pine

- 30.5mm
- 14.5mm
- Hole 9mm diameter
- 45mm
- 44mm
- 44mm
- 412mm

Reinforcing Block
Make two from 19mm thick pine

- 45mm
- 20mm
- 2 holes 4mm diameter countersunk for size 8 screws 35mm long
- 44mm
- 20mm
- 90mm
- Hole 9mm diameter

Top Cross Brace and Tie beam
Make from 19mm thick pine

- Hole 4mm diameter countersunk for size 8 screws 50mm long
- 432mm
- 10mm
- 44mm

Bottom Decorative Cross Brace
Make two from 19mm thick pine

- 20mm
- 432mm
- 75mm
- 10mm
- 30mm
- 6 Holes 4mm diameter countersunk for size 8 screws 45mm long

Back Rest Adjustable Brace Assembly Diagram

- Top Cross Brace
- Post/Strut
- Reinforcing Block
- Tie beam
- 45mm Size 8 Countersunk screws
- Bottom Decorative Cross Brace

- Fully reclined stop batten
- Semi reclined stop batten
- Upright position stop batten
- Back Rest Adjustable Brace
- Rear lateral cross member

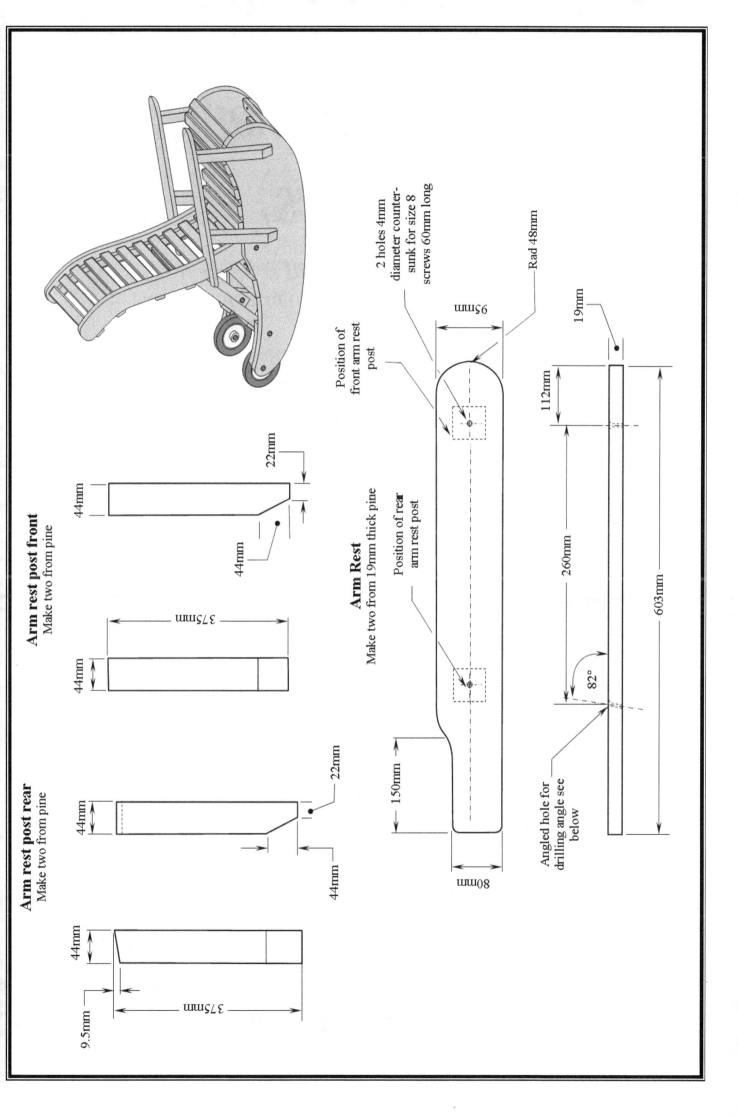

Round well planter (18 sides)

This wishing well planter will enhance the appearance of any garden, patio or conservatory

Start by assembling the eighteen segments in pairs. Apply a liberal amount of weather proof wood working adhesive to the surfaces to be joined then drive a staple between the join with a heavy duty staple tacker (as shown in picture to the left) then assemble the pairs in pairs and so on, excess glue can be planed or sanded off after the 6mm plywood base is fitted

The posts tie beam and barge boards need to be assembled then the 16mm x 16mm strip wood that the 7mm thick T & G roof is pinned to, can be cut to fit, also showing the other post tie beam and barge boards ready for assembly and the well bottom half with the 9mm plywood base fitted all cleaned up and sanded ready for the skirting and capping to be fitted

Well bottom skirting and capping fitted. The capping is then notched out to take posts

Handle crank and dowel assembled and rope drum cleaned up and sanded down

Close up showing rope drum and the disc to which the drum slats are glued and pinned, also showing post, tie beam, barge boards and T & G roof boards

Roof boards, rope drum, handle and dowel fitted, then the ridge décor was added making the overall structure aesthetically pleasing to the eye

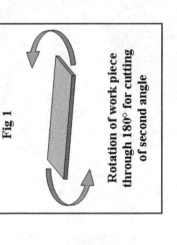

Fig 1

Rotation of work piece through 180° for cutting of second angle

Well segments

Make 18 from 67mm wide x 16mm thick x 286mm long planks

If using a table saw to cut the angles of the planks/segments, Tilt the blade of the table saw to 10 degrees then set saw fence to 67mm as measured across the top of the work piece (As shown in diagram below, Table saw set up for segment angles). Feed the plank through the saw cutting the first angle then turn the plank through 180 degrees (as shown in fig.1) feed through the saw again cutting the second angle. Repeat the afore mentioned process for the 17 remaining planks

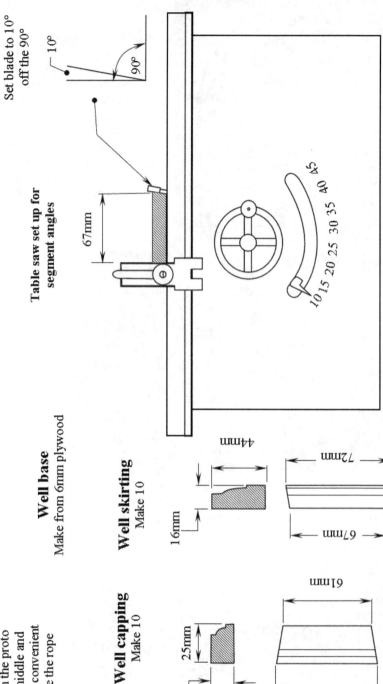

Set blade to 10° off the 90°

Table saw set up for segment angles

Well base
Make from 6mm plywood

Well skirting
Make 10

44mm
16mm
72mm
67mm

Well capping
Make 10

25mm
16mm
61mm
70mm

Well Segment (end view)
Make eighteen 286mm long

67mm
16mm
61mm

Assembling the planks

When assembling the planks, assemble in pairs then the pairs in pairs and so on. Heavy duty, staples are driven in to bridge the join (see photo and assembled segments diagram below) On the proto type banding was wrapped around the well at the top middle and bottom to strengthen the base and prevent spread then a convenient sized tub was filled with earth and placed inside before the rope drum was fitted

Plan view on assembled segments

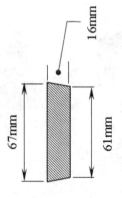

Heavy duty staples bridging join see photo

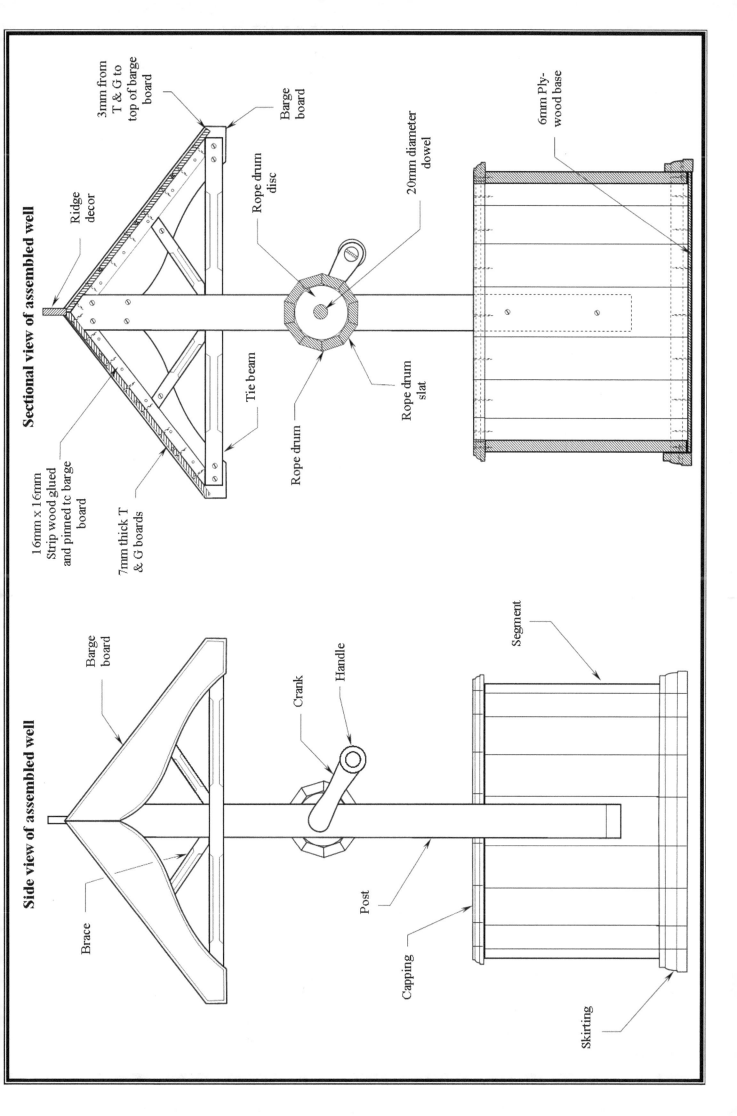

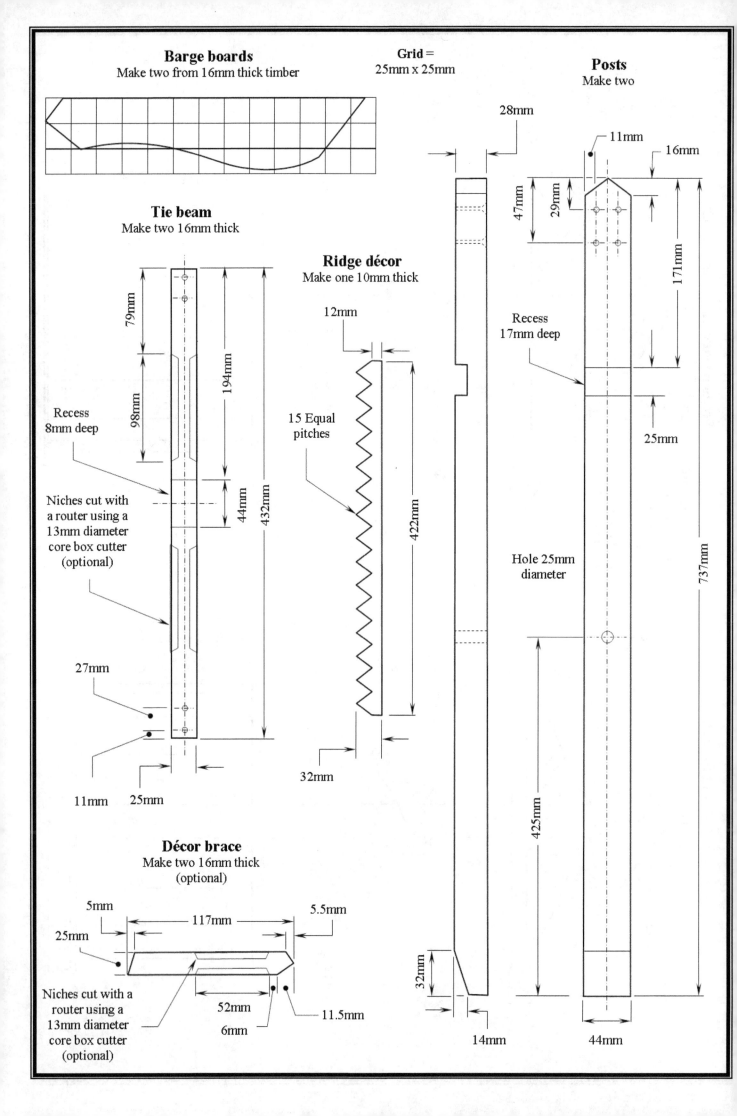

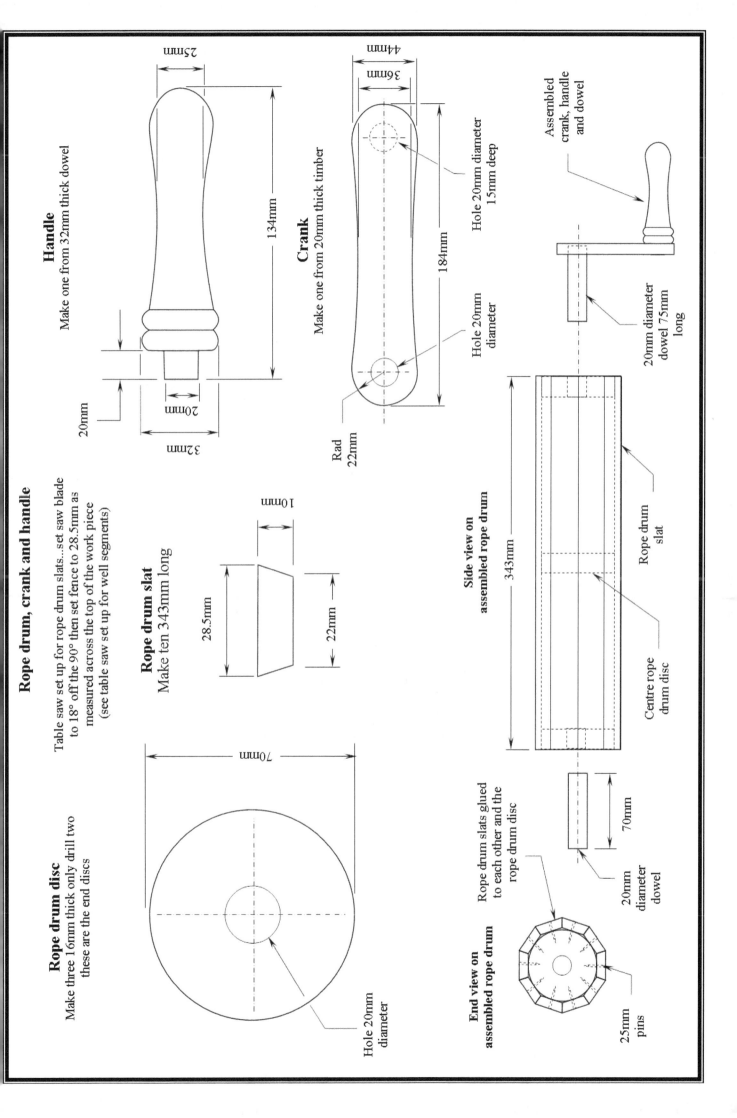

Toy and Model projects

Clock puzzle

Learn to count and tell the time clock puzzle

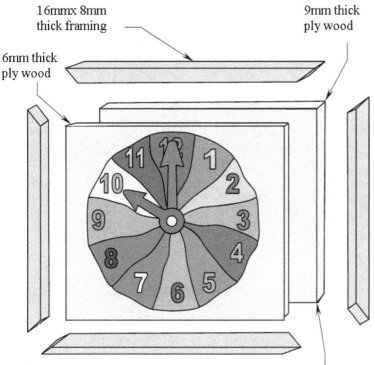

- 16mm x 8mm thick framing
- 9mm thick ply wood
- 6mm thick ply wood
- A 9mm diameter hole is drilled through the centre of the 9mm thick plywood

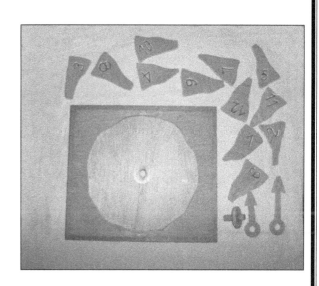

Clock hands
Make from 6mm thick plywood

Tip
Drill the holes first then cut to shape thus avoiding any drill bit break out

Tip
When drilling the holes drill half way through from one side then drill all the way through from the other side

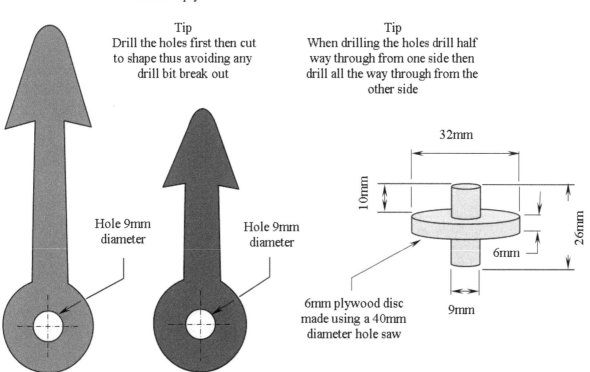

- Hole 9mm diameter
- Hole 9mm diameter
- 32mm
- 10mm
- 26mm
- 6mm
- 9mm
- 6mm plywood disc made using a 40mm diameter hole saw

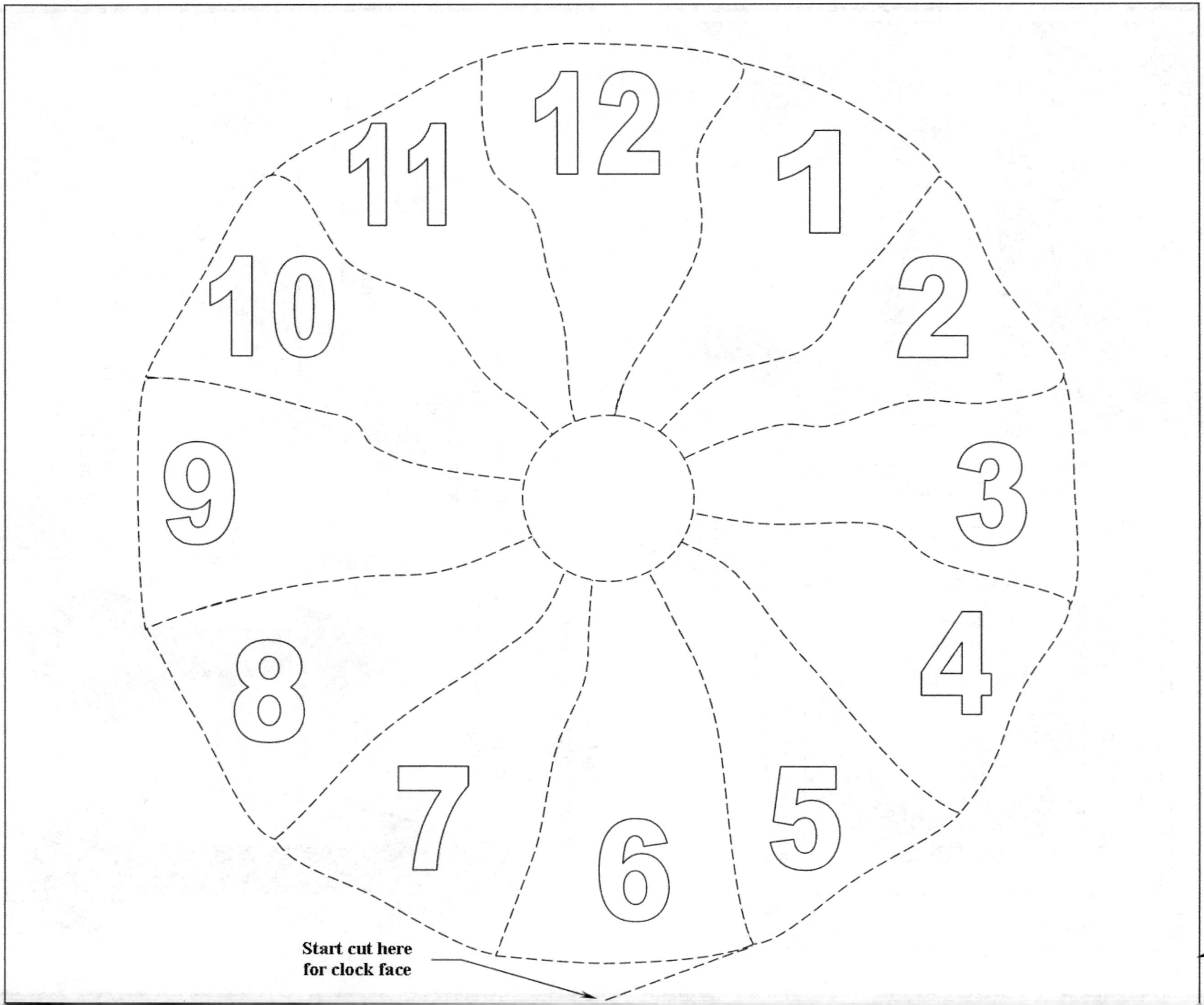

Drill the 9mm diameter hole through the centre of both pieces of 6mm plywood and 9mm plywood then cut out the clock face from the 6mm plywood starting the cut as indicated on the drawing, once this is done then the segments can be cut and sanded to remove saw marks the remaining off cut of 6mm plywood is then glued to the 9mm plywood and the starting saw cut is filled and sanded

Tip

When drilling a through hole with a spade bit, drill from one side until the bit protrudes then turn the work piece over and carefully drill all the way through thus no drill break out and a cleaner hole

6mm thick plywood

Start cut here for clock face

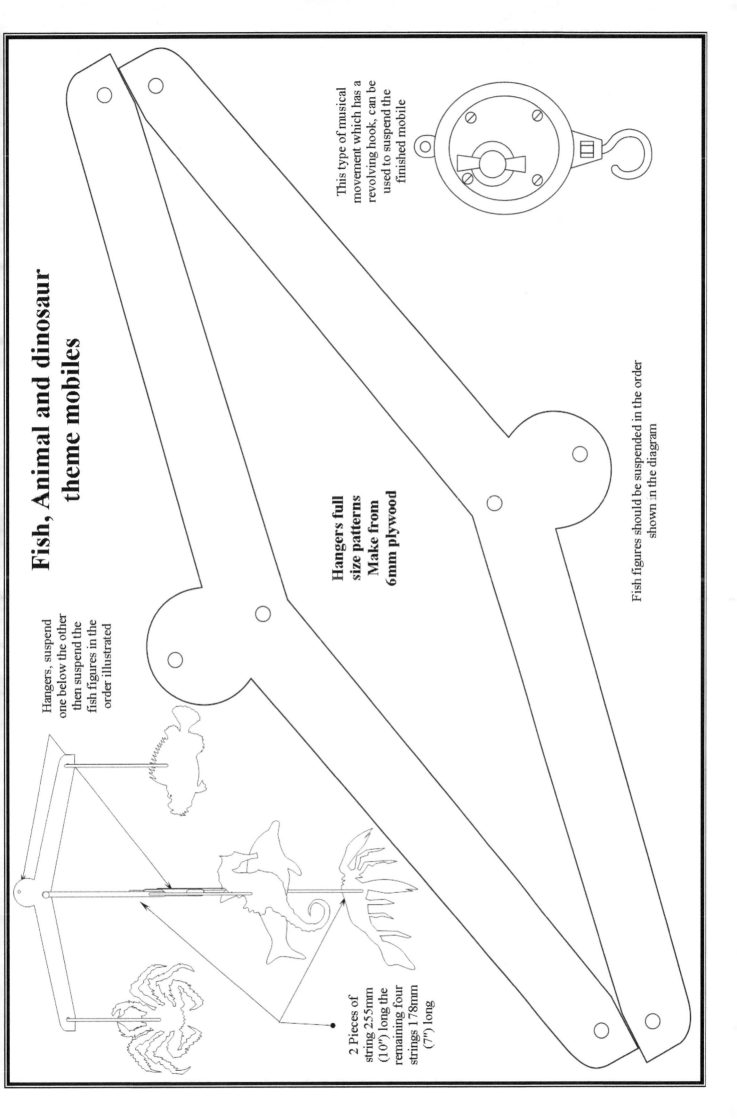

Toy Wheel barrow or planter

Children's wheel barrow can also be made as a planter
860mm long x 380mm wide

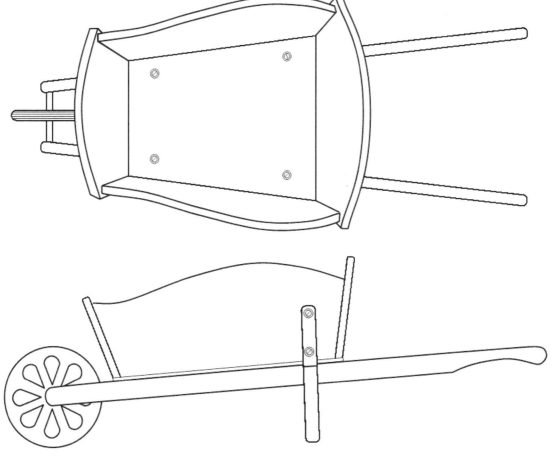

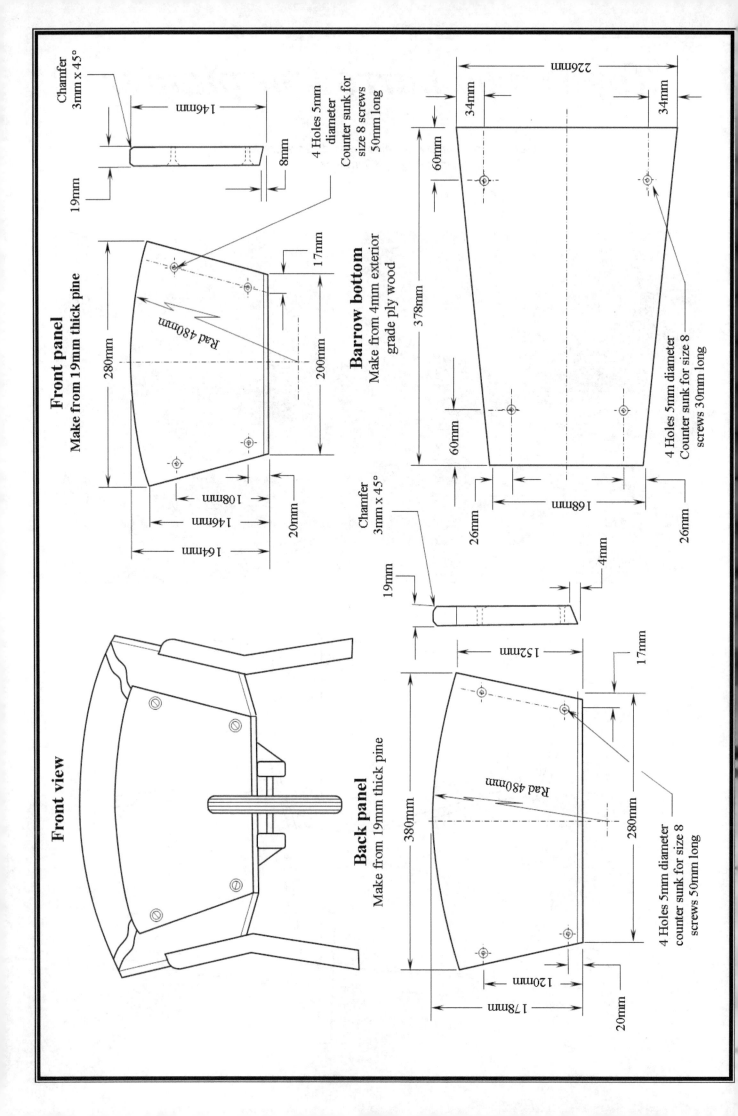

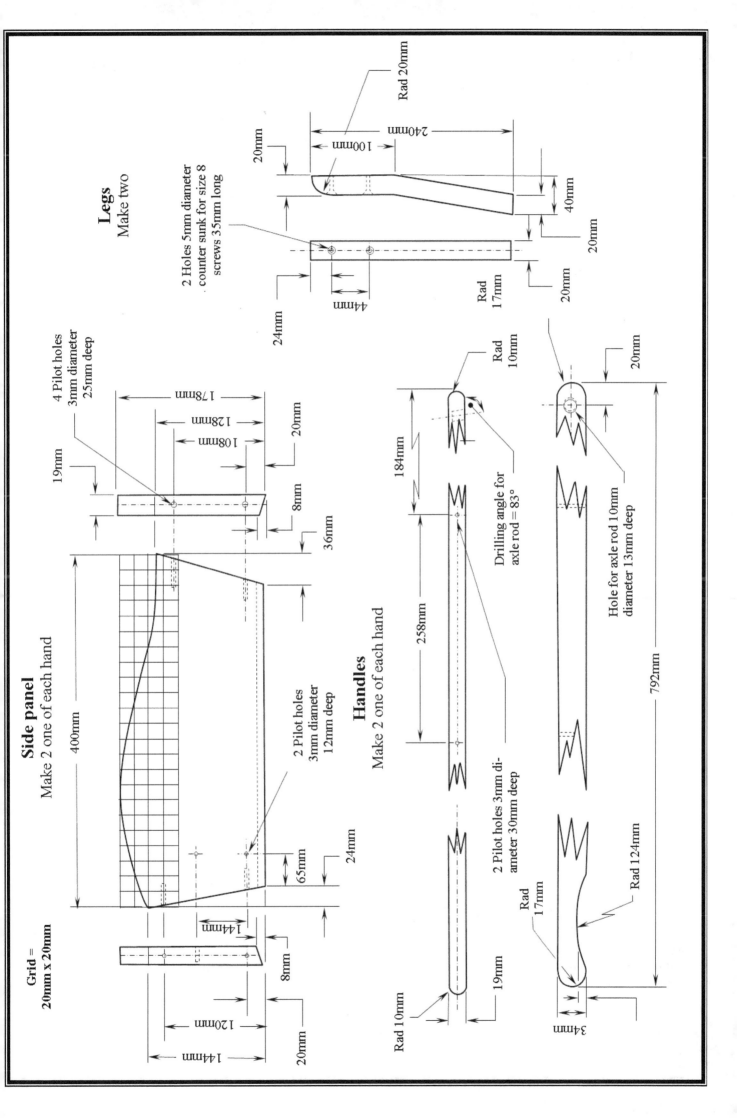

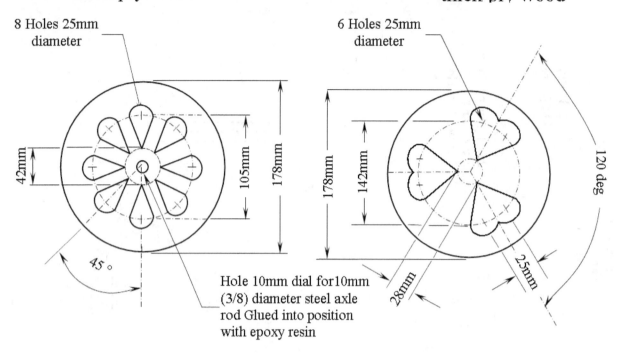
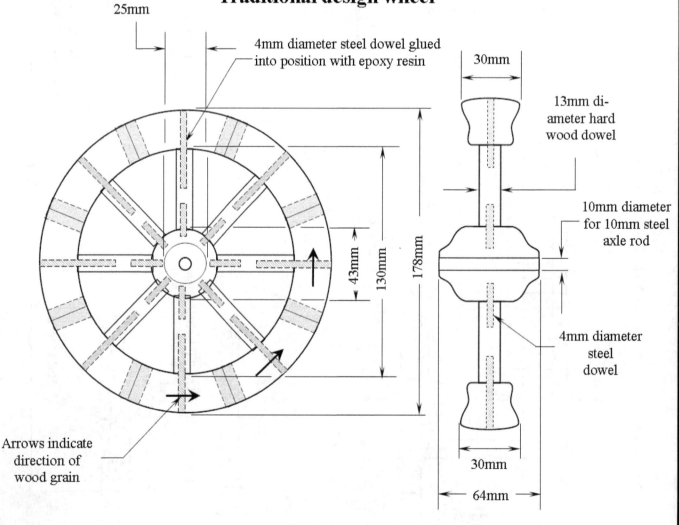

Pine Piano and Stool

This delightful pine piano was designed with an electronic key board in mind and was fitted with a children's electronic key board then key board spacers were cut to fill in the gap either end to fit a key board that' had dimensions of 150mm (5⅞") wide x 660mm(26") long x (2") high but room for alterations to take a wider keyboard have been allowed for.

Close up of the cut down stair spindle which is fixed at the top with a 4mm diameter steel dowel 20mm long made from a 75mm (3") nail and screwed from the under side of the foot with a size 8 screw 50mm long

This picture shows the keyboard spacers adapted to accommodate the keyboard also showing the 10mm x 10mm fixing strip pinned to the rear batten. The keyboard lid hinge batten is fixed to the top of the rear batten with dowels. The key board holder front batten is fixed to the keyboard holder ends with 6mm diameter dowels and the keyboard rear batten is screwed

This particular keyboard was inset so the keys were level with the front batten

N.B

Key board holder can be made wider if necessary by cutting the grooves that house the back panel further back, remember to purchase a suitable key board and make the key board holder to suit it is wise to test fit all parts before any gluing up takes place

Finished piano with key board fitted so the piano keys are level with the front batten

This picture shows the piano top fixing block

The prototype was made from varnish and stain grade flooring boards 19mm thick for the sides and stool and 7mm thick T&G v groove boards for the back panel

Key board holder pictorial assembly diagram, lid and bottom omitted for clarity

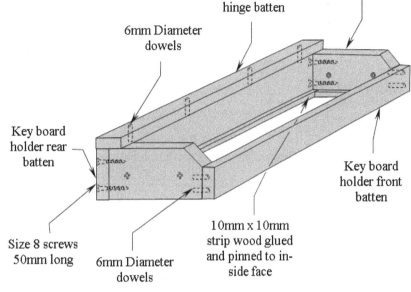

- Piano lid hinge batten
- Key board holder end
- 6mm Diameter dowels
- Key board holder rear batten
- Size 8 screws 50mm long
- 6mm Diameter dowels
- Key board holder front batten
- 10mm x 10mm strip wood glued and pinned to inside face

Front view on piano

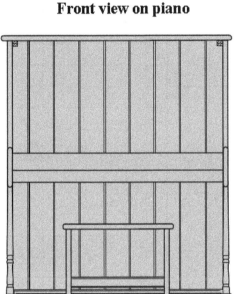

Key board holder assembly diagram

Piano and Stool Assembly diagram

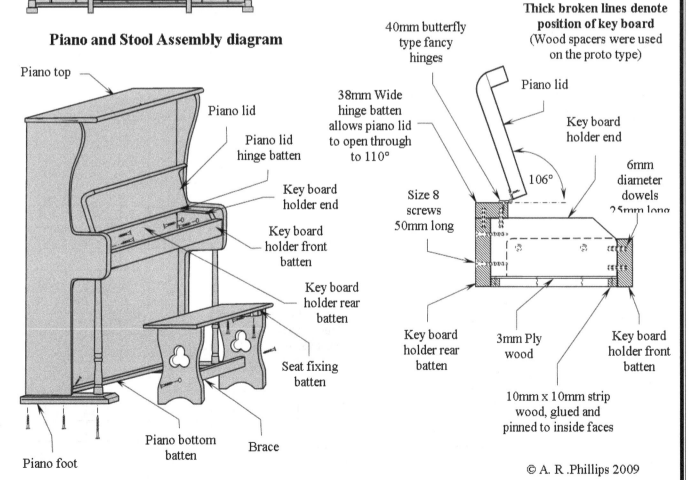

- Piano top
- Piano lid
- Piano lid hinge batten
- Key board holder end
- Key board holder front batten
- Key board holder rear batten
- Seat fixing batten
- Piano foot
- Piano bottom batten
- Brace

- 40mm butterfly type fancy hinges
- 38mm Wide hinge batten allows piano lid to open through to 110°
- Size 8 screws 50mm long
- Key board holder rear batten
- 3mm Ply wood
- 10mm x 10mm strip wood, glued and pinned to inside faces

Thick broken lines denote position of key board (Wood spacers were used on the proto type)

- Piano lid
- Key board holder end
- 106°
- 6mm diameter dowels 25mm long
- Key board holder front batten

© A. R. Phillips 2009

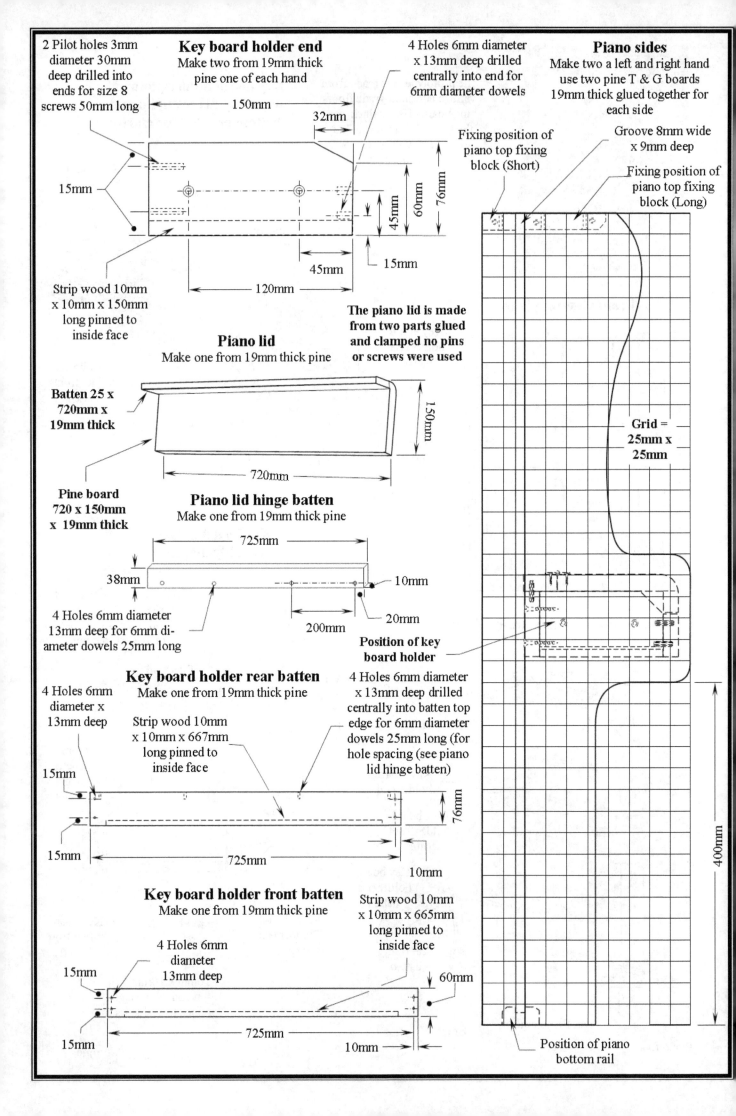

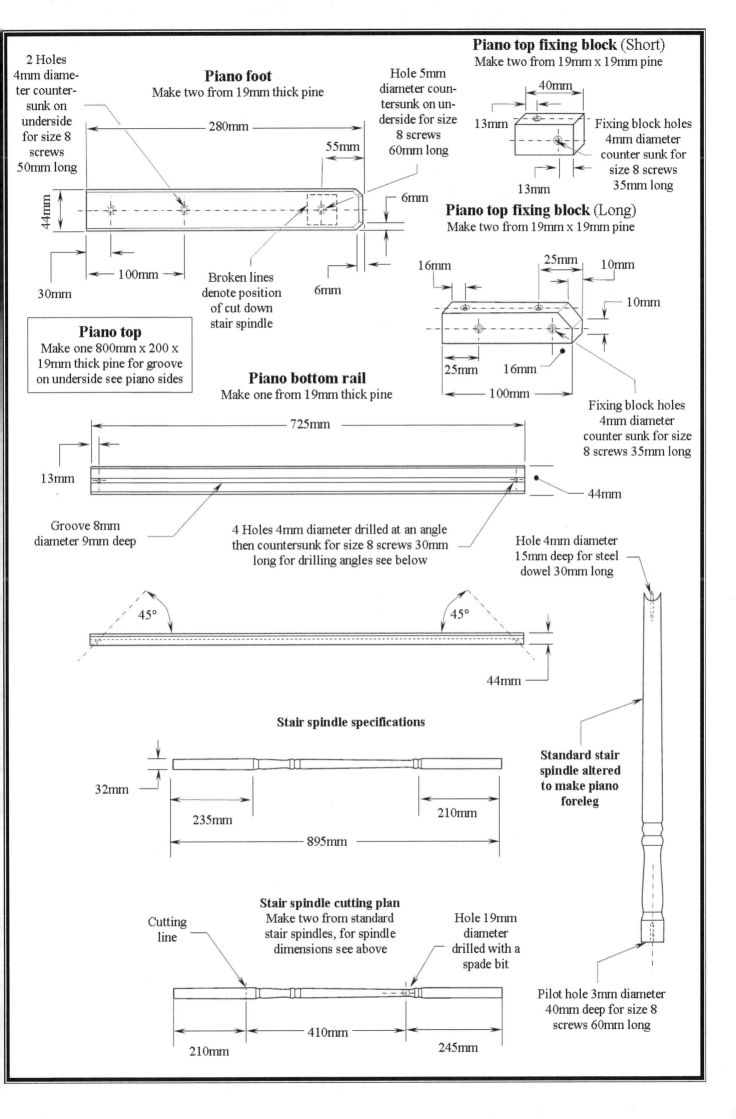

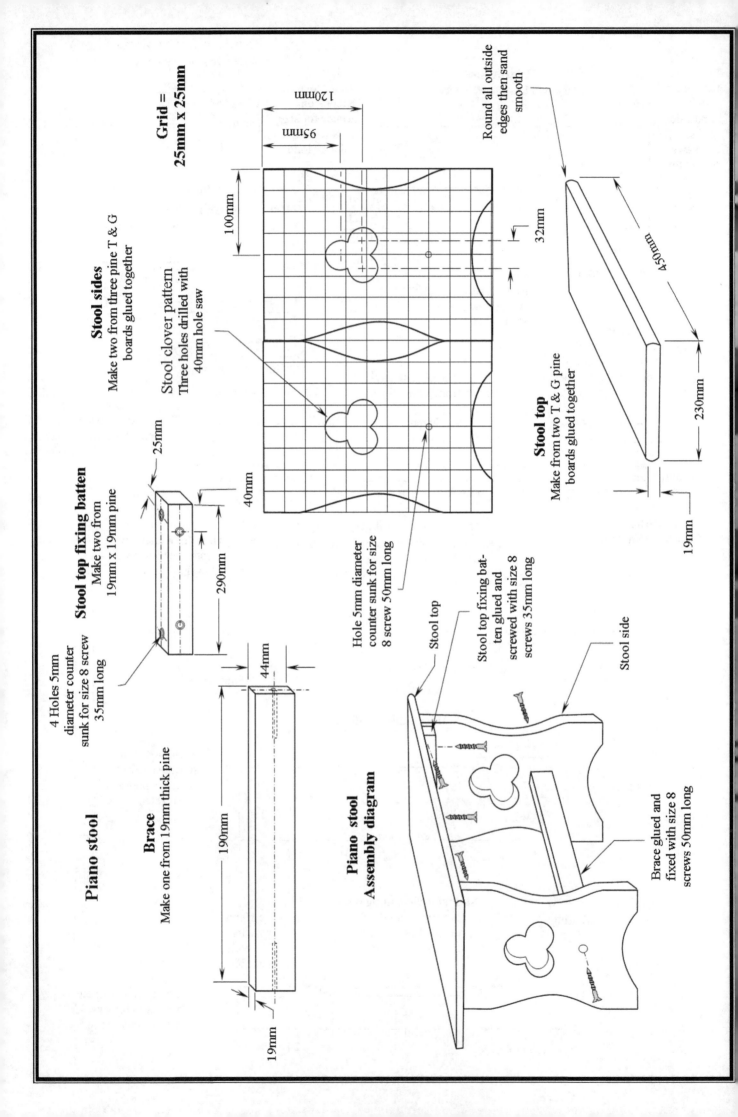

Tractor and trailer

A sturdy tractor with tipper trailer and hinged tail gate ideal toy for a sand pit

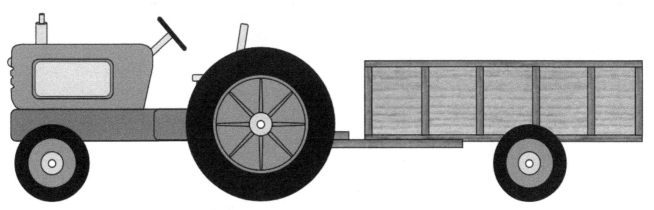

Tip up trailer with hinged tail gate

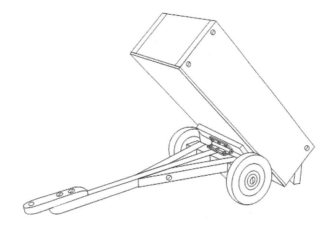

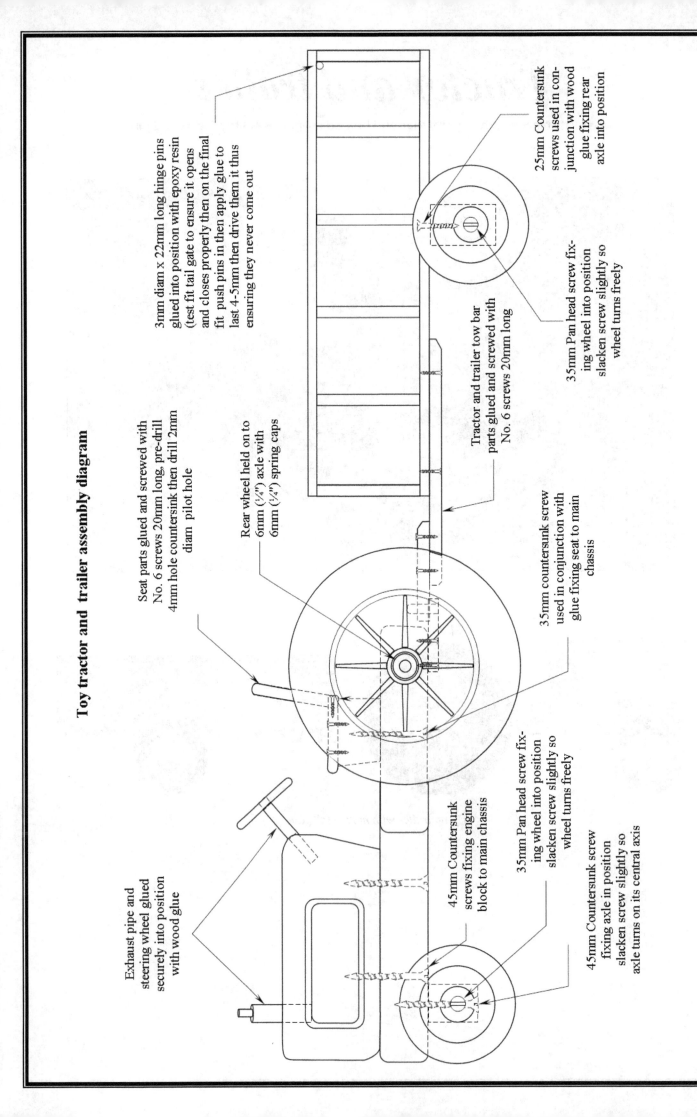

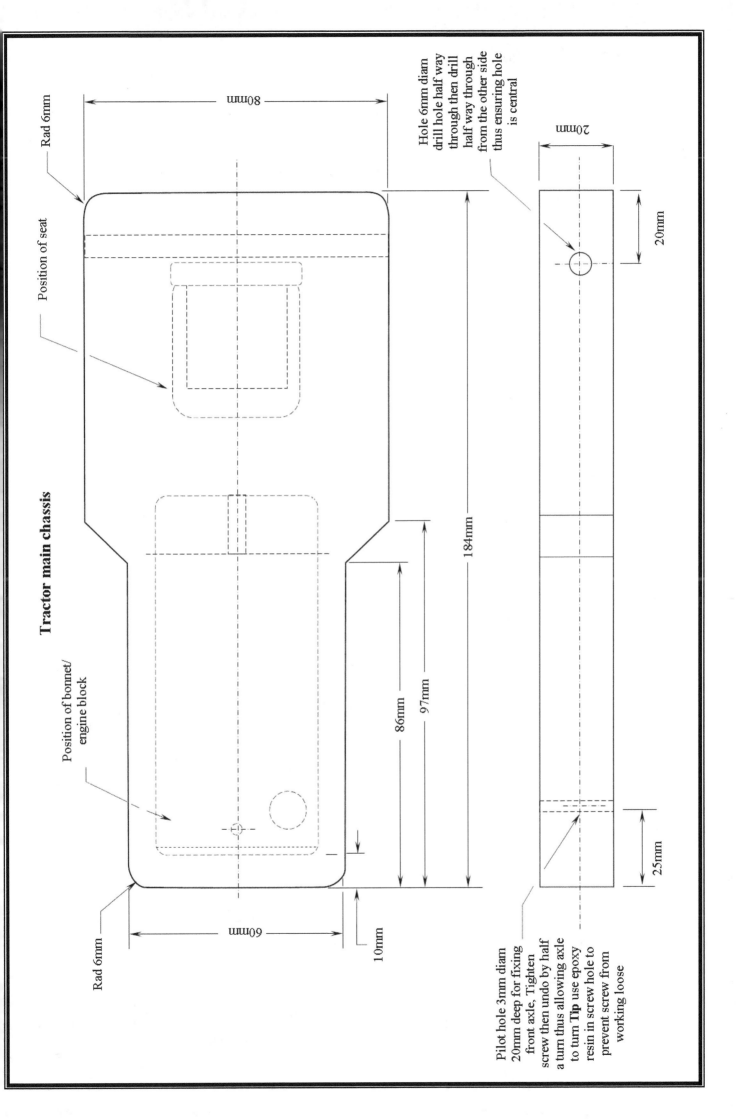

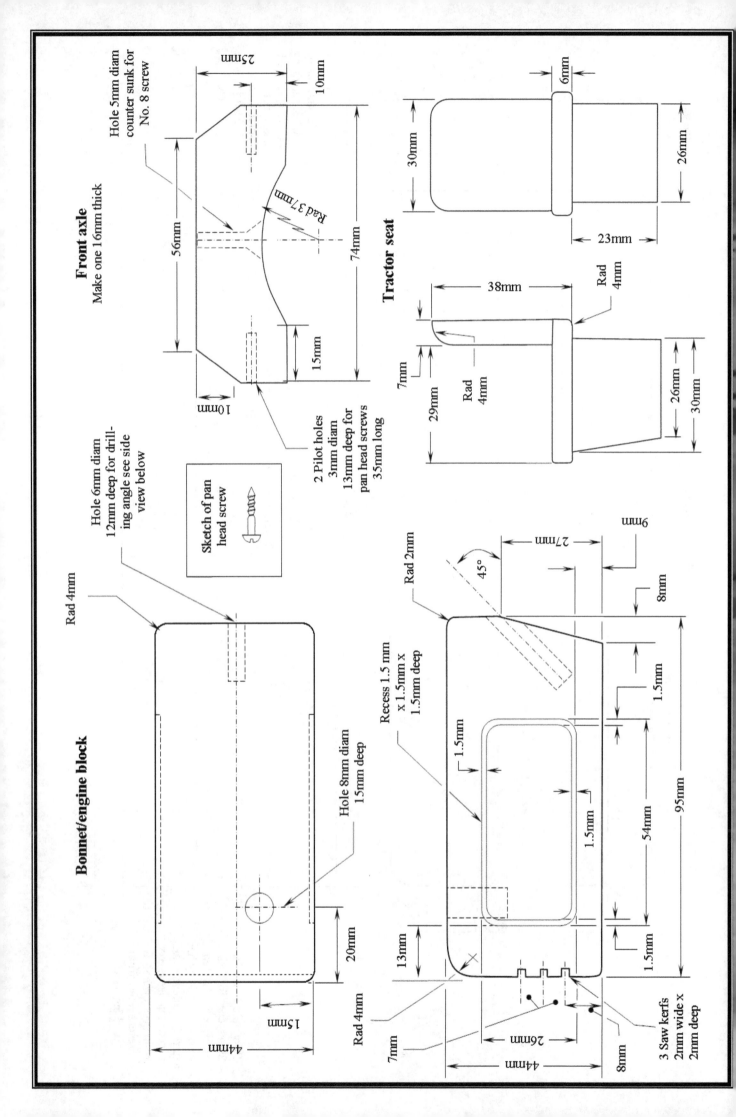

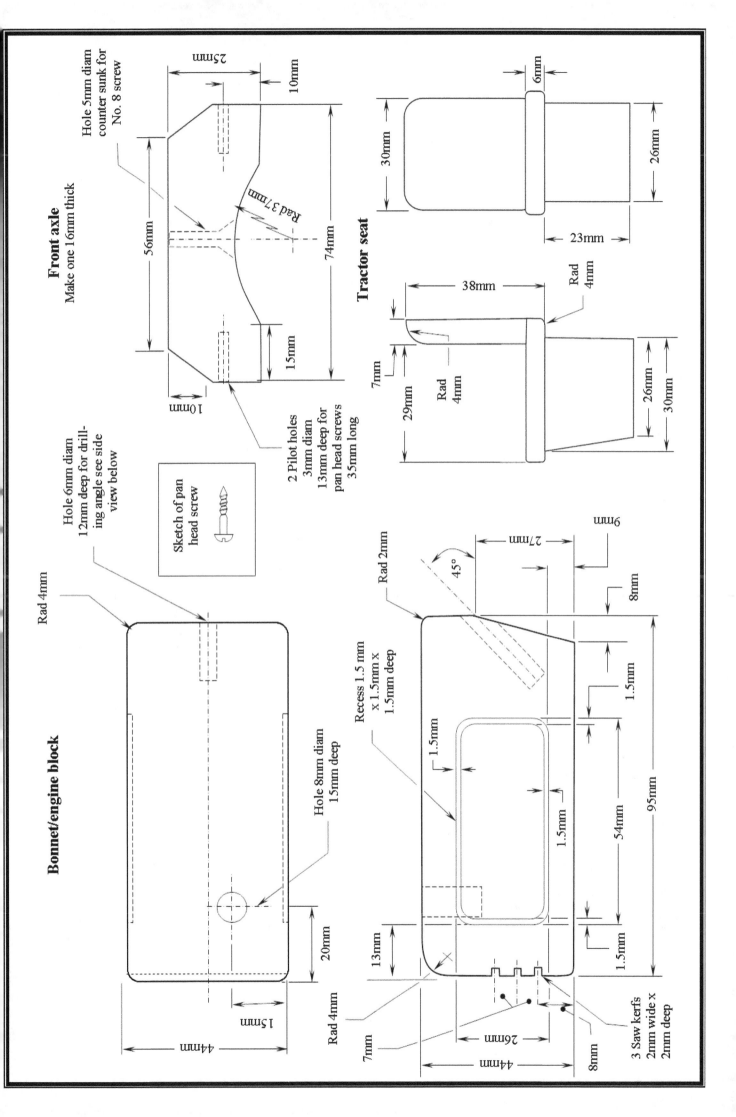

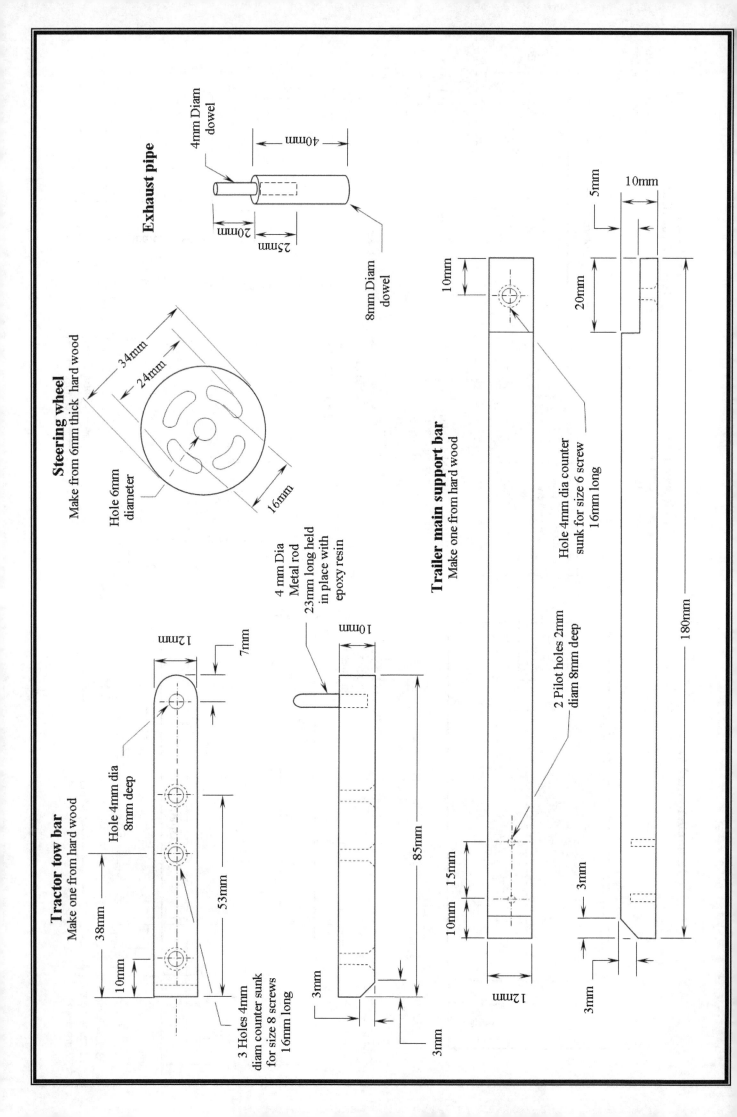

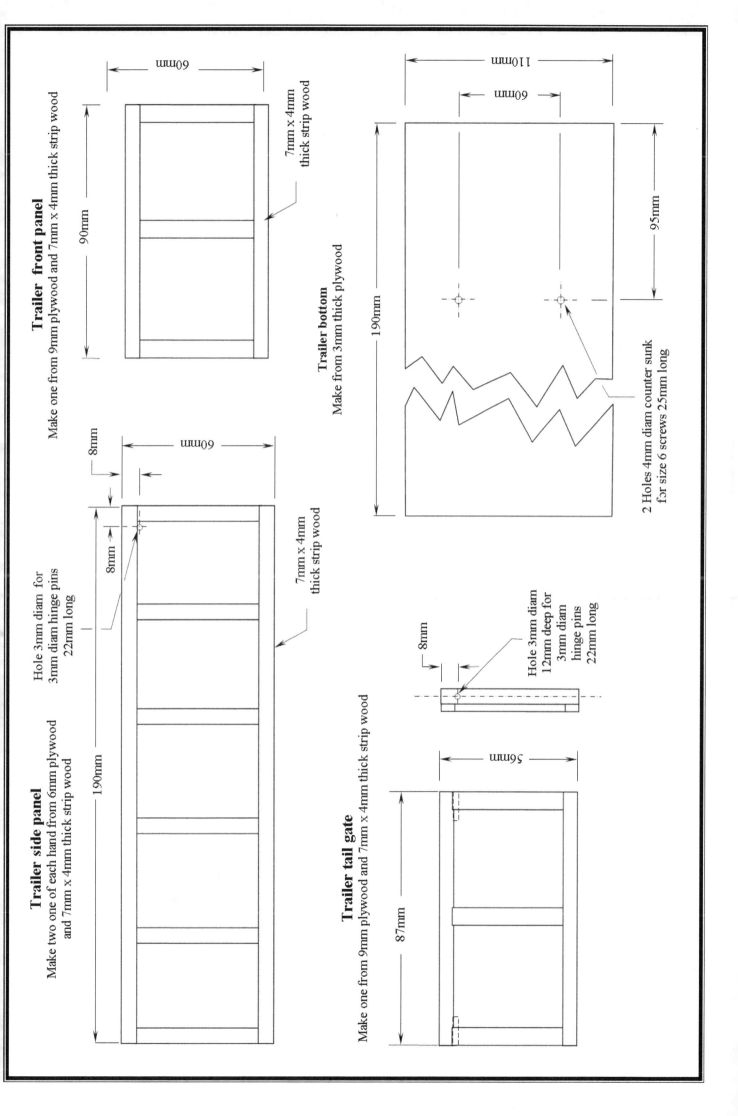

Trailer axle
Make one from hard wood
(see also (Trailer parts/assembly diagram))

Pilot hole 3mm diam 20mm deep for 35mm long pan head screws holding wheels in place. on the final fit place epoxy resin into the screw hole this will prevent screws working loose

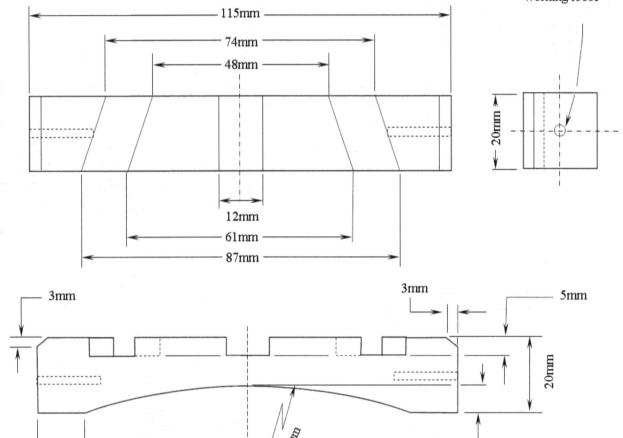

Head Lamps
Make two from 8mm diameter dowel

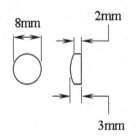

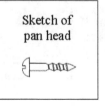

Sketch of pan head

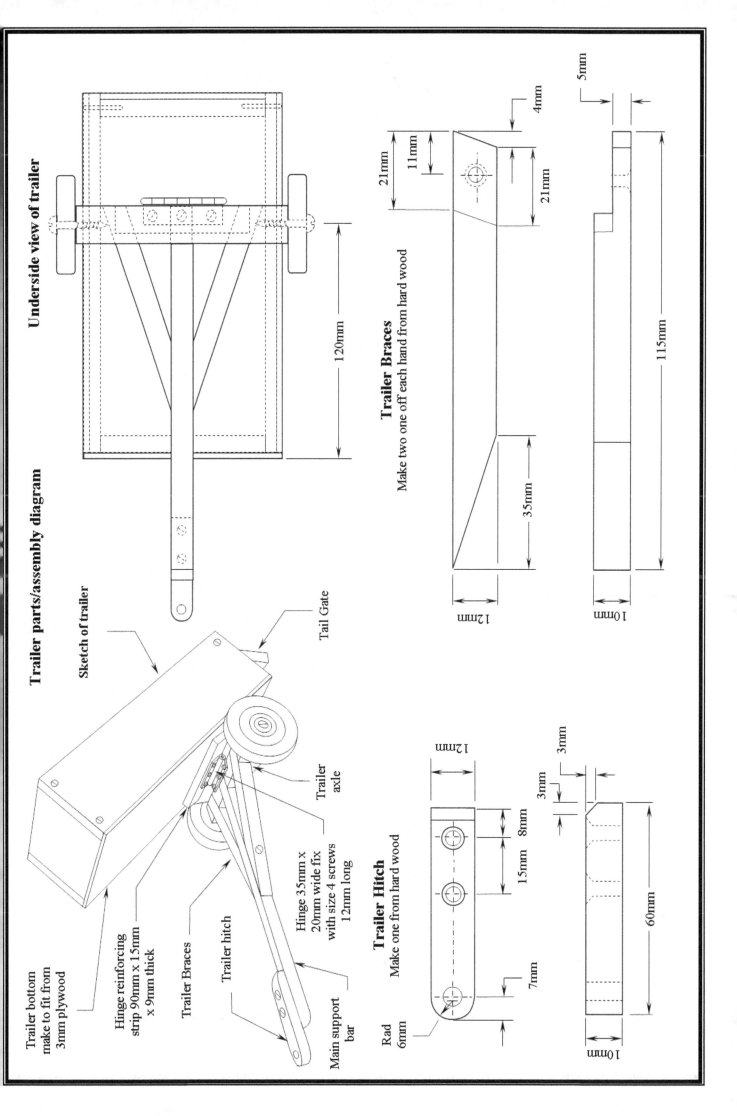

Toy Helicopter

This toy helicopter is loosely based on the famous bell huey and has a toothed wheel at the rear of the fuselage, which when turned with ones thumb spins the rotor blades,. The main parts were made from pine a block of 75mm x 75mm (3" x 3") was used for the fuselage and a block of 63mm x 38mm (2½" x 1½") was used for the tail, 3mm plywood was used for the front wind screen and door side panels

Wind screen panels and door panels made from 3mm plywood

The rotor blades and skids are made from beech and the skid supports made from 3.5mm diameter steel rod

Any discrepancies are filled and then a coat of undercoat applied then sanded smooth ready for the top coat

Helicopter painted and front and rear seats fitted

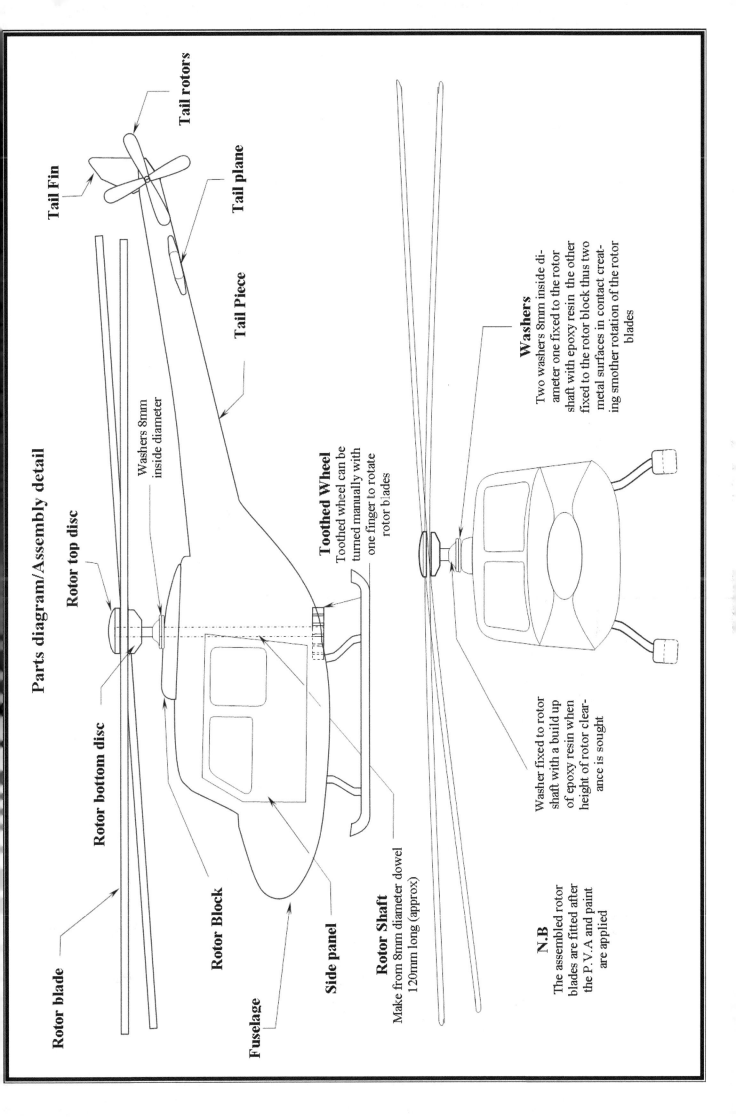

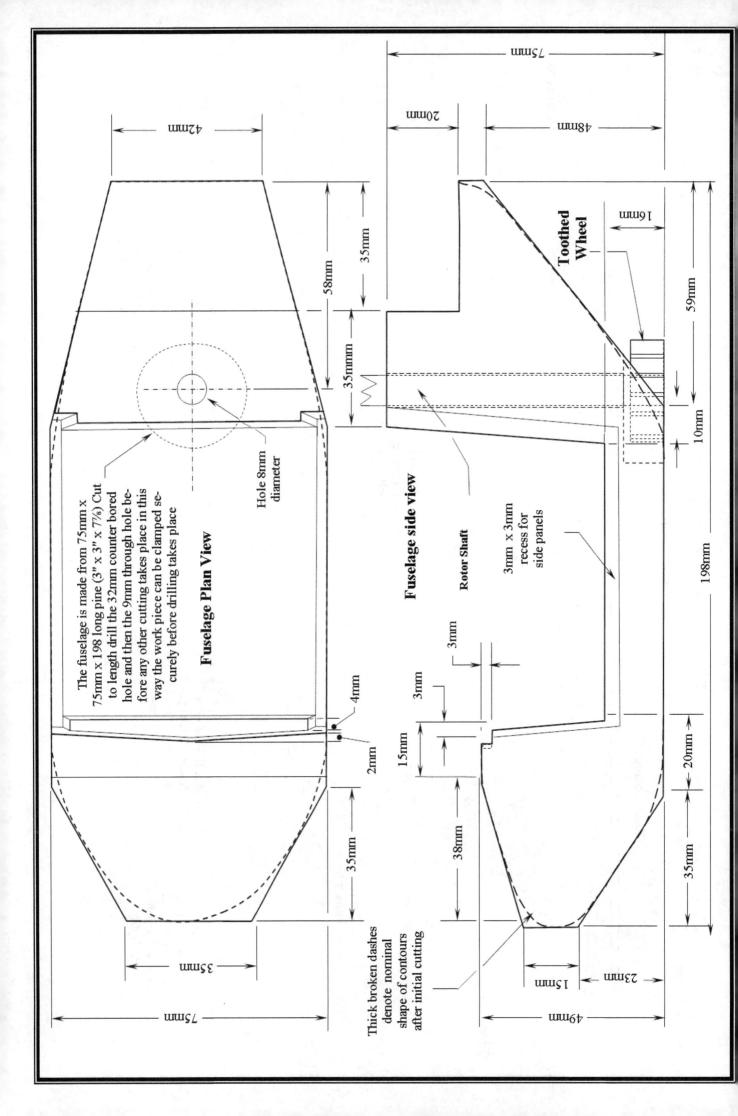

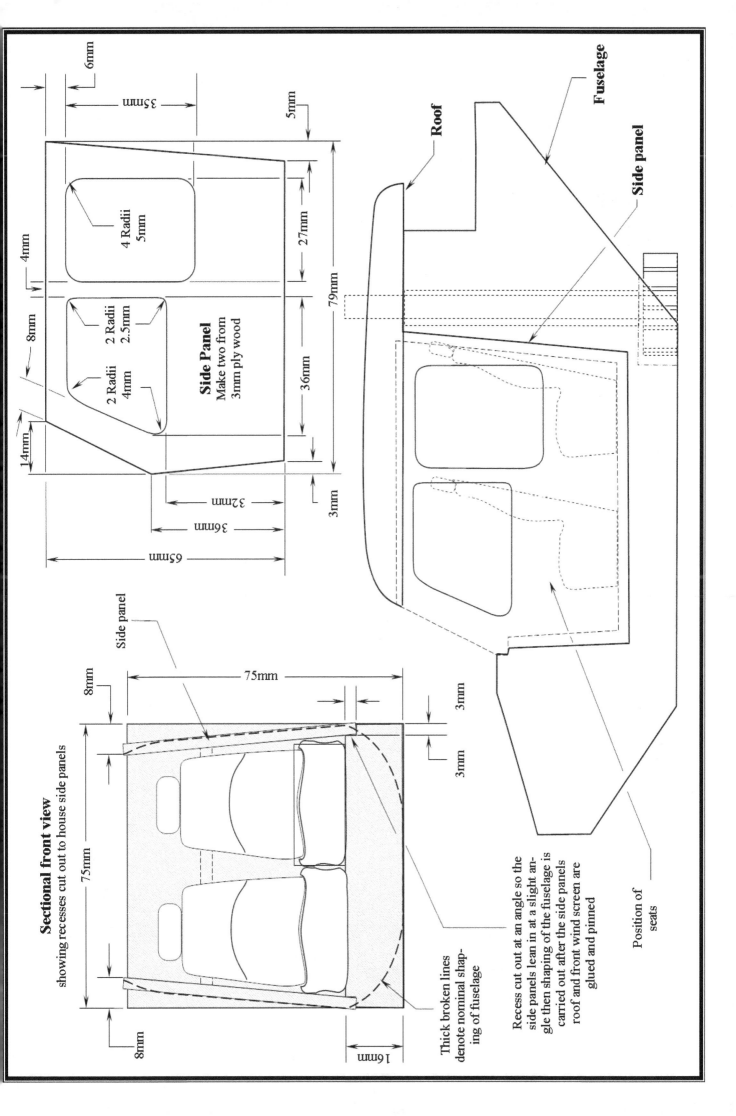

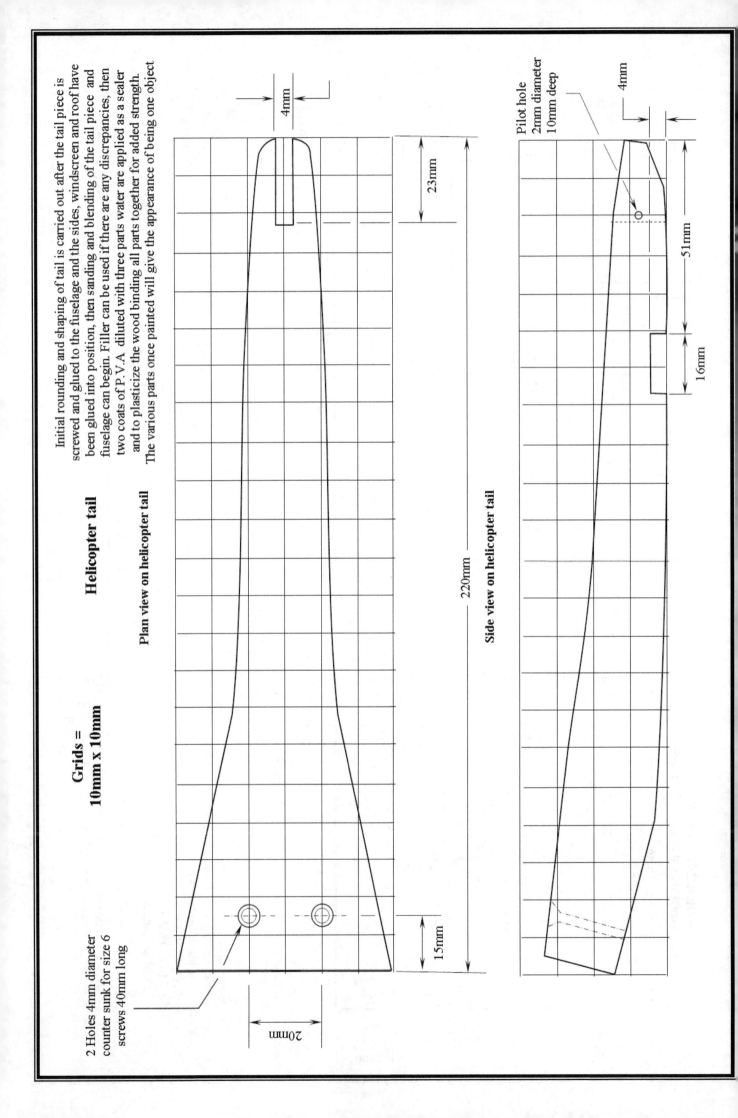

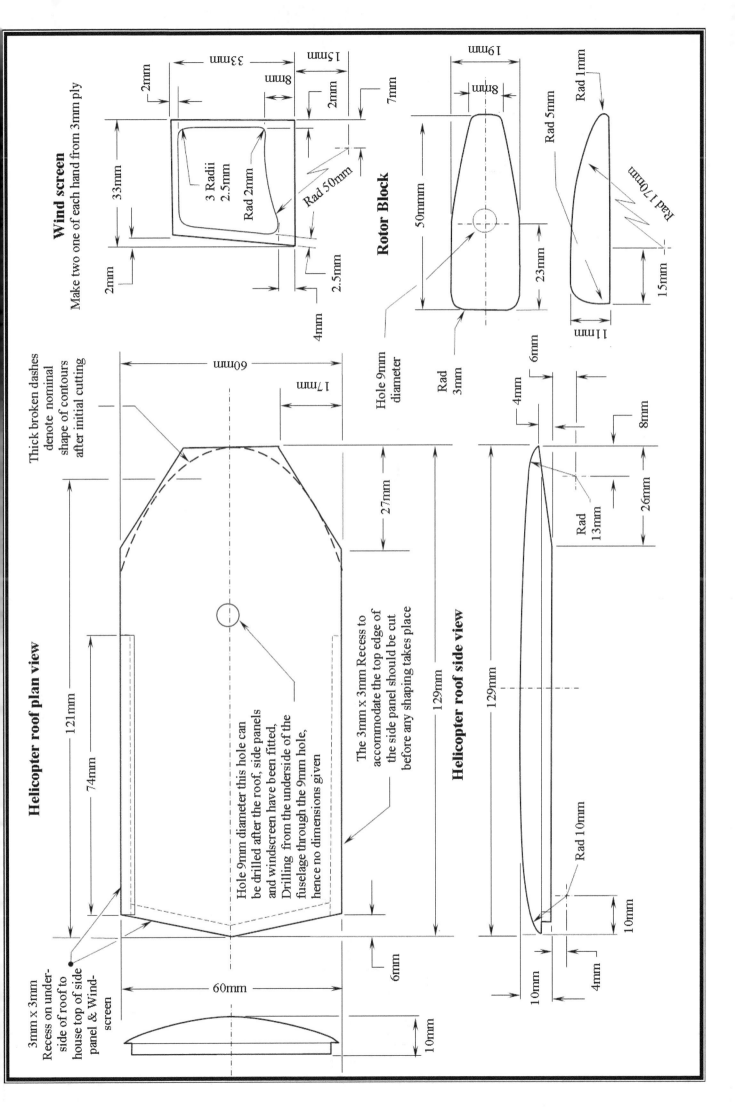

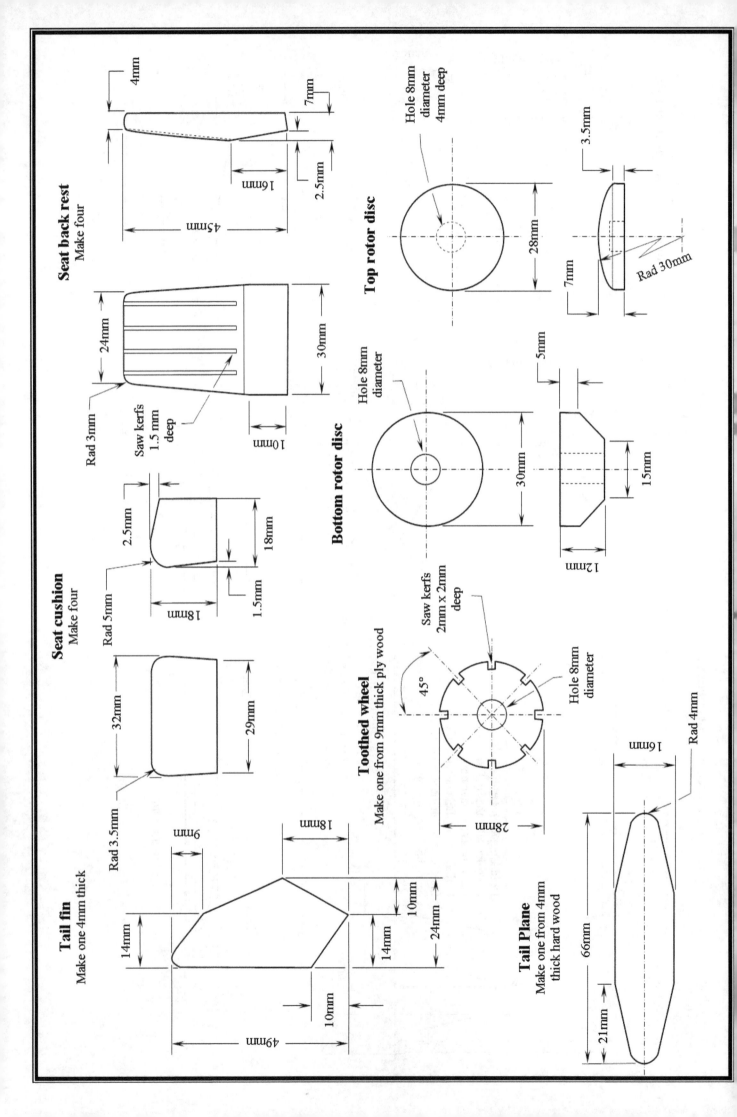

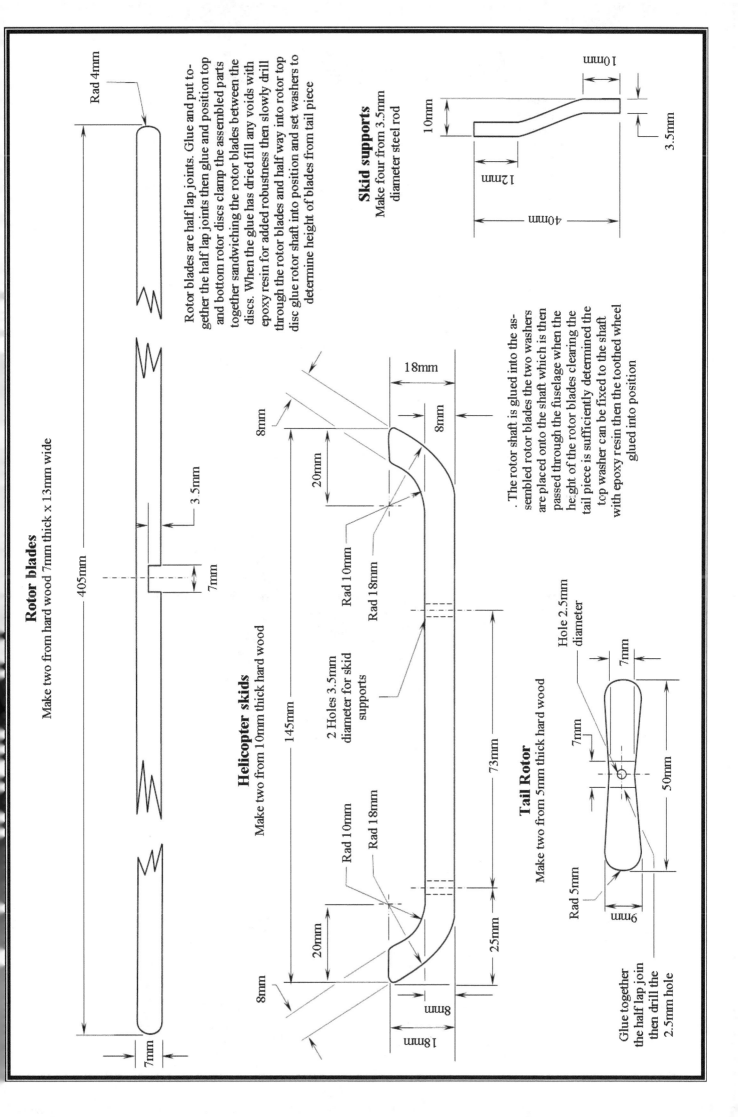

Small oak chair

The proto type of this chair was made for my grand daughter when she was born.
A brass plaque with her birth details engraved into it, was inset into the back rest.
Now its in my daughters conservatory proudly displaying a potted plant

Small oak chair assembly diagrams

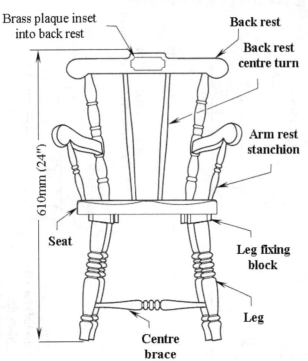

Labels: Brass plaque inset into back rest; Back rest; Back rest centre turn; Arm rest stanchion; Seat; 610mm (24"); Leg fixing block; Leg; Centre brace

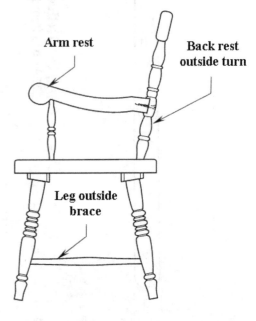

Labels: Arm rest; Back rest outside turn; Leg outside brace

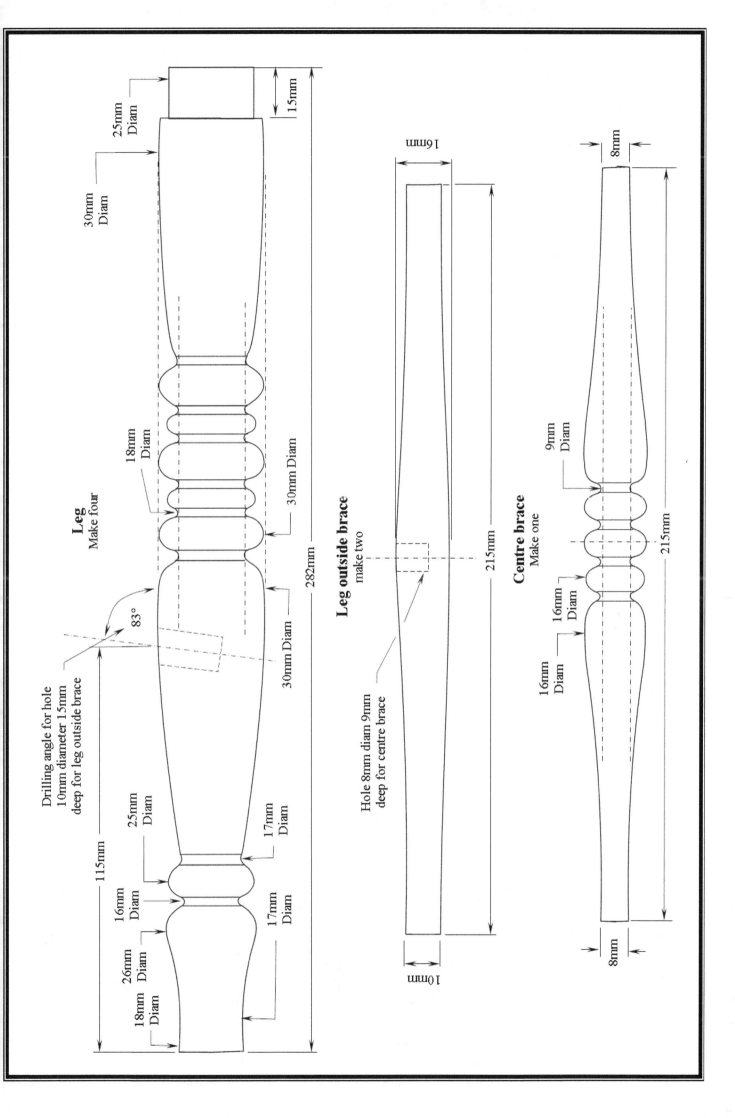

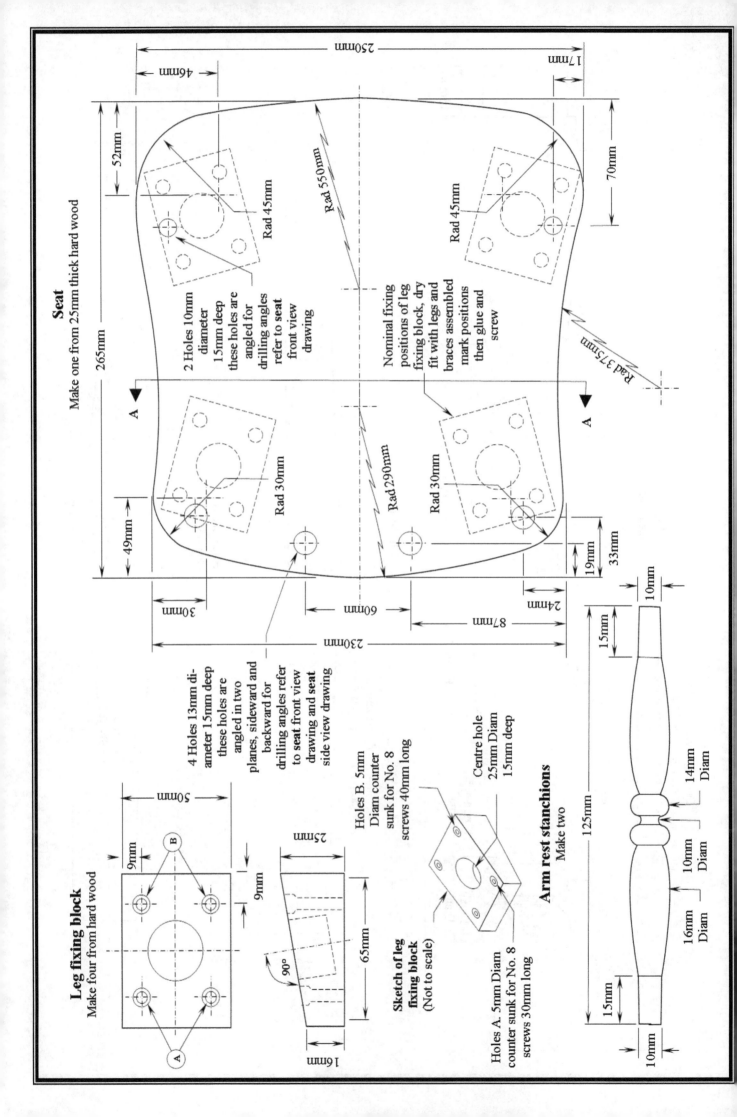

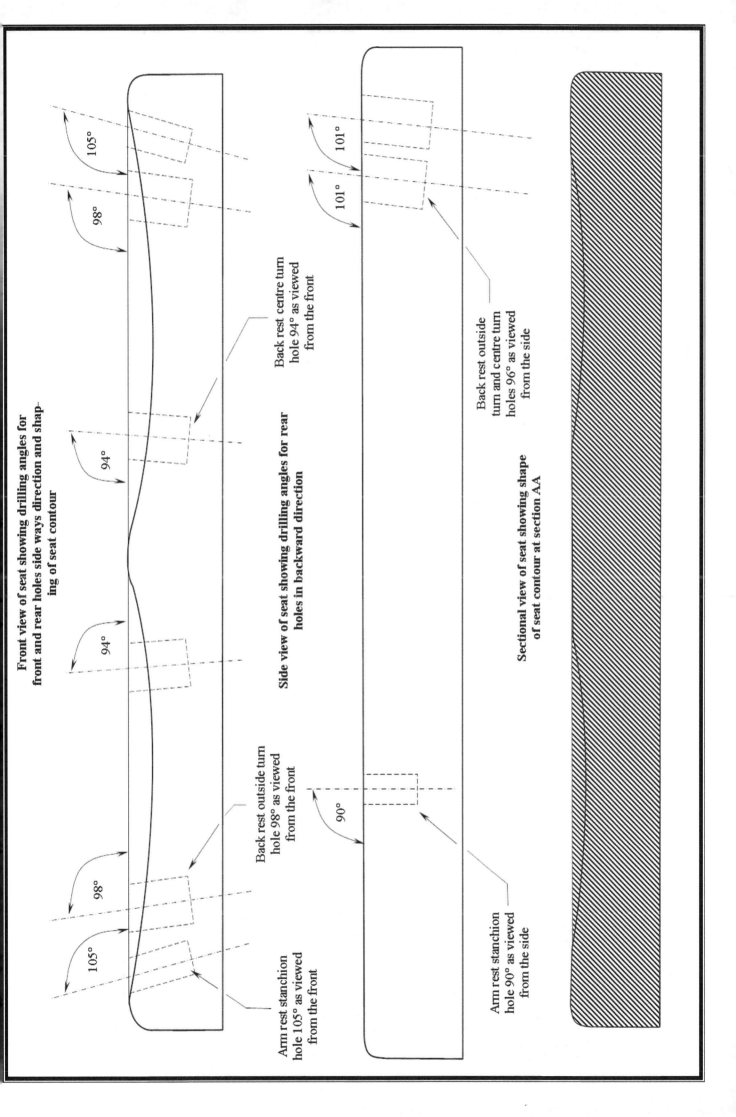

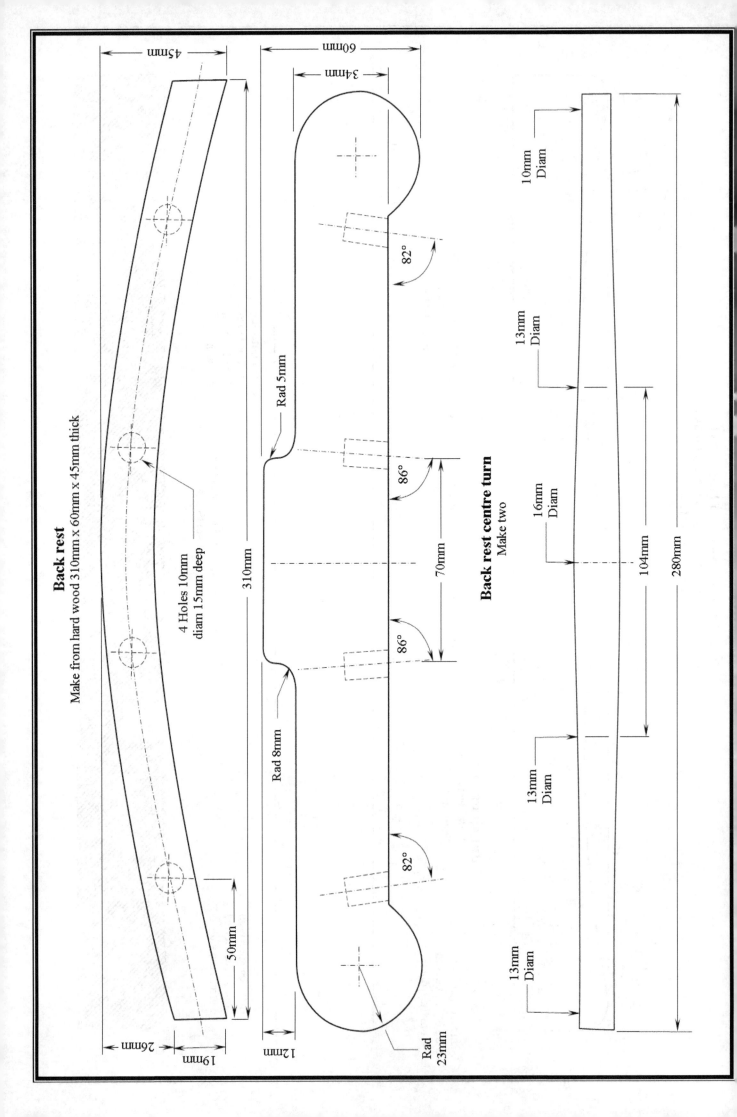

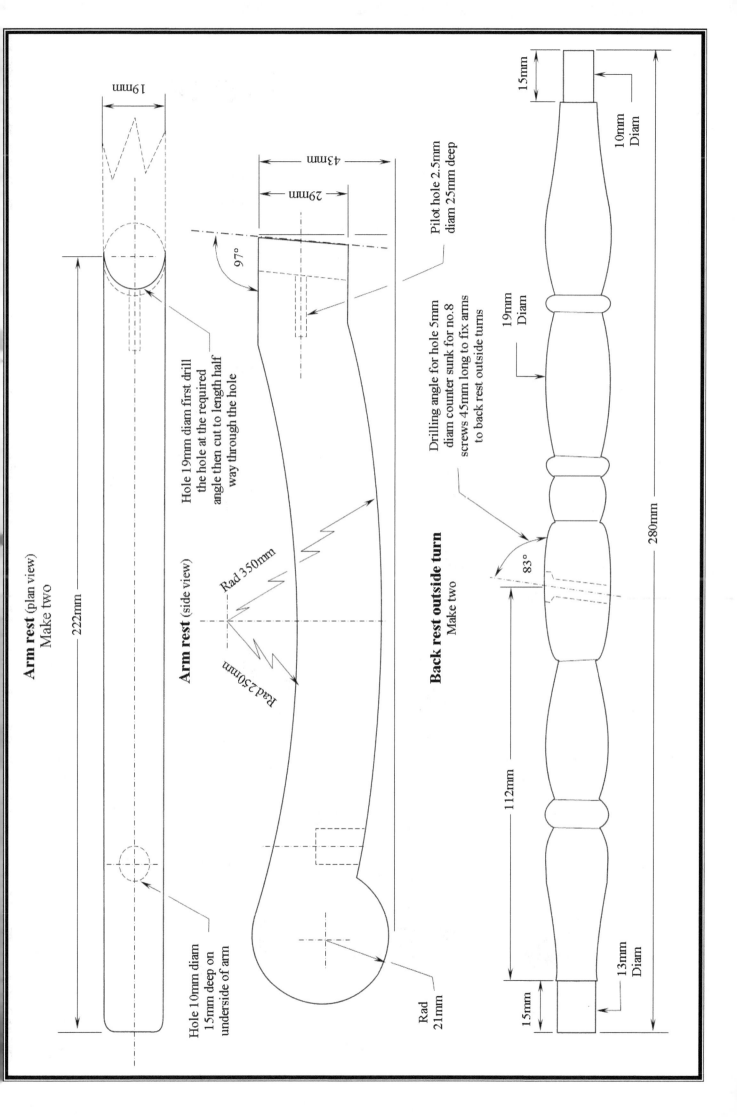

Toy tow truck/crane

This tow truck has 100mm (4") wheels a winding hook, and jib that turns around its axis. This can be removed making this toy sit and ride

This picture shows the two sanding sticks used to clean up the front wind screen after initial cutting. Emery cloth was glued to a 20mm diameter dowel with contact adhesive for the corners and to a piece of batten for cleaning up the straight bits, the vice jaws are a good guide for keeping a straight line, the wooden jaws on this vice were never added for this reason

View of chassis and chassis strengtheners, the chassis strengthener also makes up the step just inside the door.

Bonnet and cab assembled and fitted. Rear side panels, doors and chassis infill ready for fitting

Underside view showing the 9mm ply wood wheel spacers cut using a 30mm hole saw, also showing chassis strengtheners and cross members. The assembled bonnet top, sides and front are screwed to and level with the front cross member

Radiator parts glued to the bonnet front and bonnet bulge glued to bonnet top, On this occasion the doors will be glued back into position after the interior has test been fitted. In my experience hinged doors soon come off during rough and rigorous play with this being a sit and ride boys toy, when the boom is removed, I think this is the best option

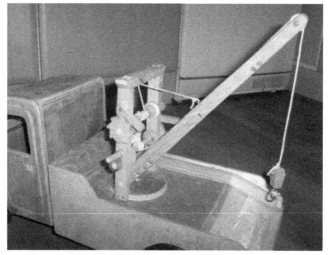

This picture shows the gantry and boom attached to the lorry bed with a small bolt and wing nut that can be easily be removed turning this toy into a sit and ride truck

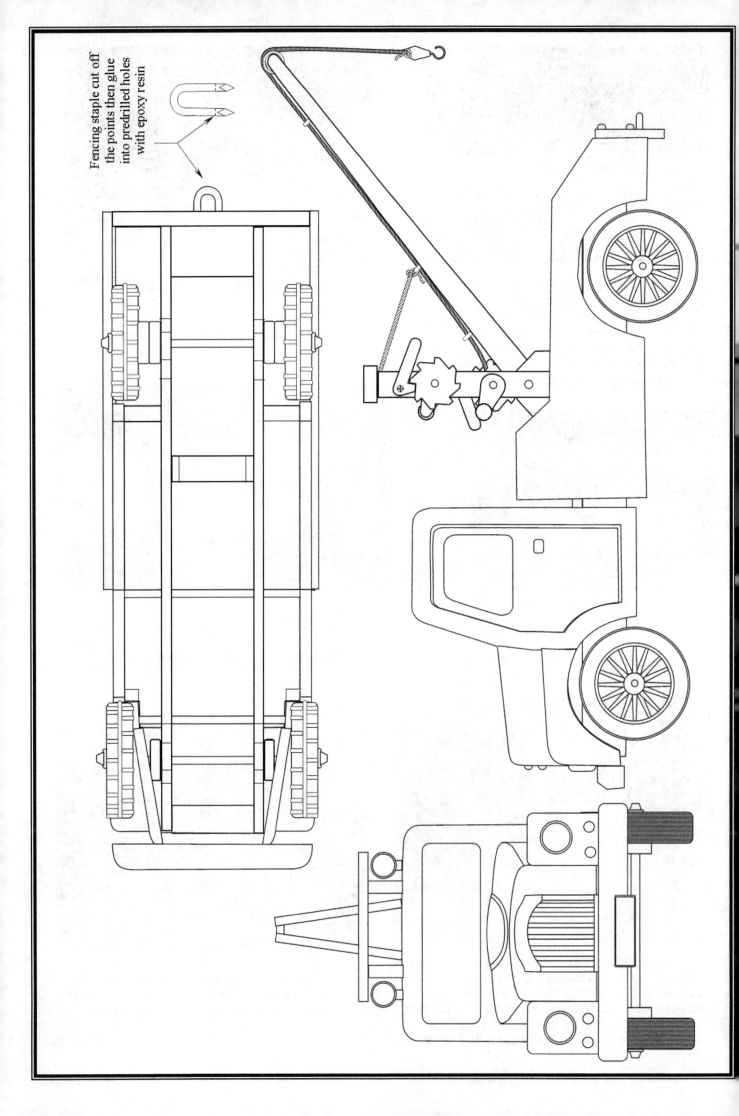

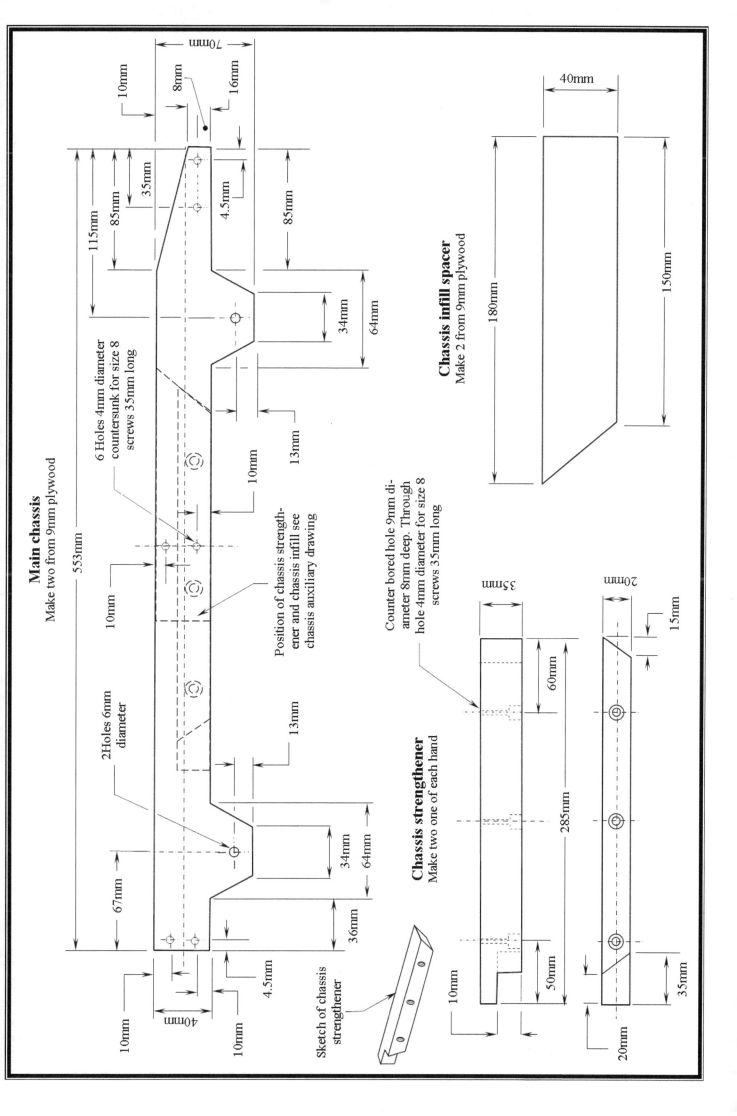

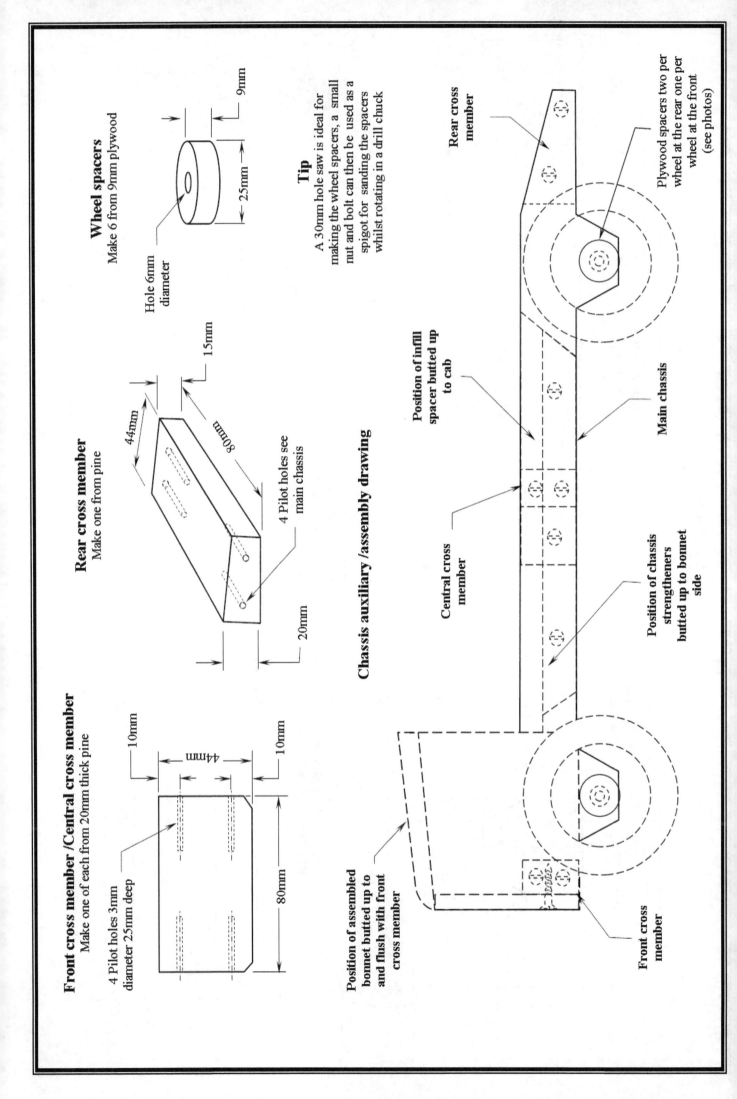

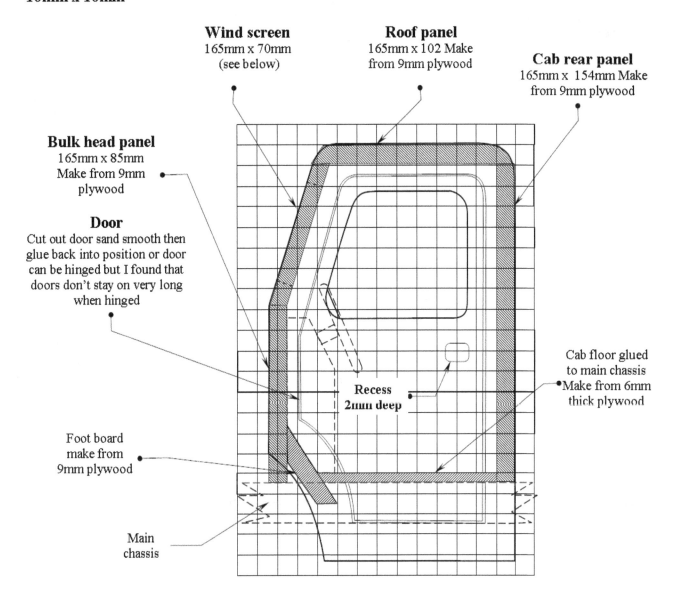

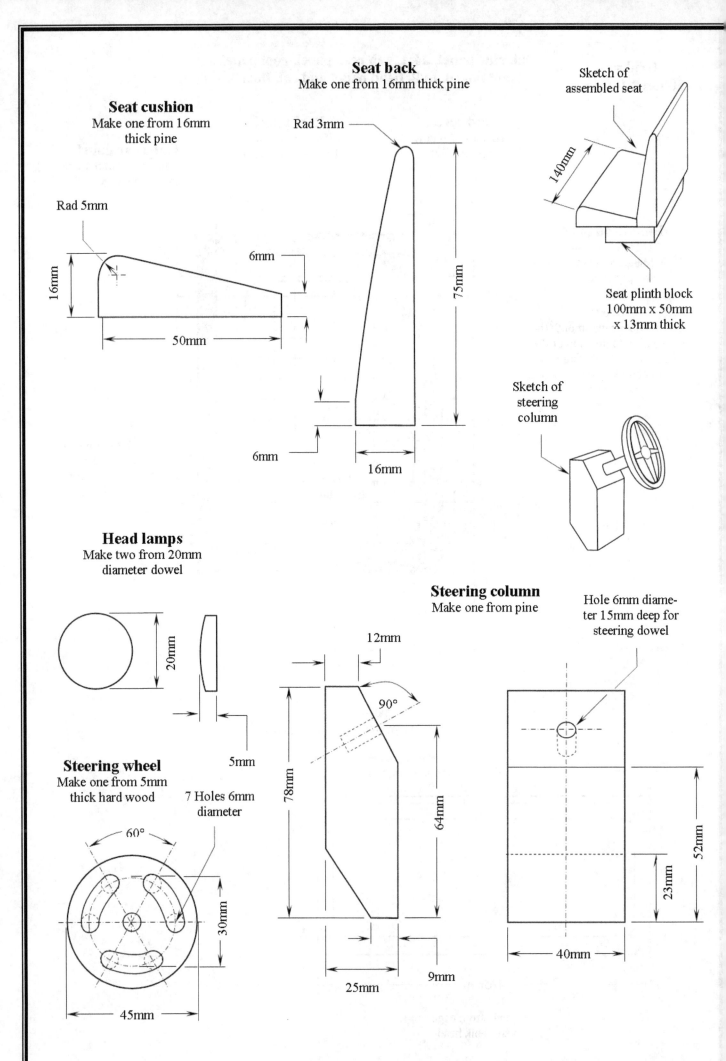

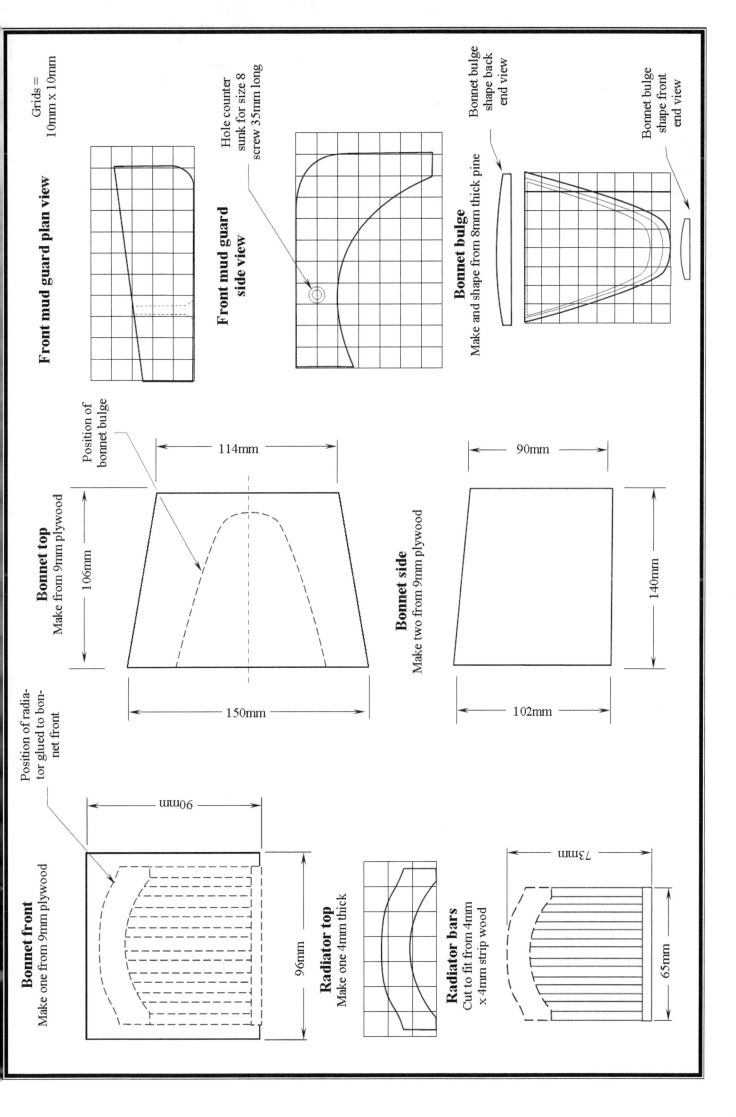

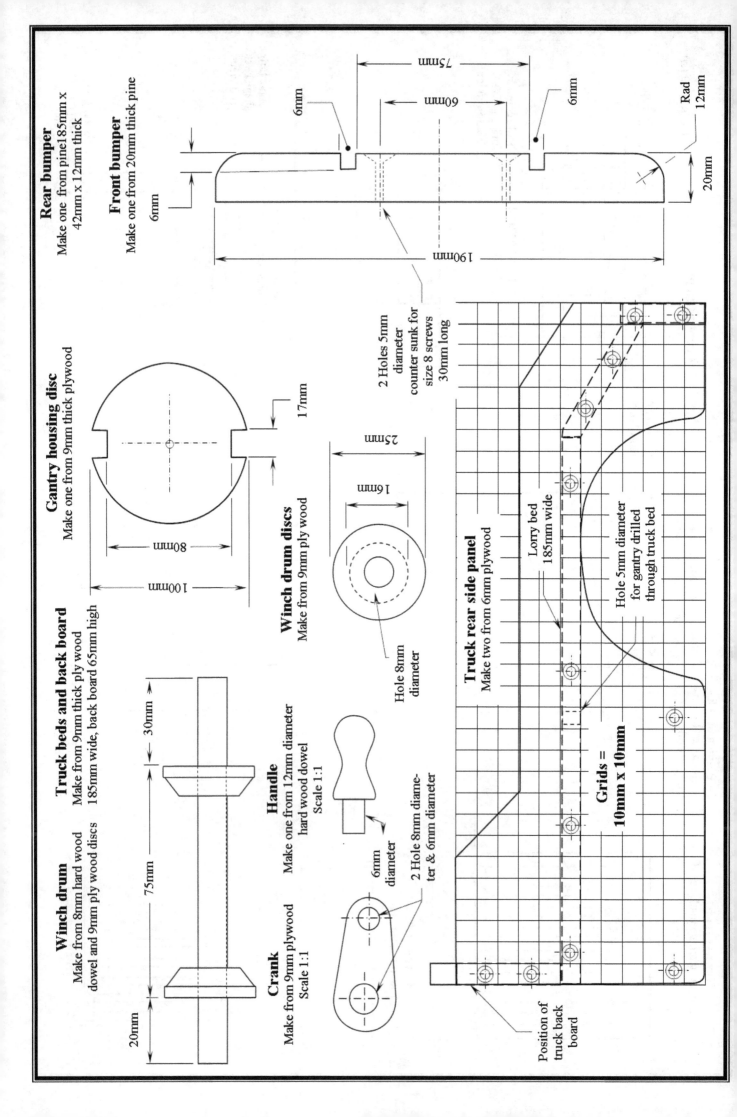

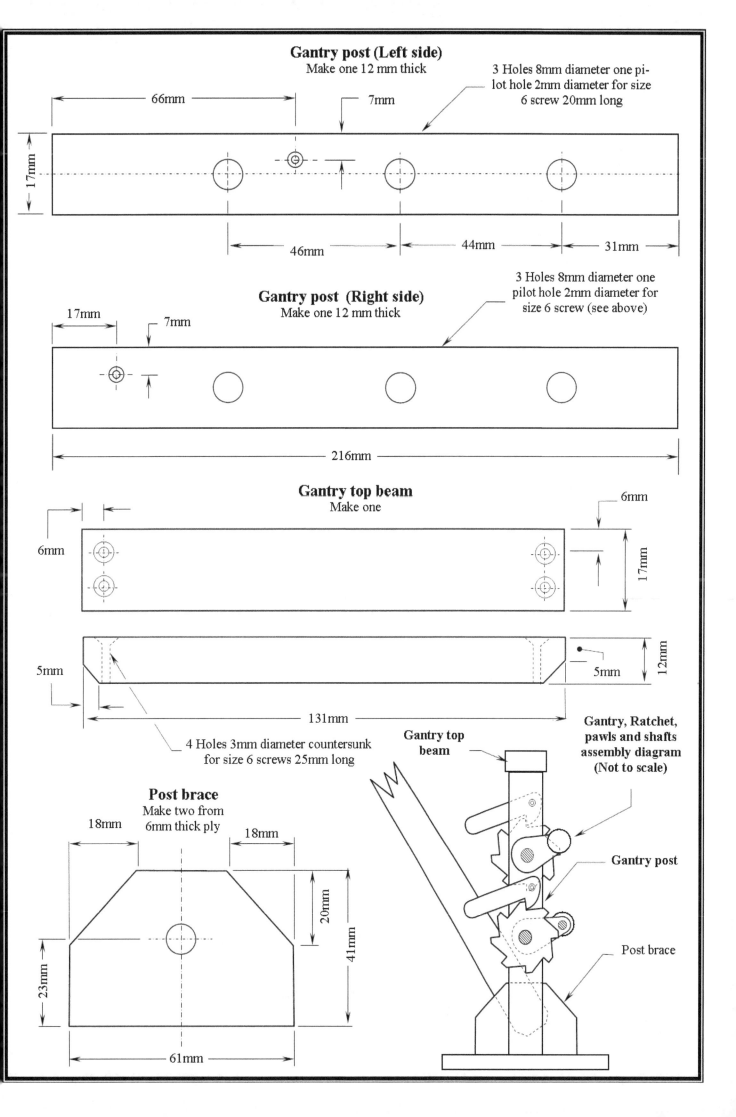

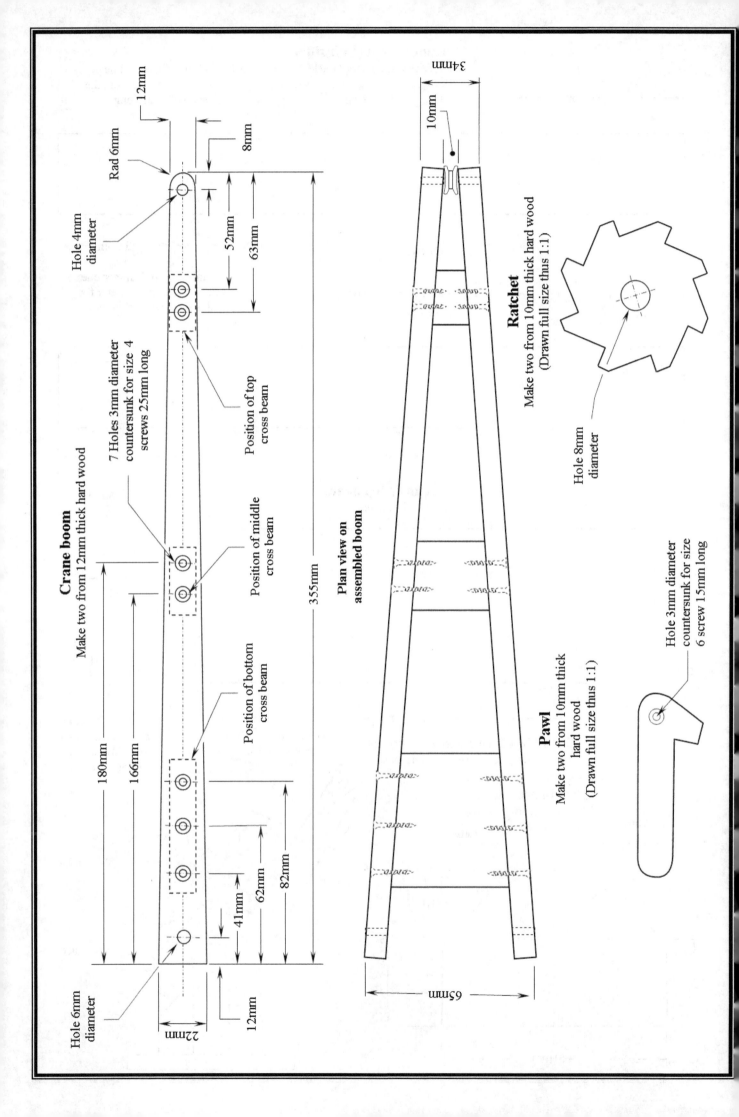

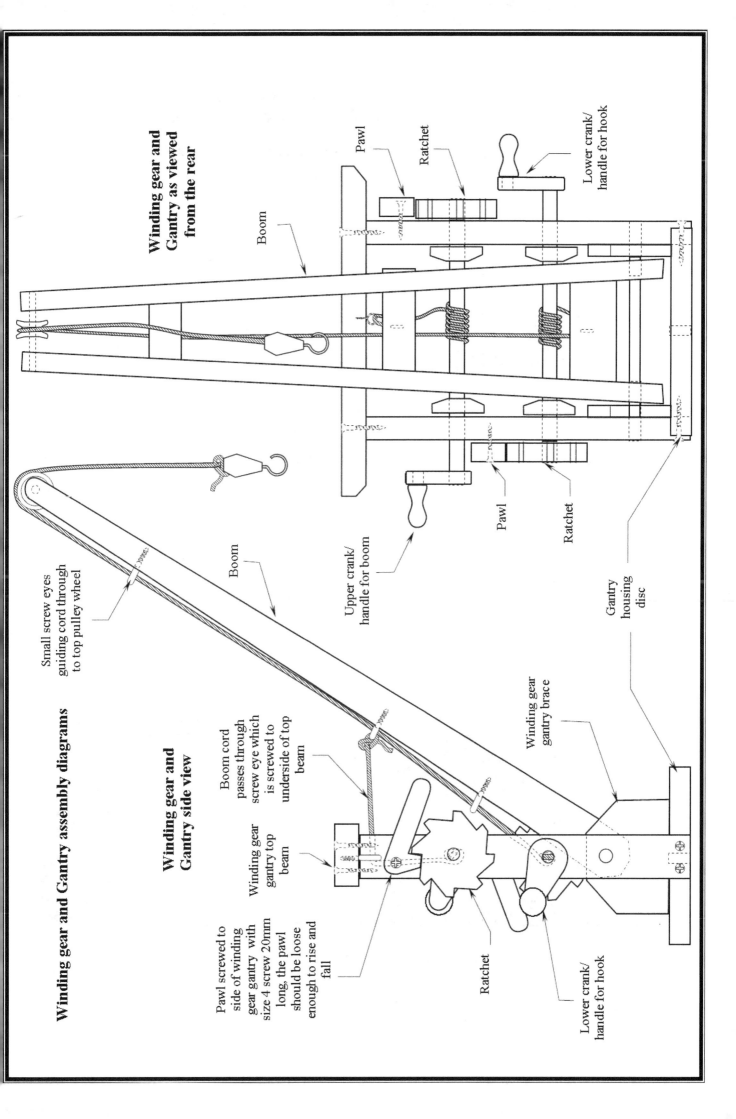

Camper van dolls house
(Sit and ride with removable back)
(533mm long 194mm wide 297mm high (21" x 7⅝" x 11" high)

Camper van dolls house sit and ride

Sit and ride camper van dolls house 533mm long x 194mm wide x 297mm high (21" x 7⅝" x 11" high)

Finished camper van fitted with 76mm (3") diameter x 18mm (¾"approx) thick, 6mm(¼") bore, plastic moulded wheels and sprincaps

Window and door trims fitted the window trims form a rabbet for the 1mm thick plexi glass

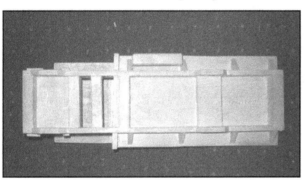

Under side view showing chassis and cross members

Side view showing bulk head bed board and fuel tank that acts as door stop and step riser

Side view showing cab and chassis filled, sanded smooth and ready for undercoat

Under coat applied, sanded smooth and ready for the top coat

Furniture made and fitted

Inside through rear window

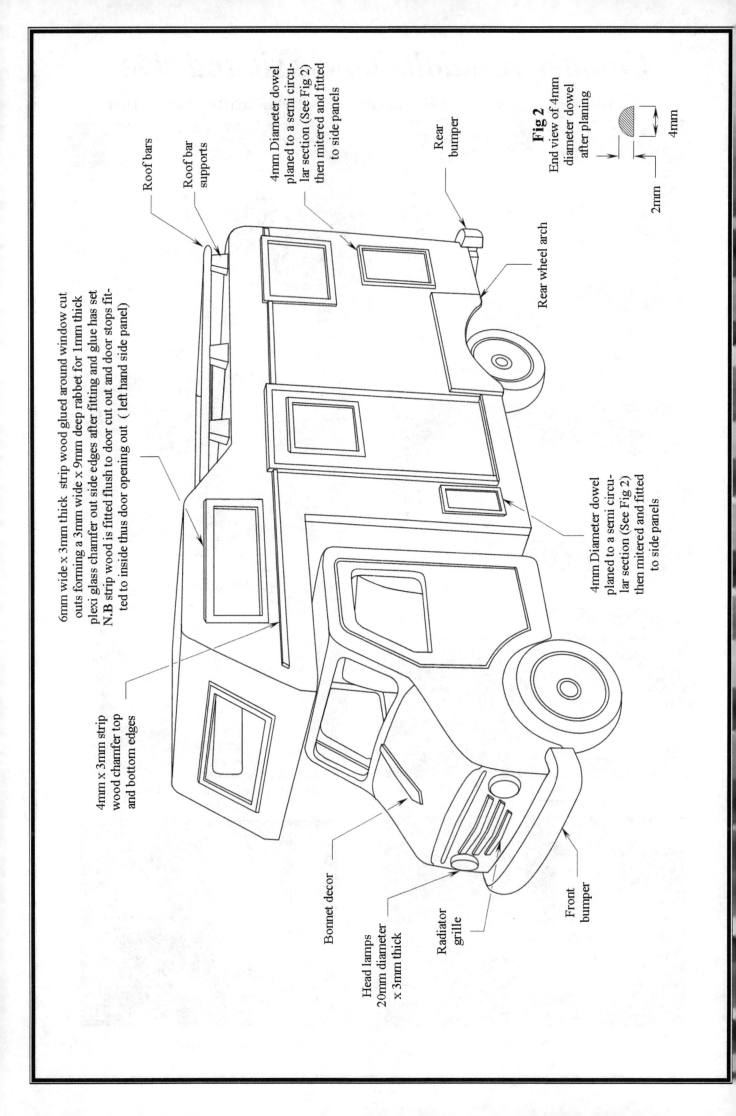

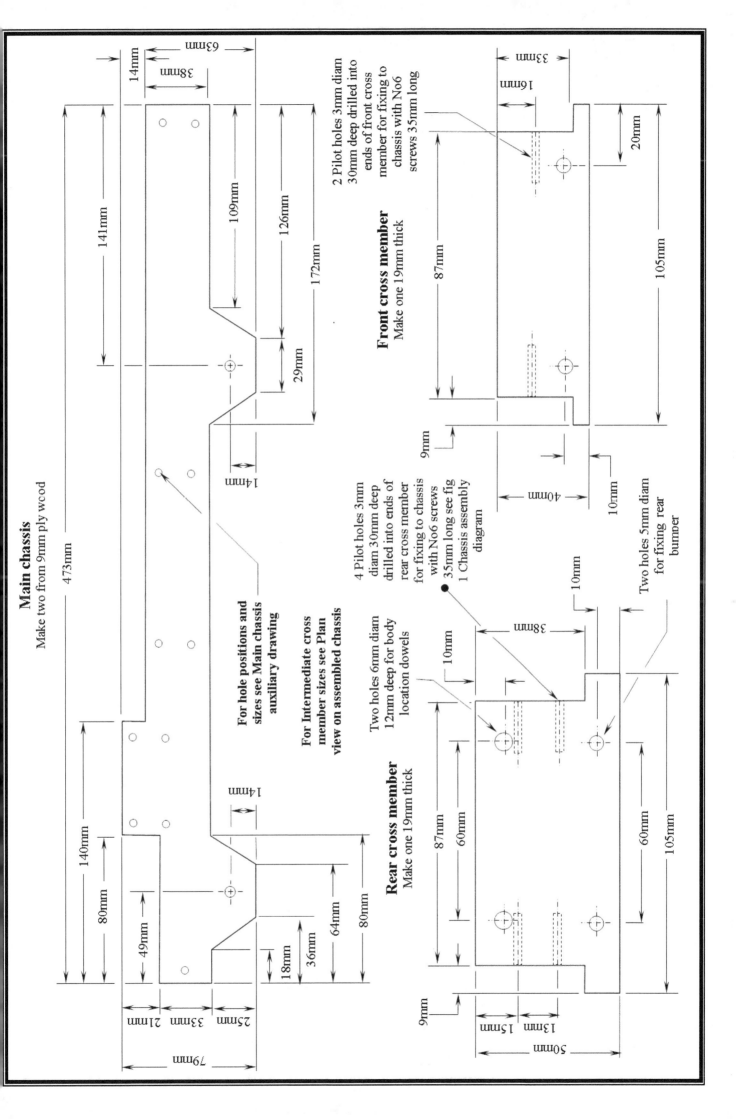

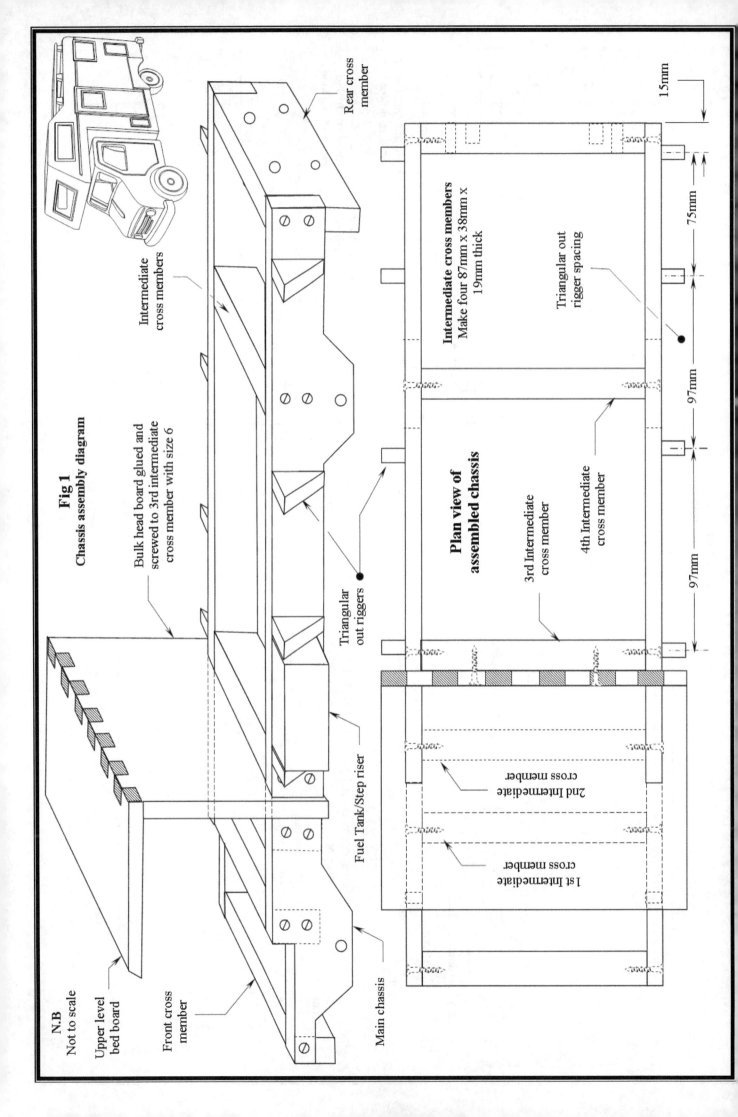

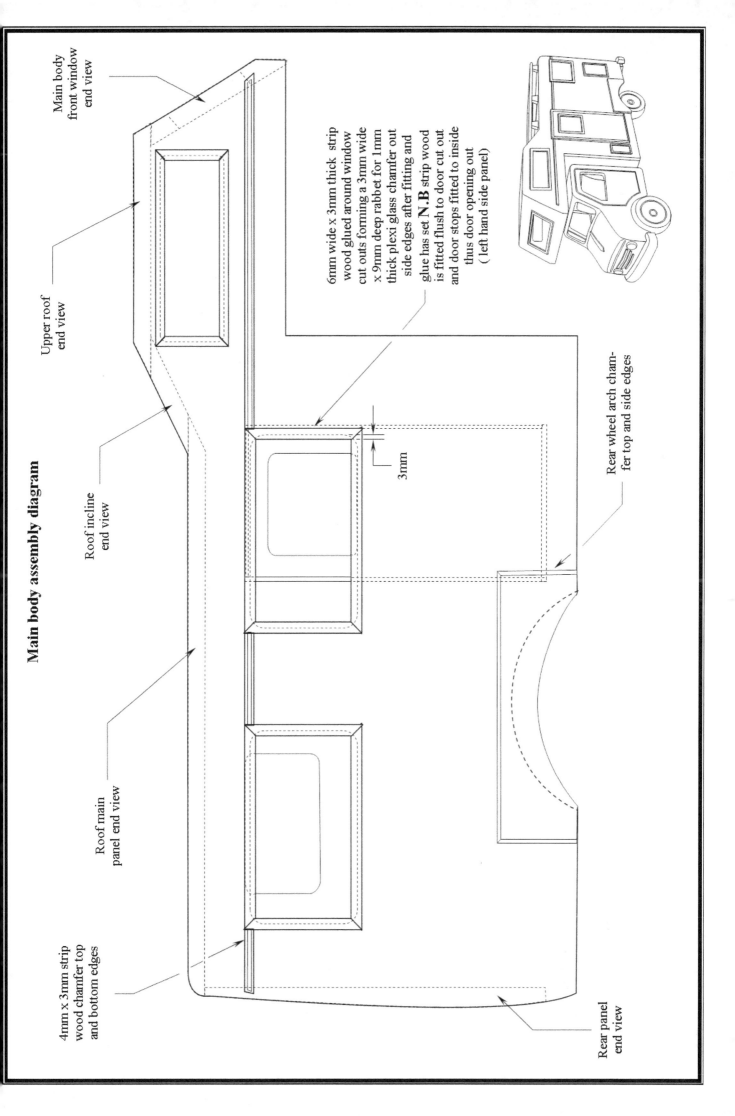

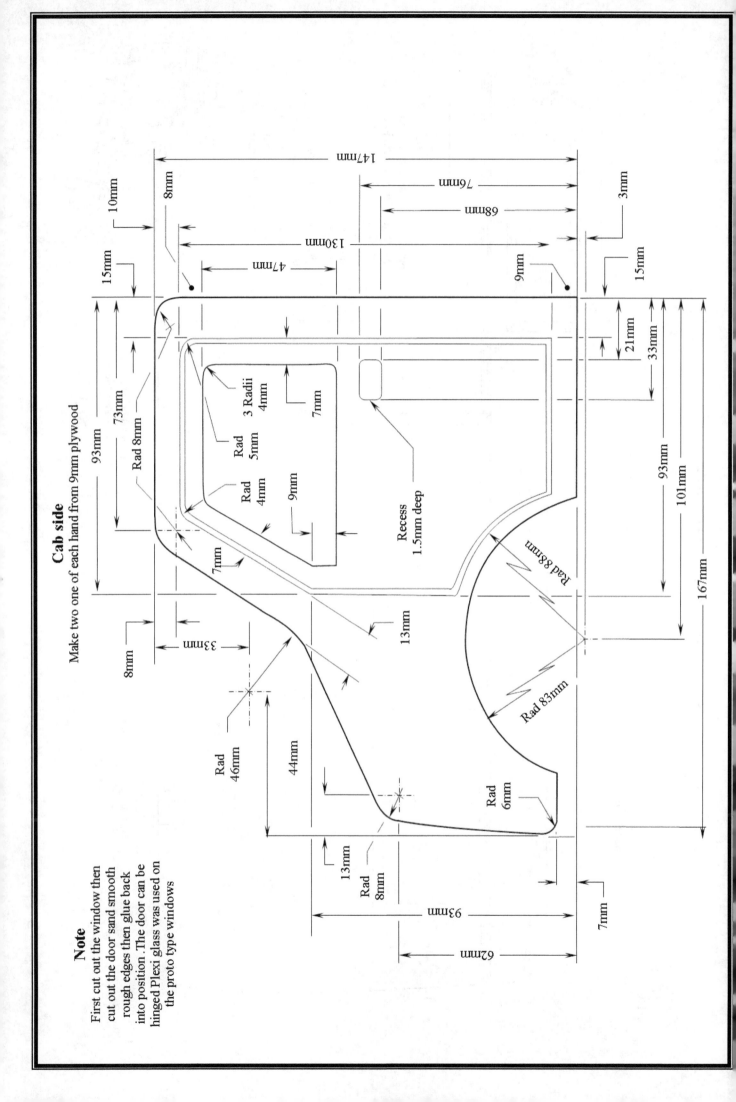

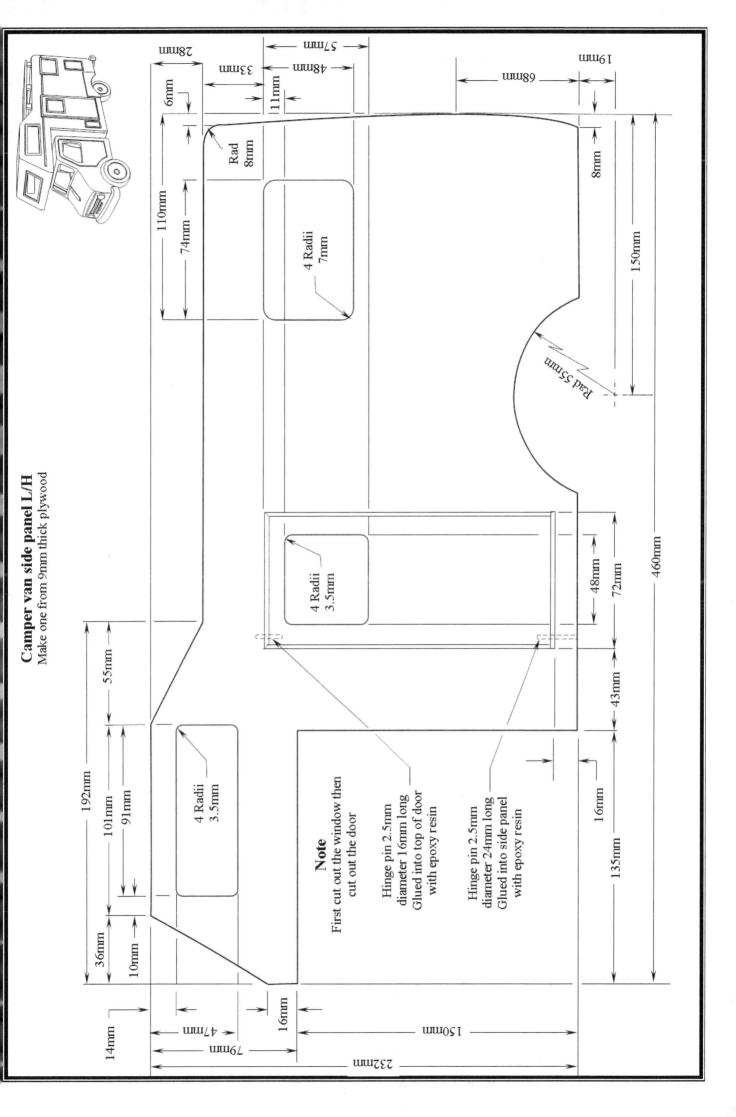

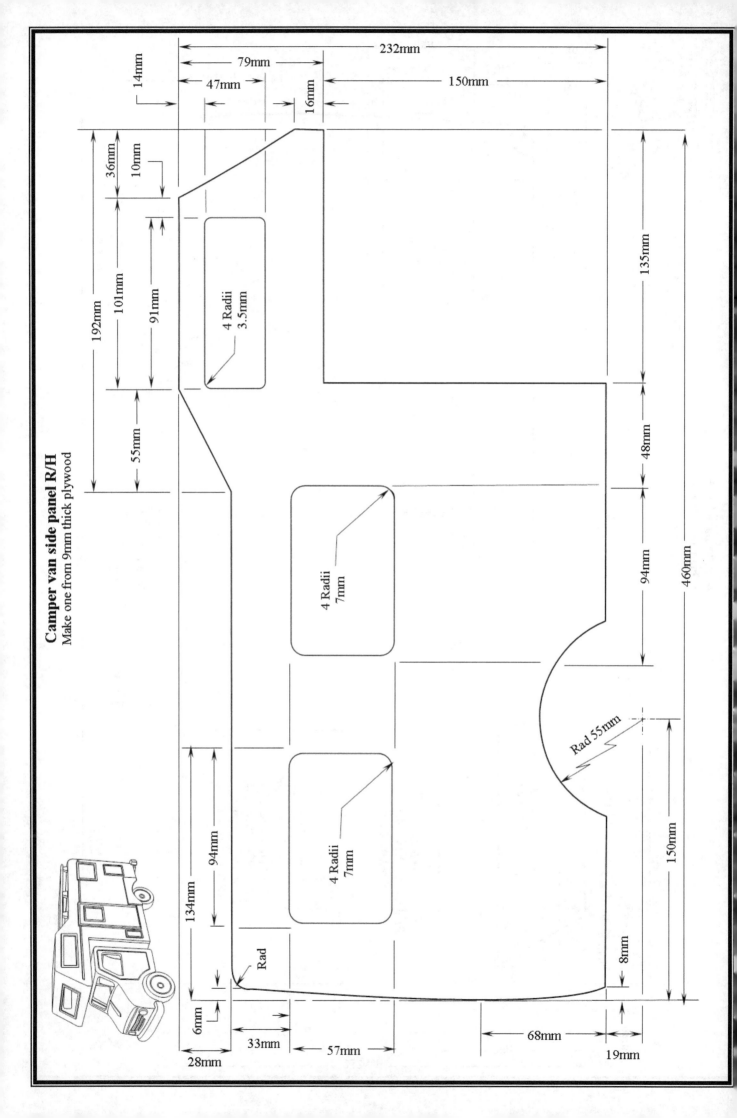

Main body front window
Make one from 9mm thick ply wood

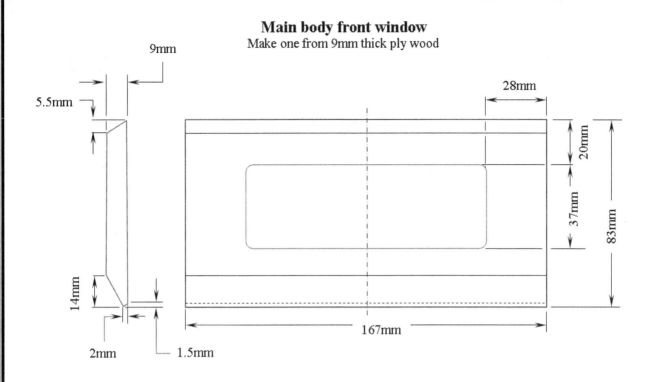

Rear panel
Make one from 9mm thick ply wood

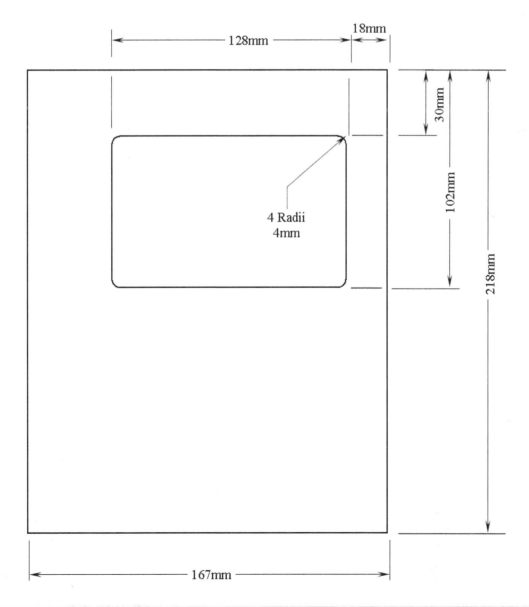

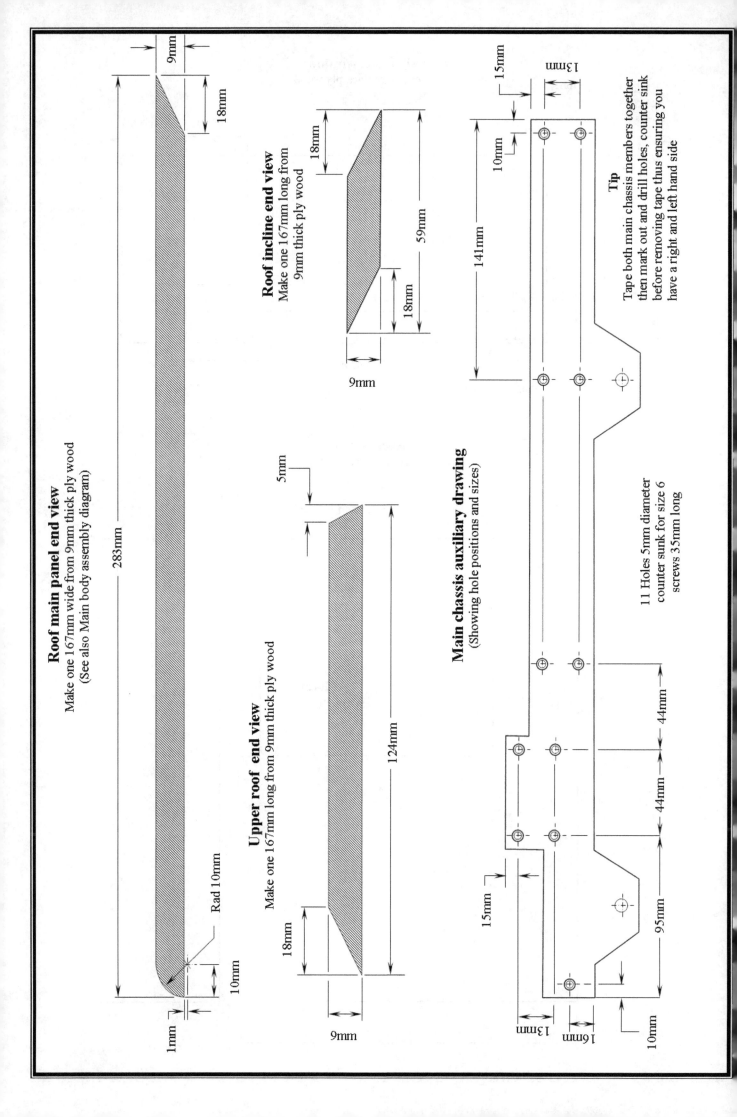

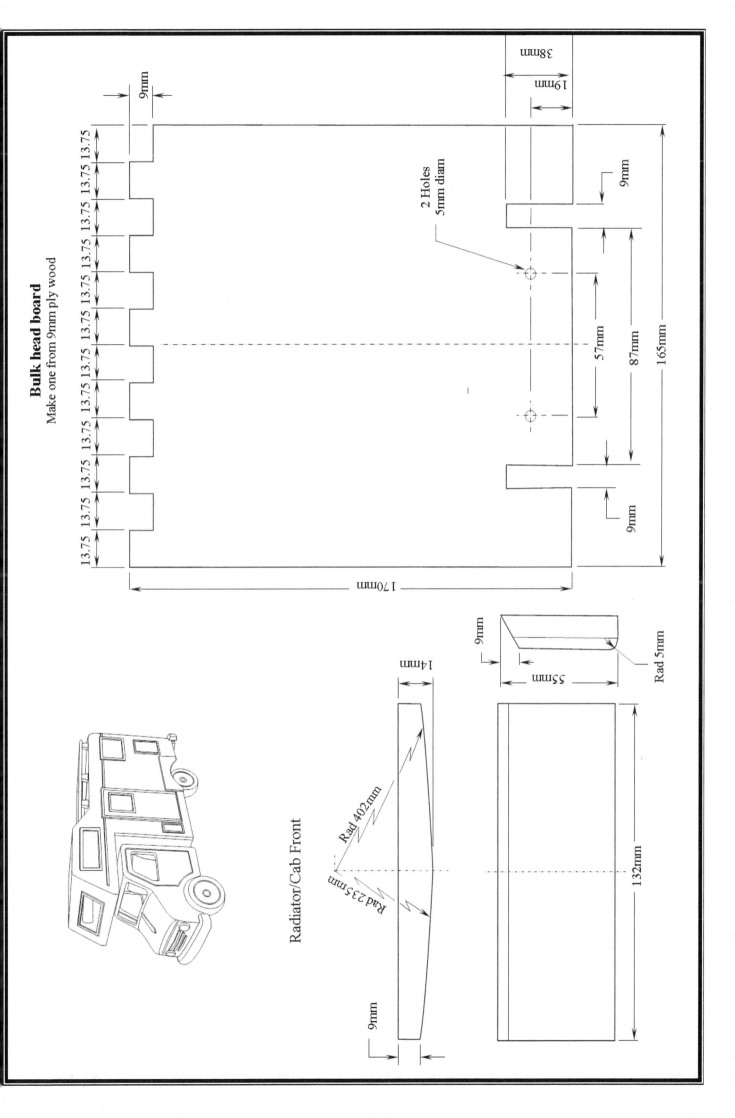

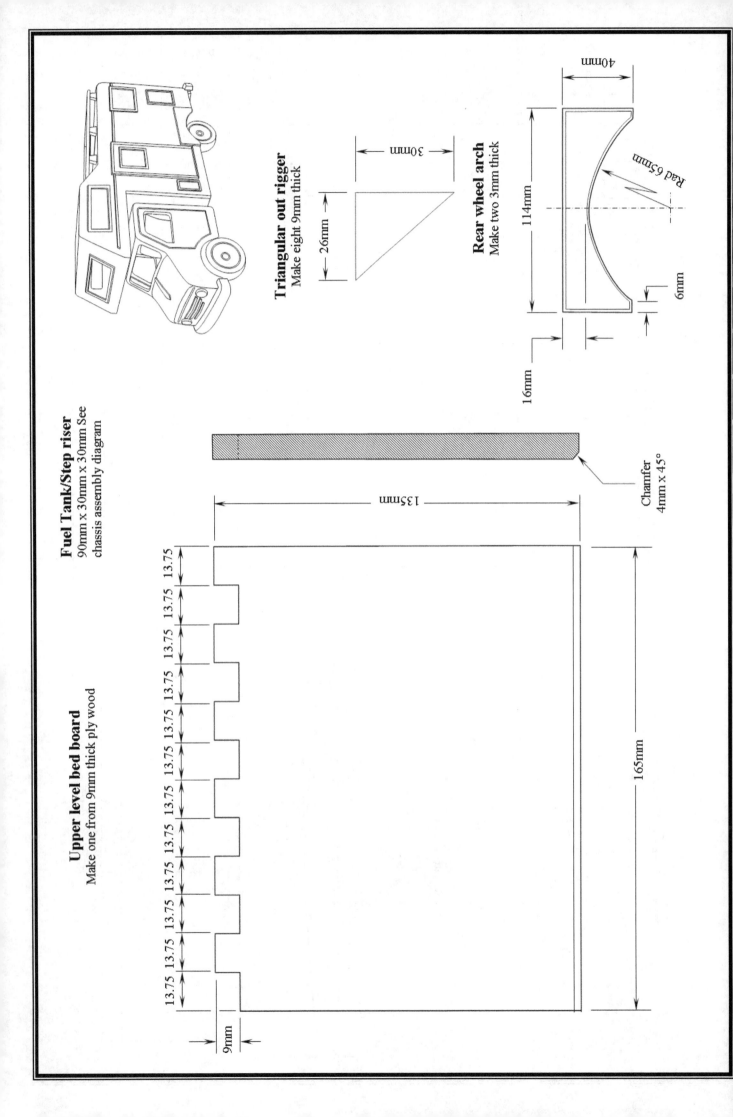

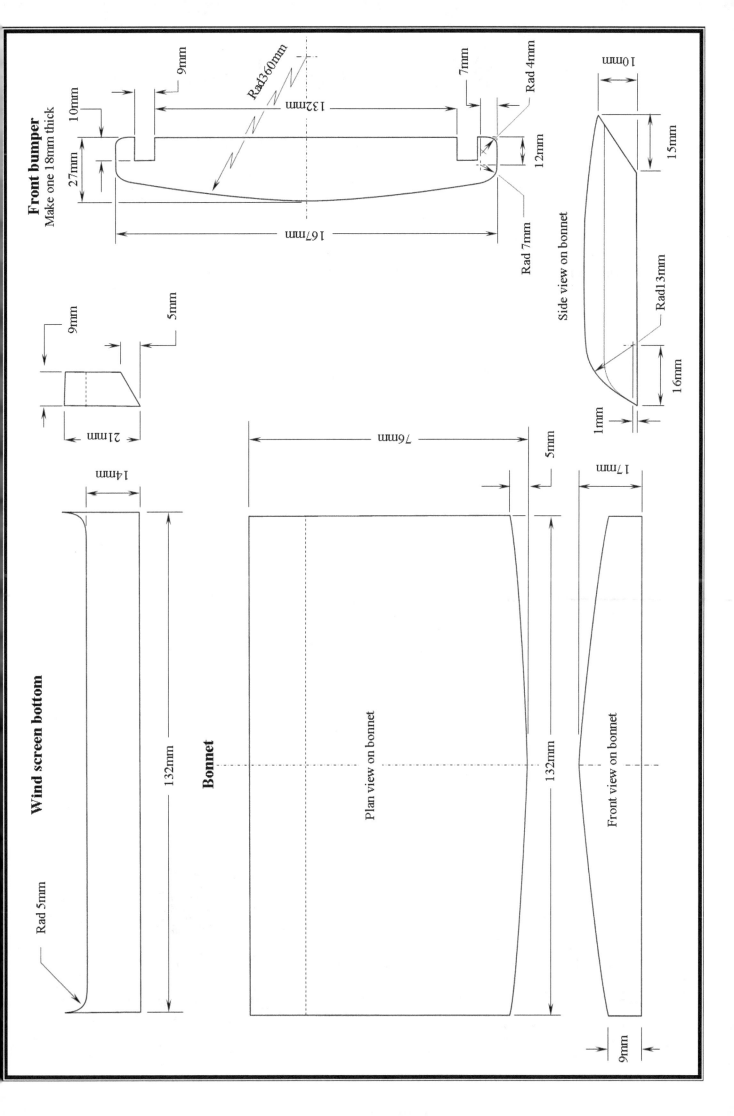

1942-1945 Model Army Jeep
355mm (14")long

A brief history of the 1943-1945 US Army Jeep

The Bantam Car Company won the opening round of the contest to satisfy the US army's 1940 specification for a light general purpose four wheel drive vehicle but Willys Overland won the battle and, some would say, the war. To ensure supply in war time the Army decided on a second supplier Ford. Between 1941 and 1945 Willys and Ford built about 700,000 of these vehicles. The main difference between the two is that the Willys chassis front cross member is tubular, whereas the Ford cross member is an inverted U section. The model jeep is mainly based on the ford, although this project is made mainly from wood metal has been used on the model where wood is inappropriate or doesn't have the strength

This picture shows the front spring hanger riveted to the chassis with brass dome head pins

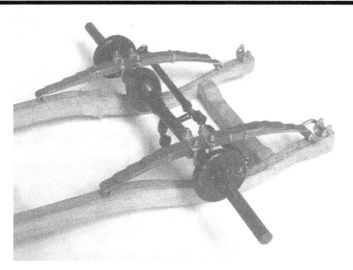

Front spring hanger riveted to chassis then the spring and front axle is test fitted to find the position of front spring rear hanger

The fire wall and fire wall top are glued between the side panels then the mud guards and inner wings are glued to these

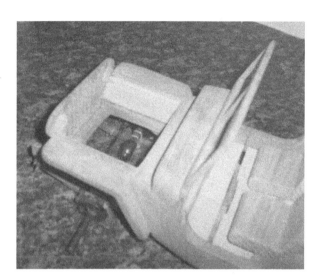

On the final fit the radiator grille is glued to the chassis front cross member.

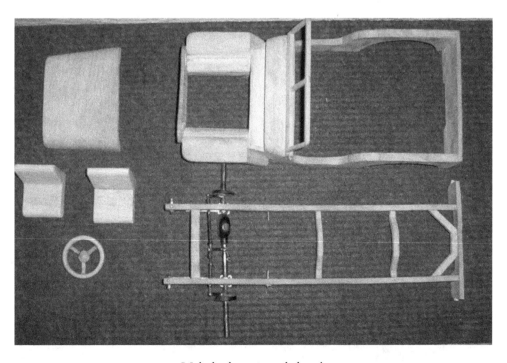

Main body parts and chassis

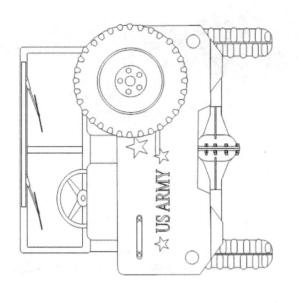
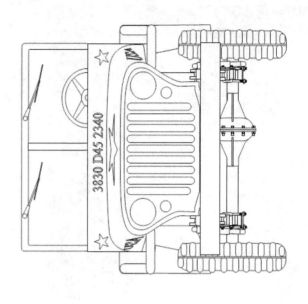
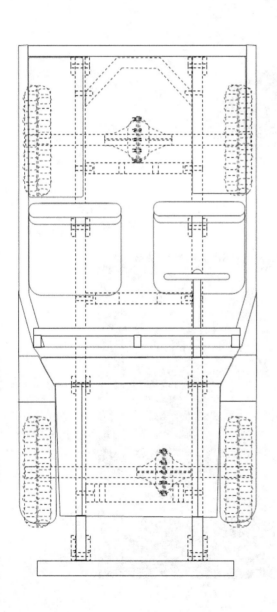
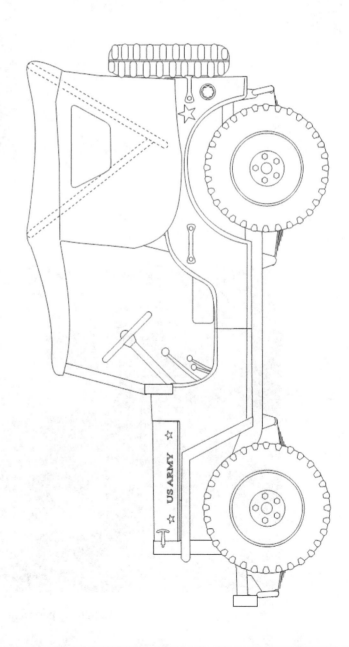

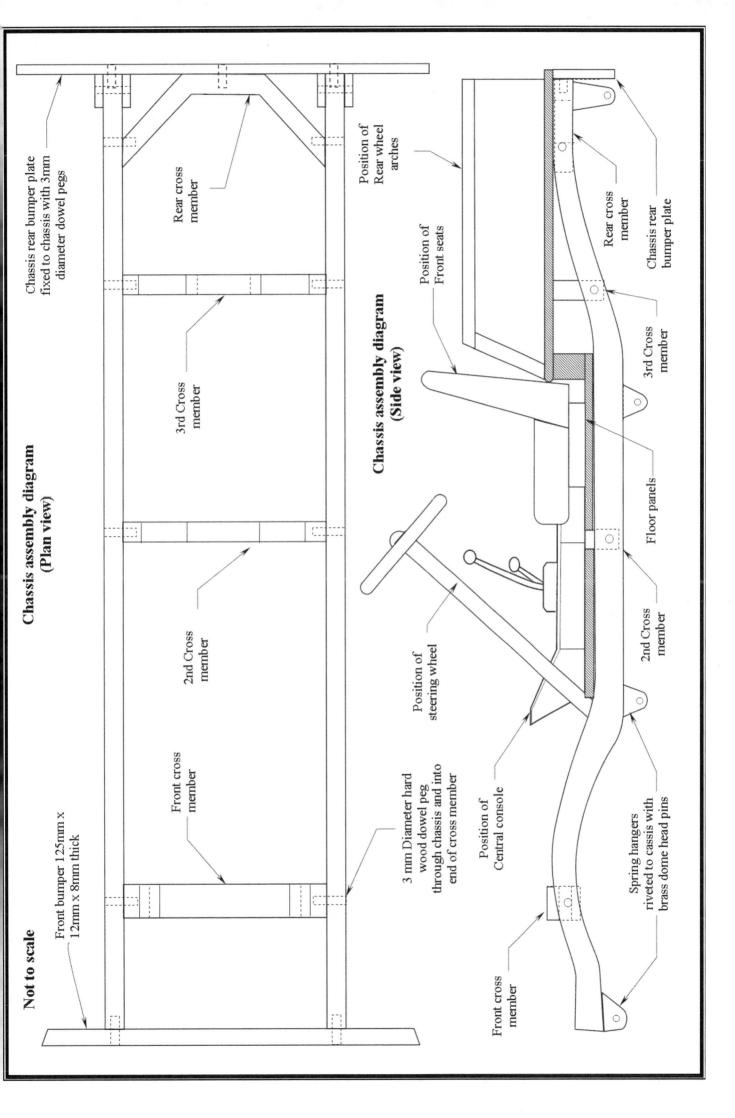

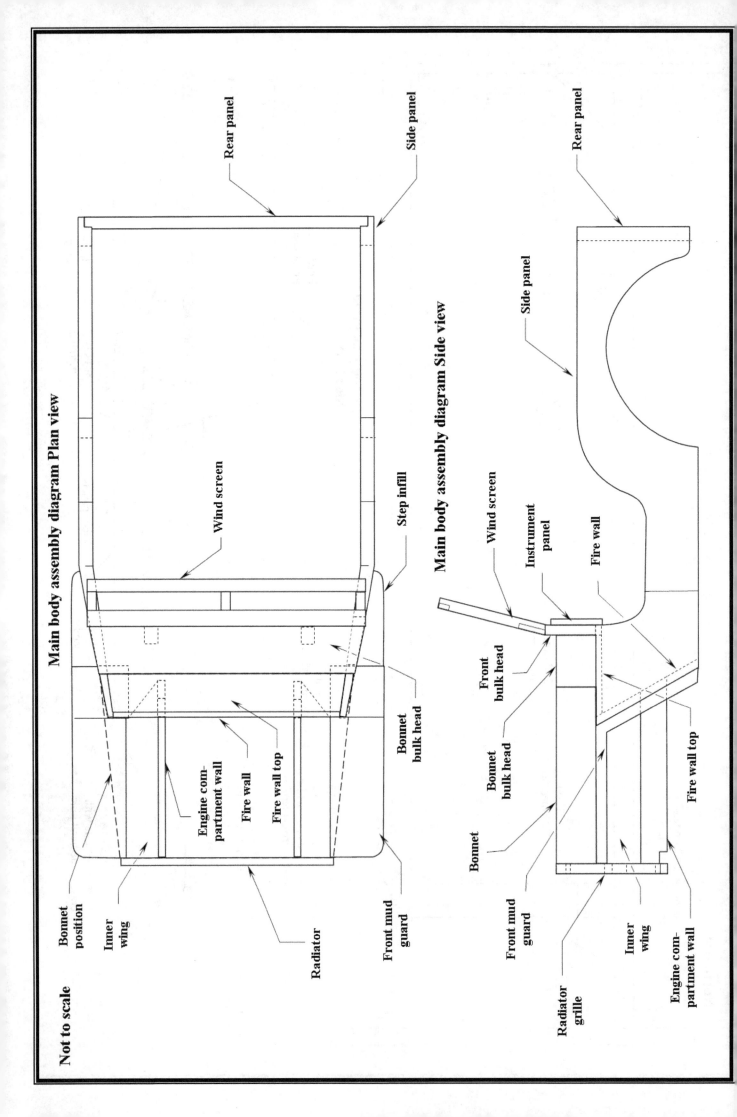

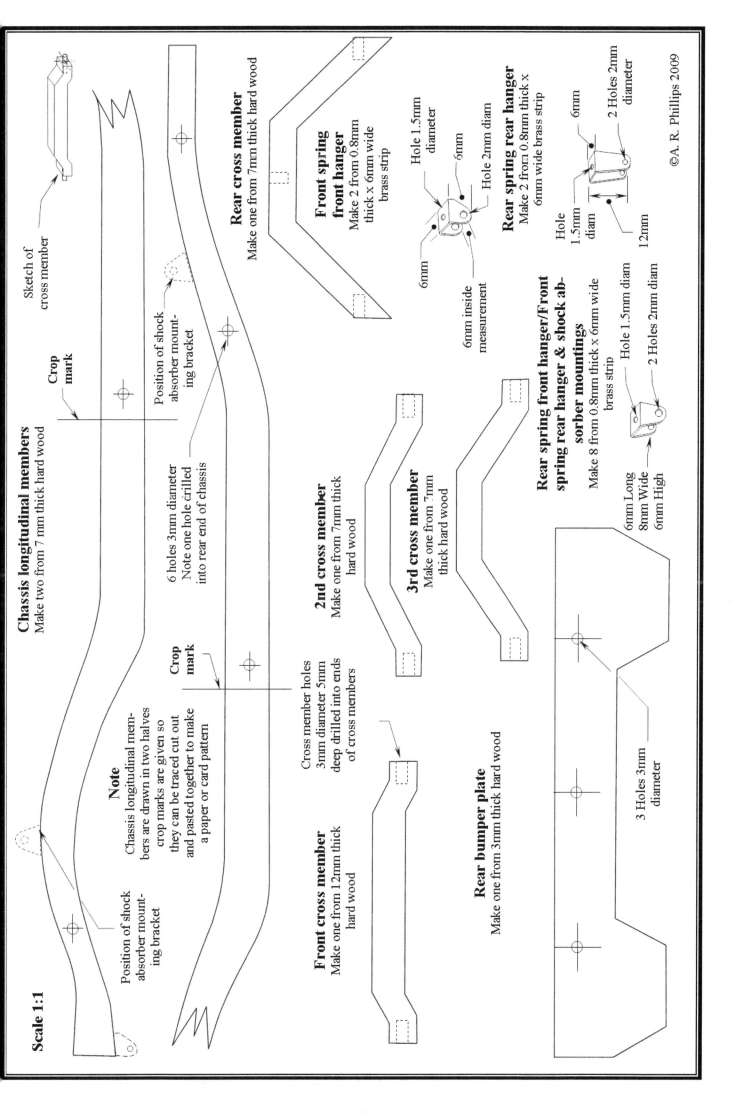

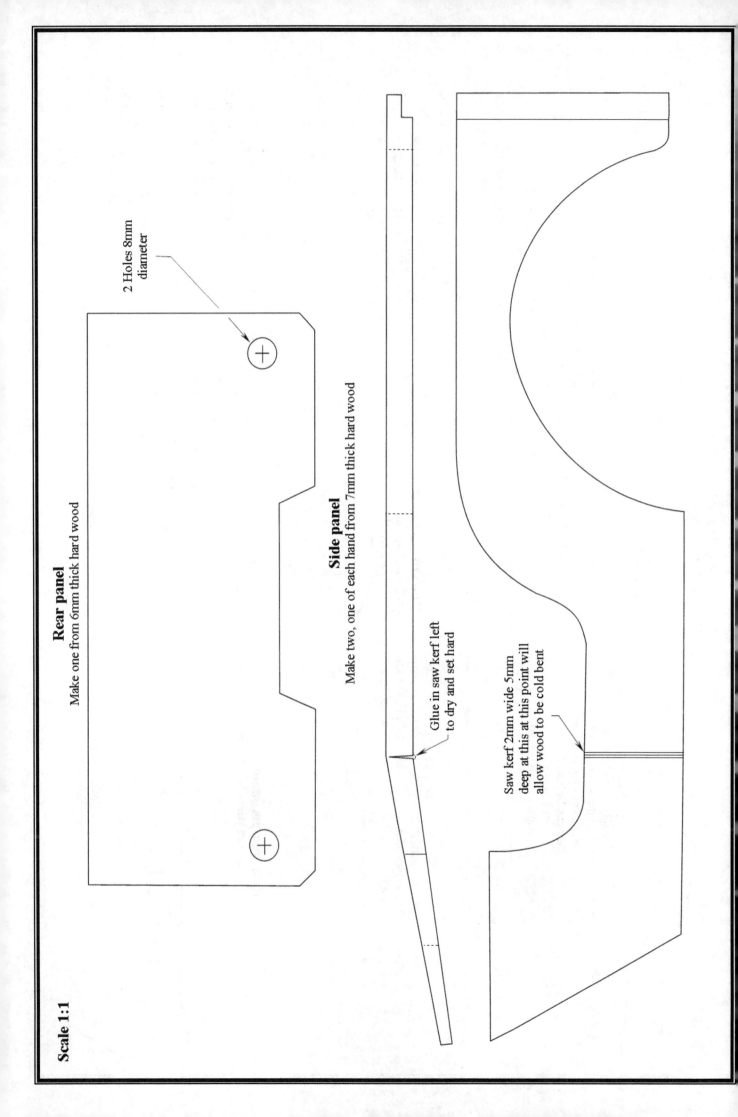

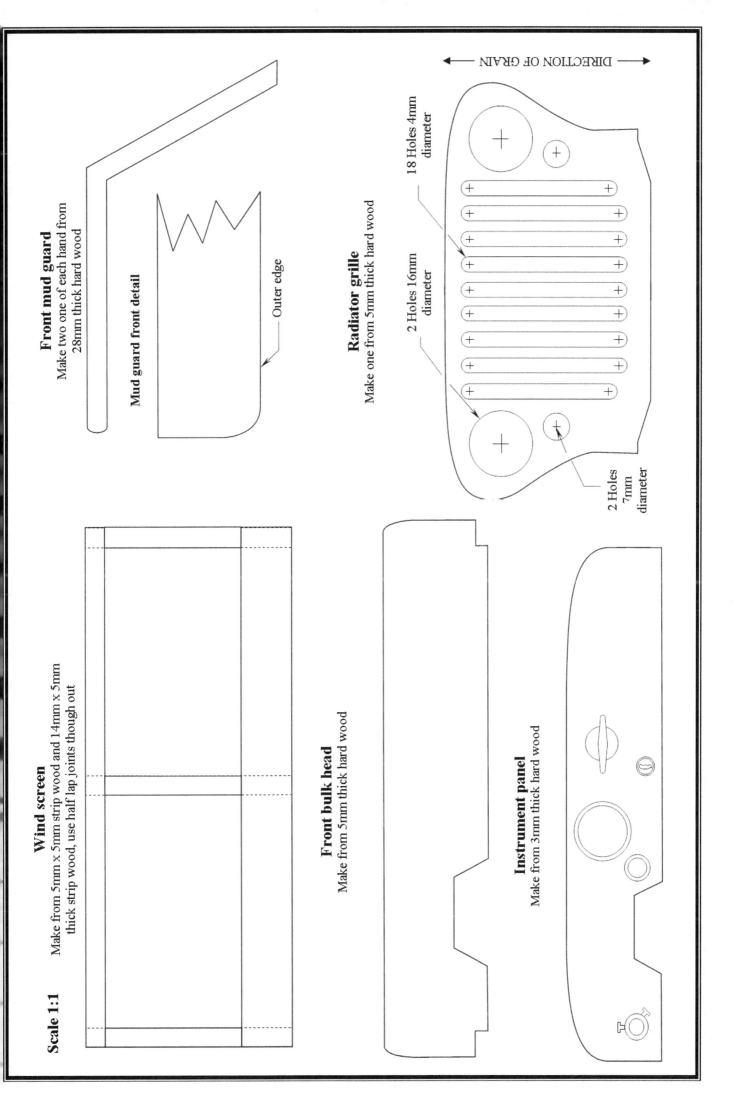

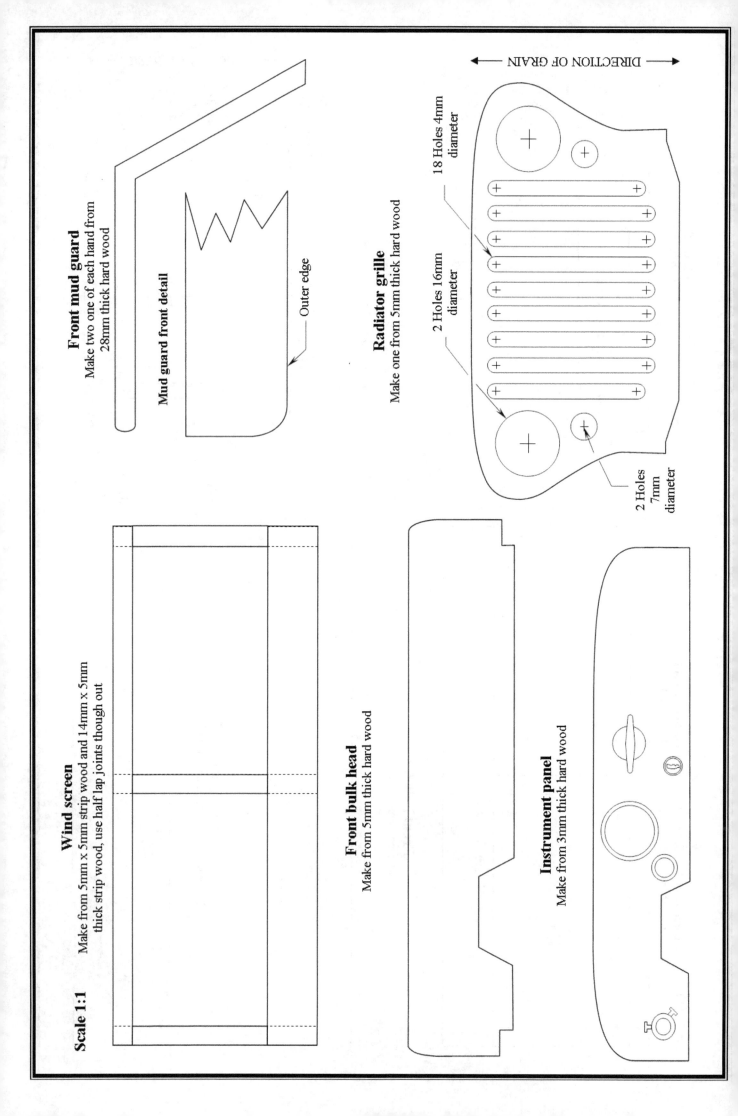

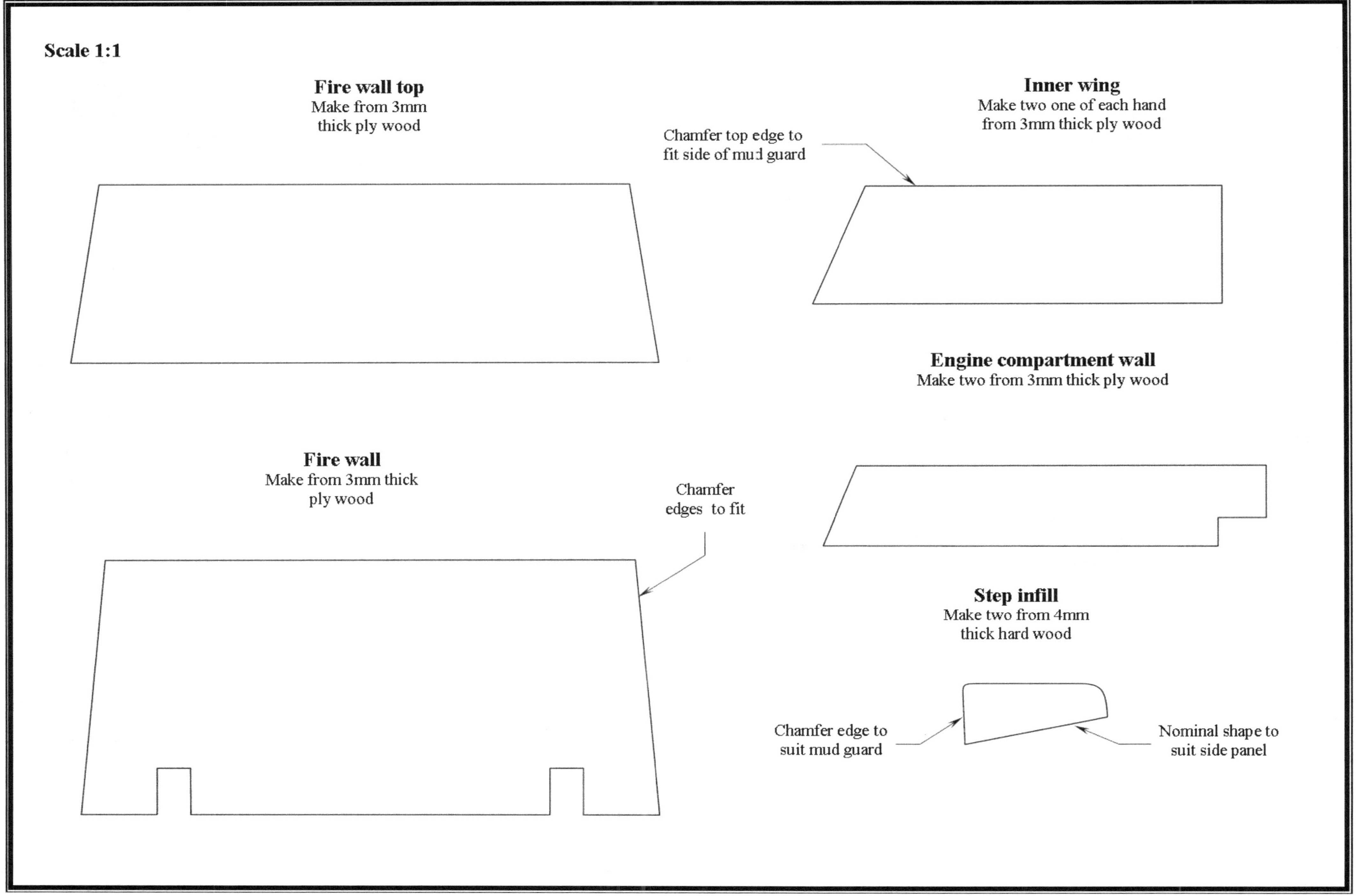

Scale 1:1

Inner wing
Make two one of each hand from 3mm thick ply wood

Chamfer top edge to fit side of mud guard

Engine compartment wall
Make two from 3mm thick ply wood

Step infill
Make two from 4mm thick hard wood

Nominal shape to suit side panel

Chamfer edge to suit mud guard

Fire wall top
Make from 3mm thick ply wood

Chamfer edges to fit

Fire wall
Make from 3mm thick ply wood

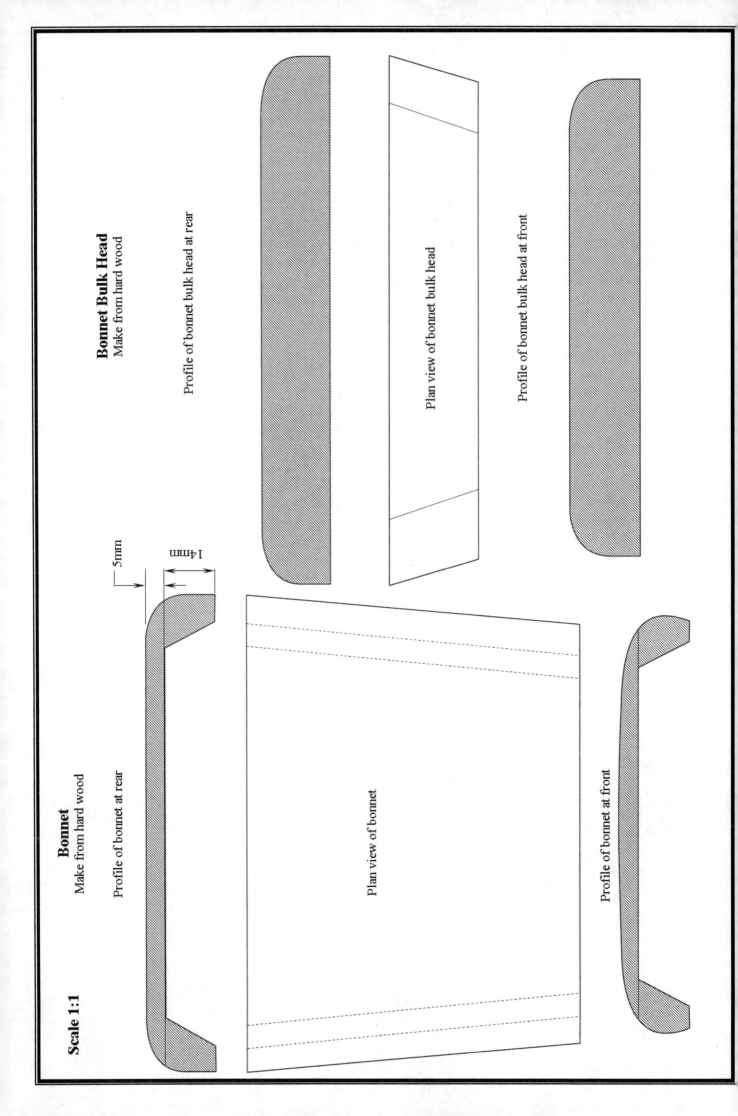

Front floor panel
Make from 3mm thick plywood

Centre floor panel
Make from 3mm thick plywood

Rear floor panel
Make from

8mm x 8mm strip wood glued to underside

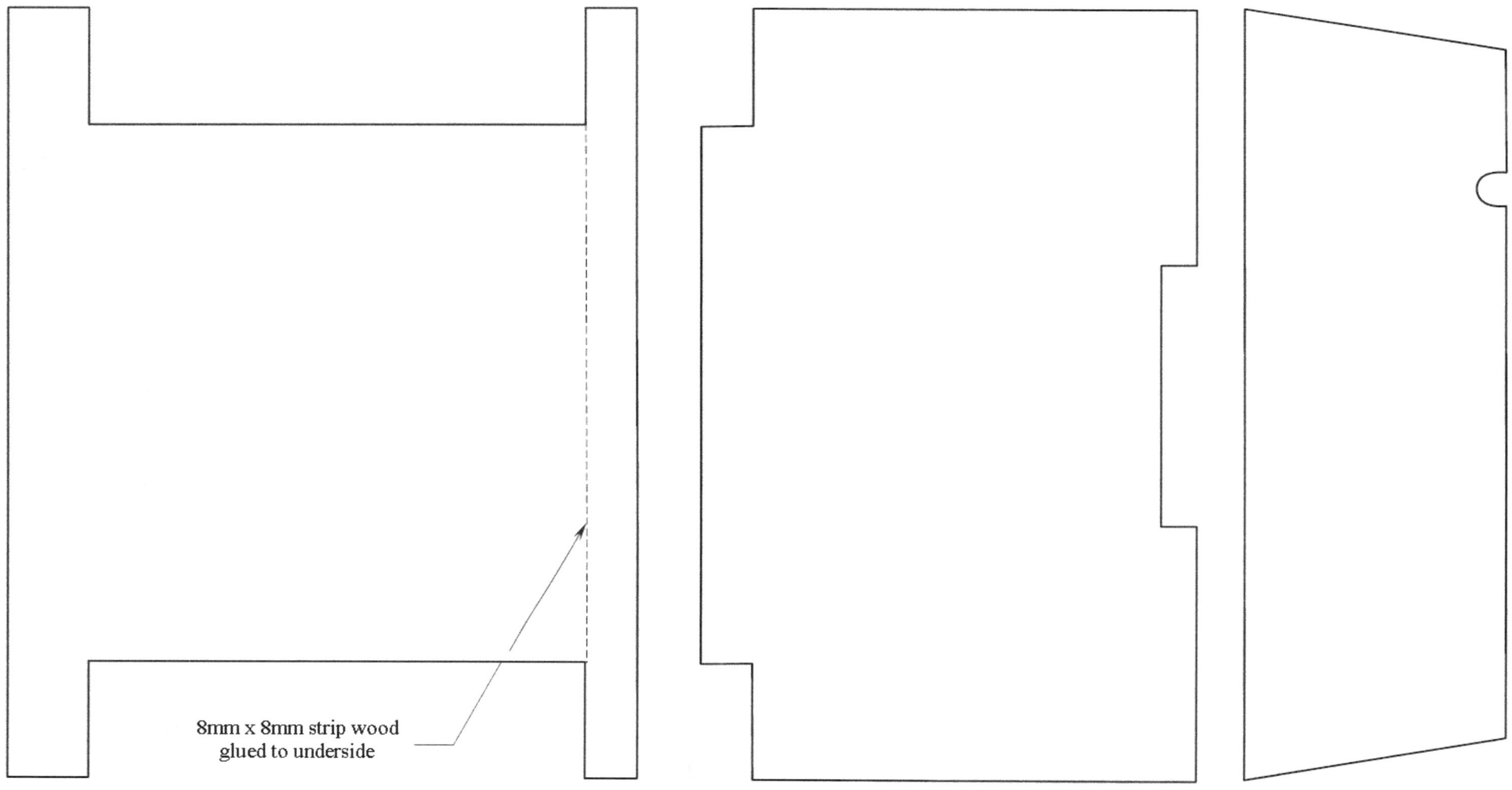

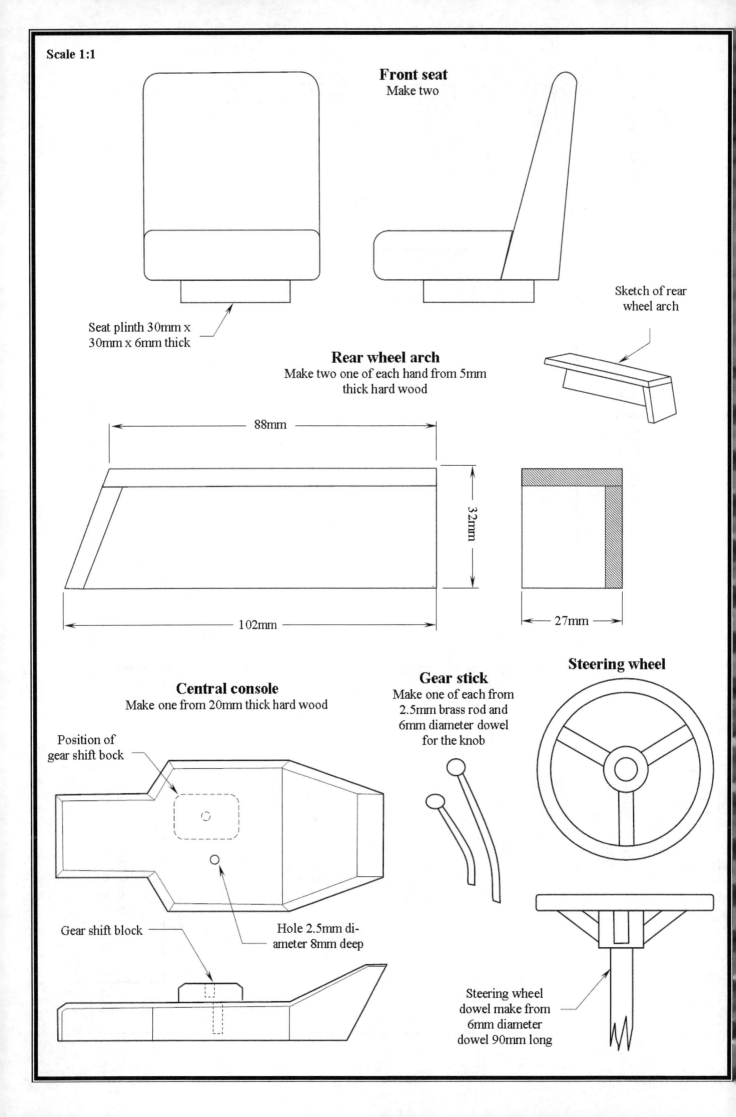

Scale 1:1

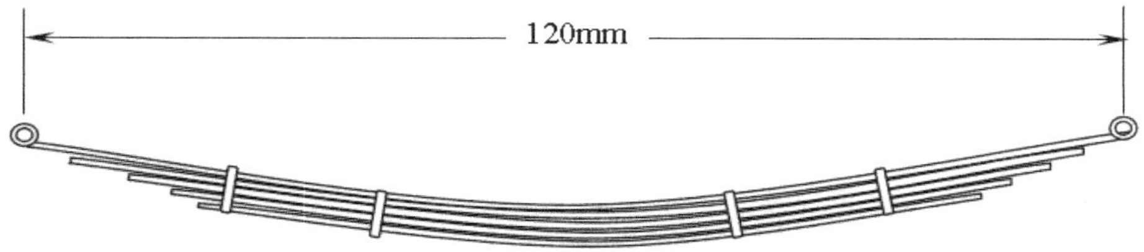

Rear spring
Make two from .08mm thick x 6mm wide brass strip

100mm

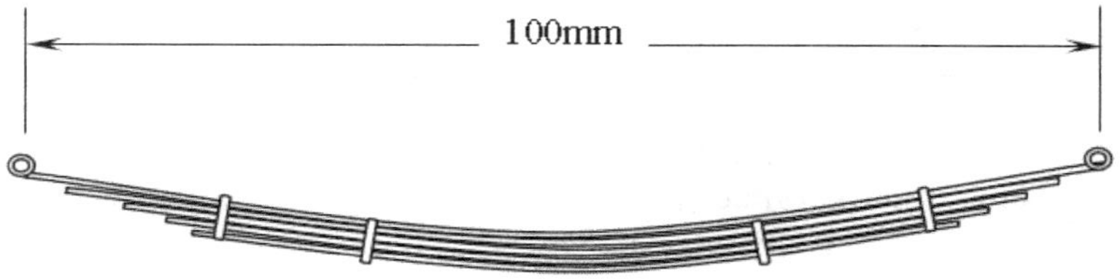

Wheel
Make four from 18mm thick hard wood

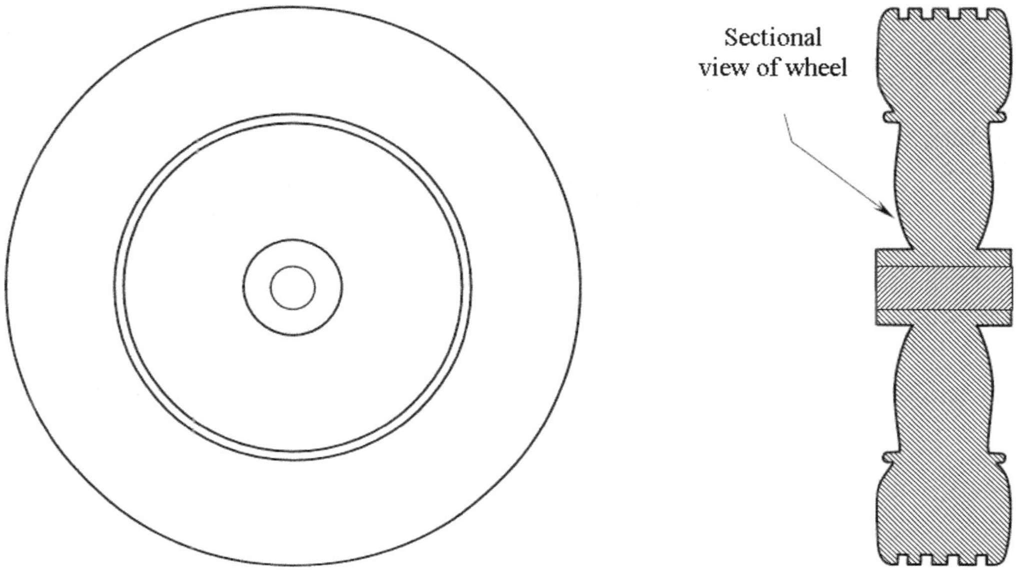

Sectional view of wheel

Front spring
Make two from .08mm thick x 6mm wide brass strip

120mm

NOTE
The wheels are held on to the axles by drilling a 3mm diameter hole down the end of the axle then a cut down felt nail/clout nail with a 10mm diameter head is glued into the hole with epoxy resin see drawing below

Rear axle

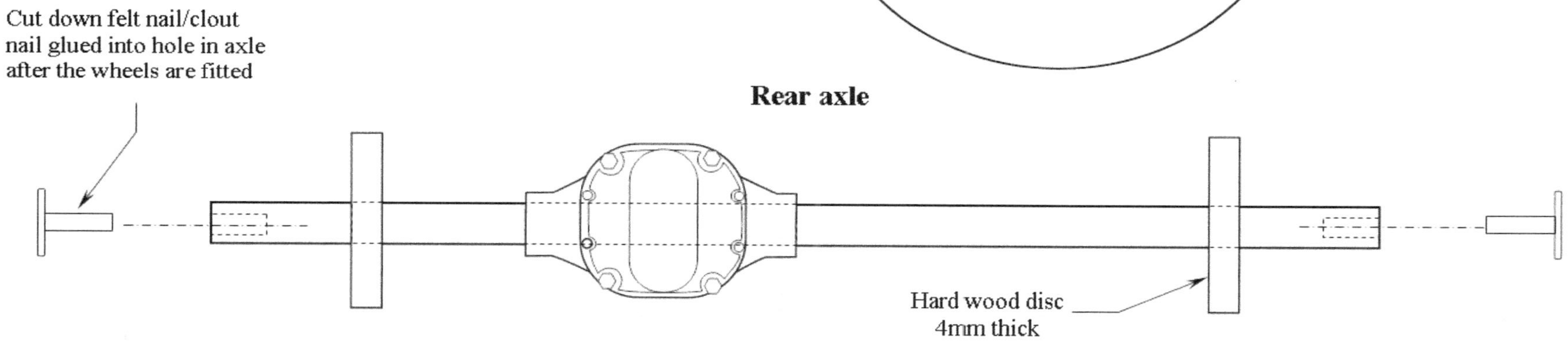

Hard wood disc 4mm thick

Cut down felt nail/clout nail glued into hole in axle after the wheels are fitted

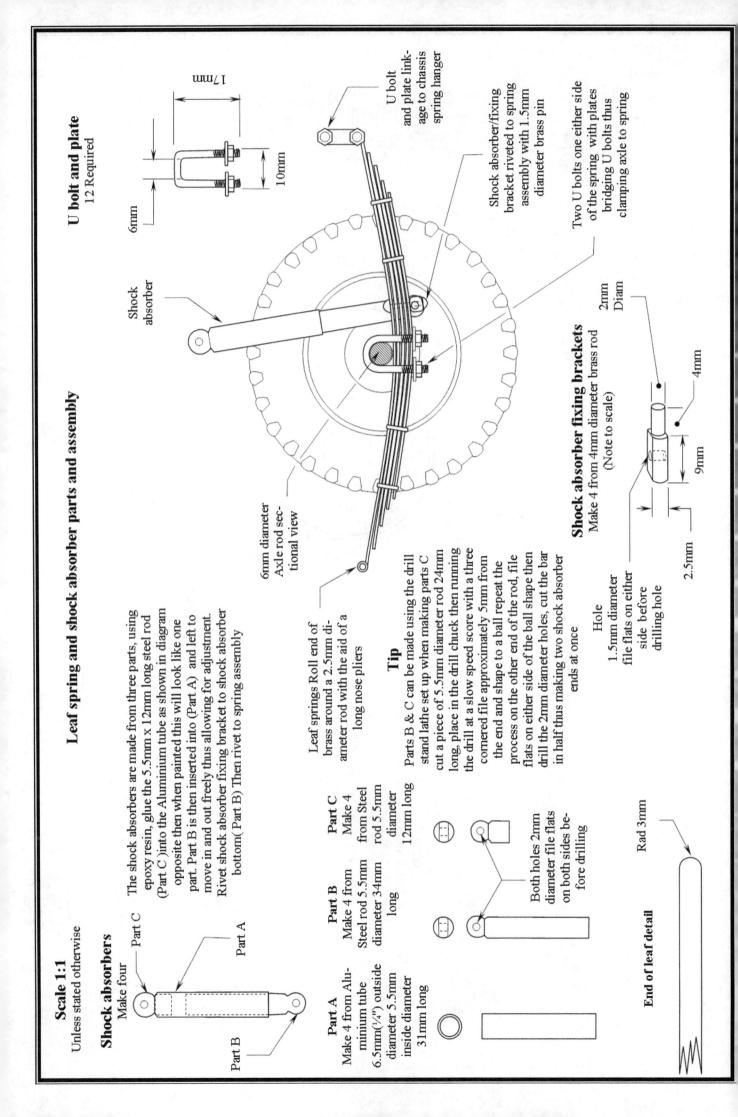

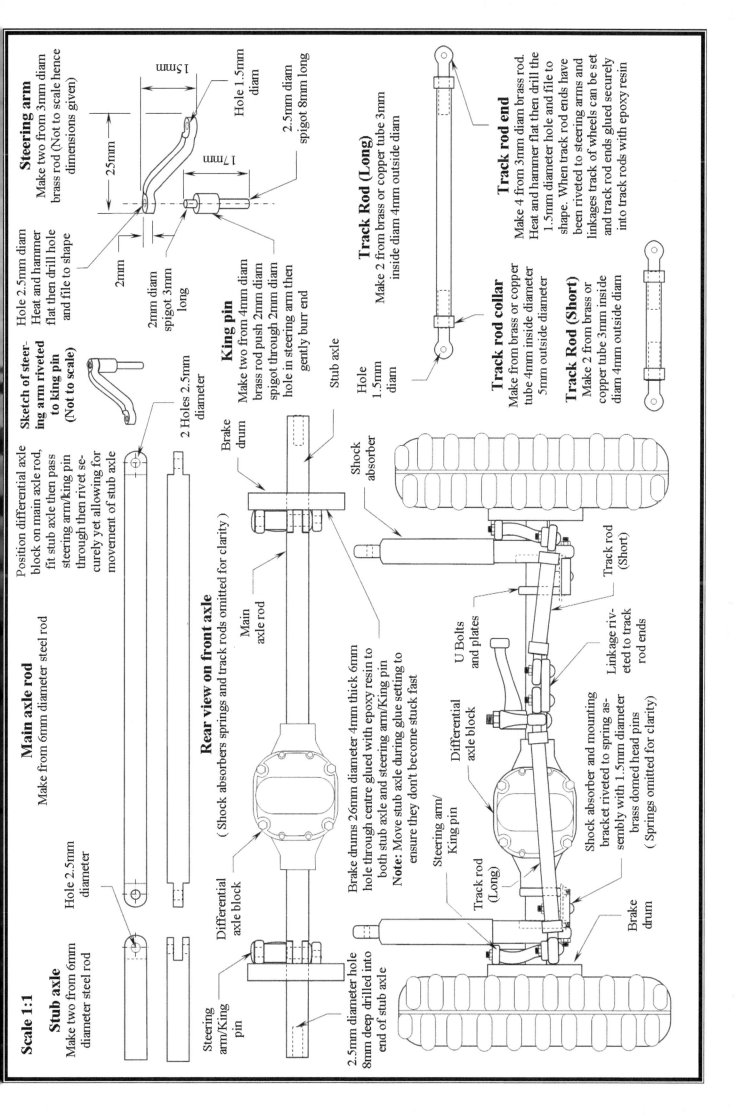

1912 Packard Victoria

355mm (14")long

James Ward Packard and electric equipment manufacturer knew he could build a better car than the Winton he had just bought. In 1899 he began building single cylinder cars. By 1903 the first four cylinder appeared. A year later the model L four cylinder was produced featuring Packard's distinctive yolk shaped radiator. By 1912 the first six cylinder appeared in the form of the Packard Victoria earning Packard a reputation for building luxury cars. The model is based on this

Plan view on completed car

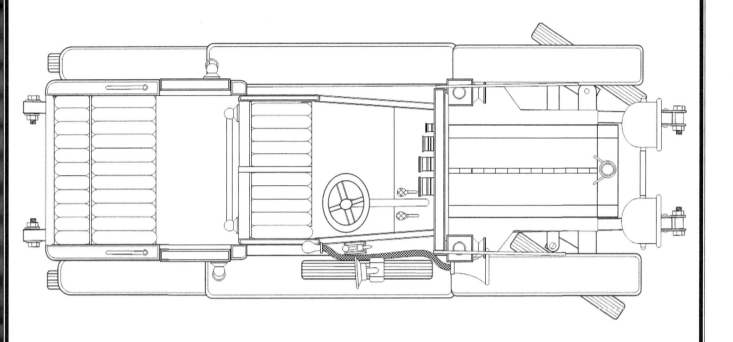

Side view on completed car

Plan view on completed car

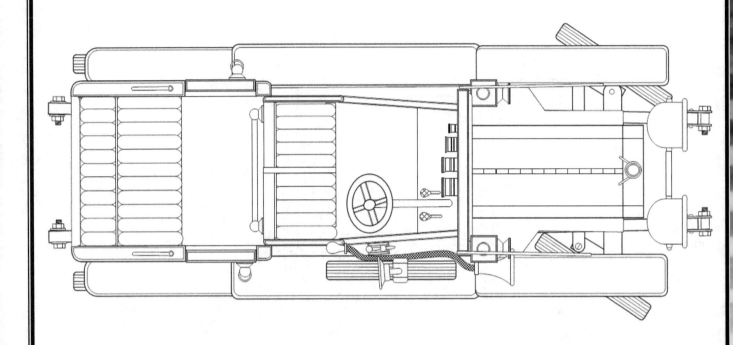

Side view on completed car

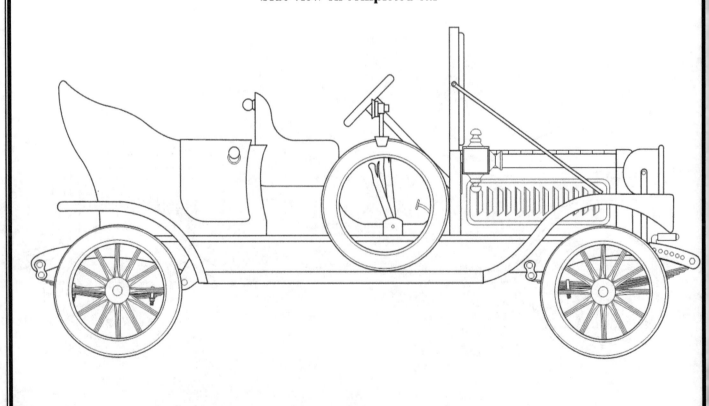

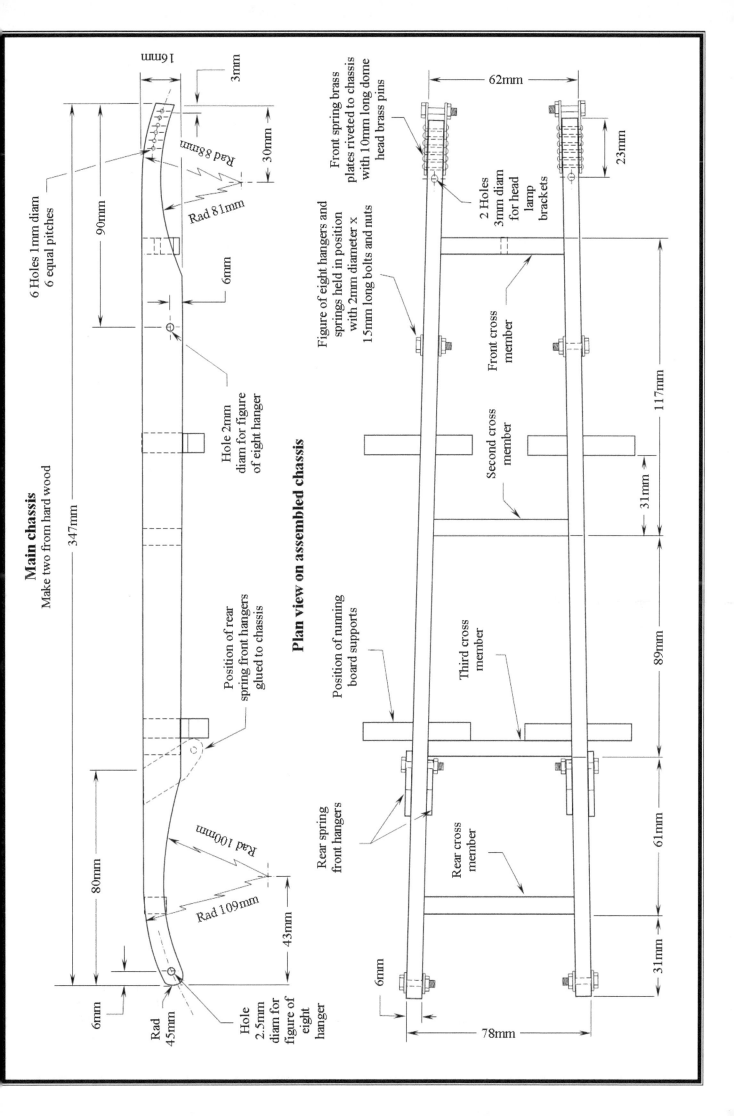

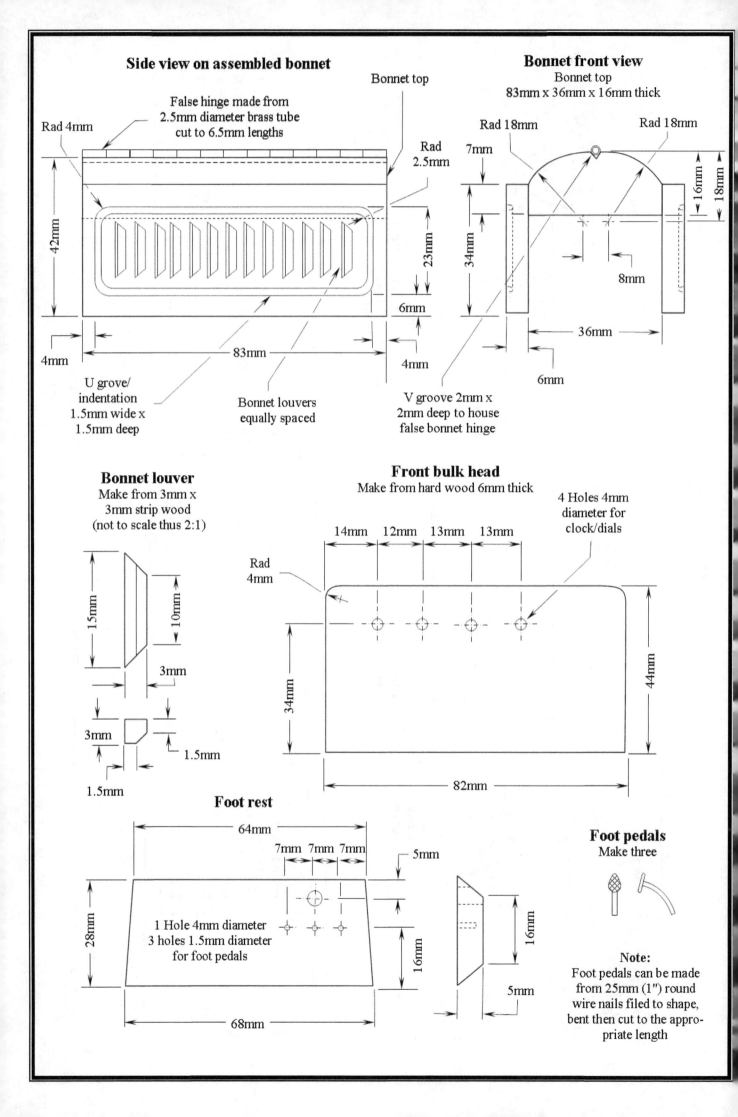

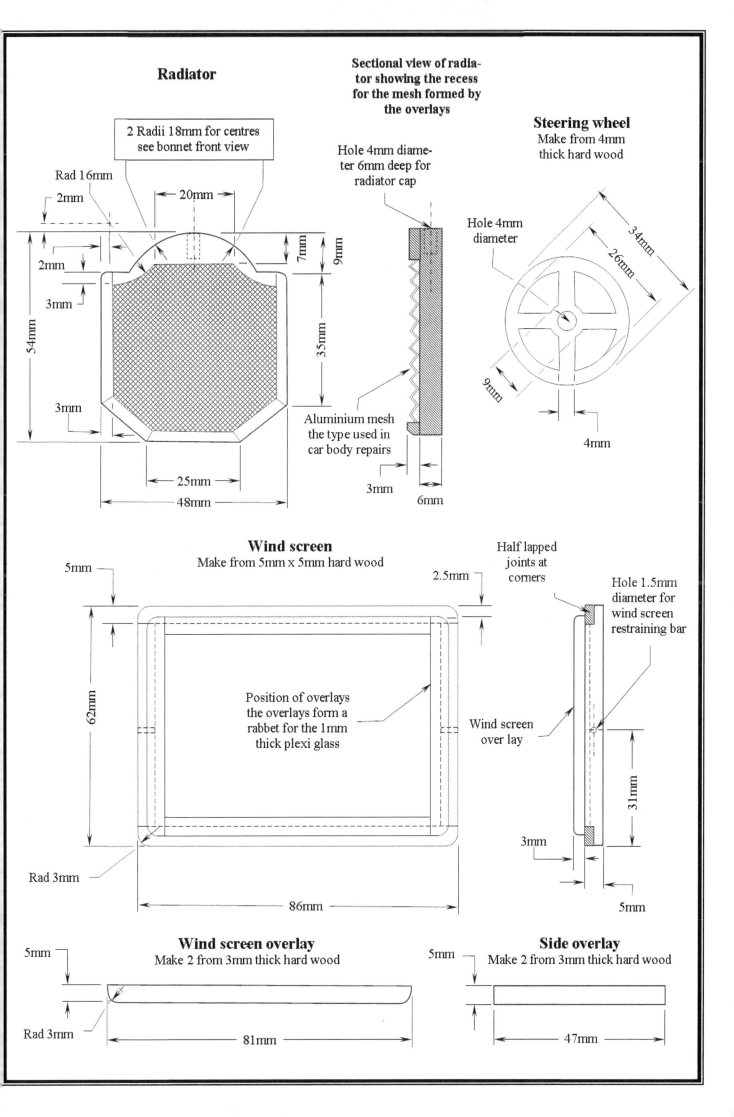

Assembled front body, plan view
Seats and seat cushions omitted for clarity

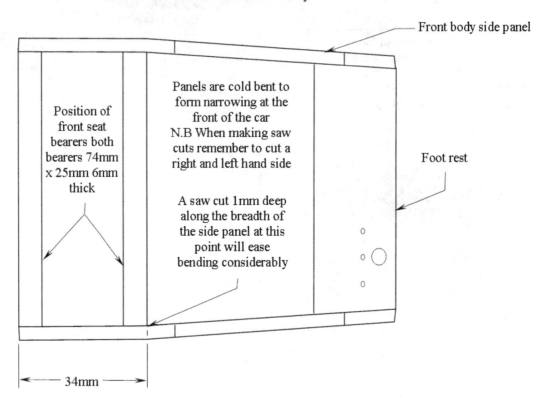

Front body side panel
Make two from 3mm thick hard wood

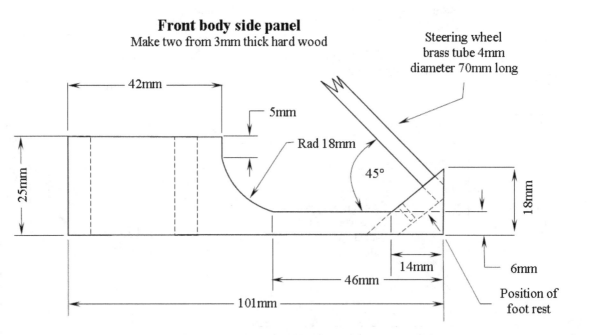

Rear seat plinth

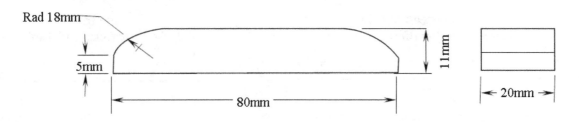

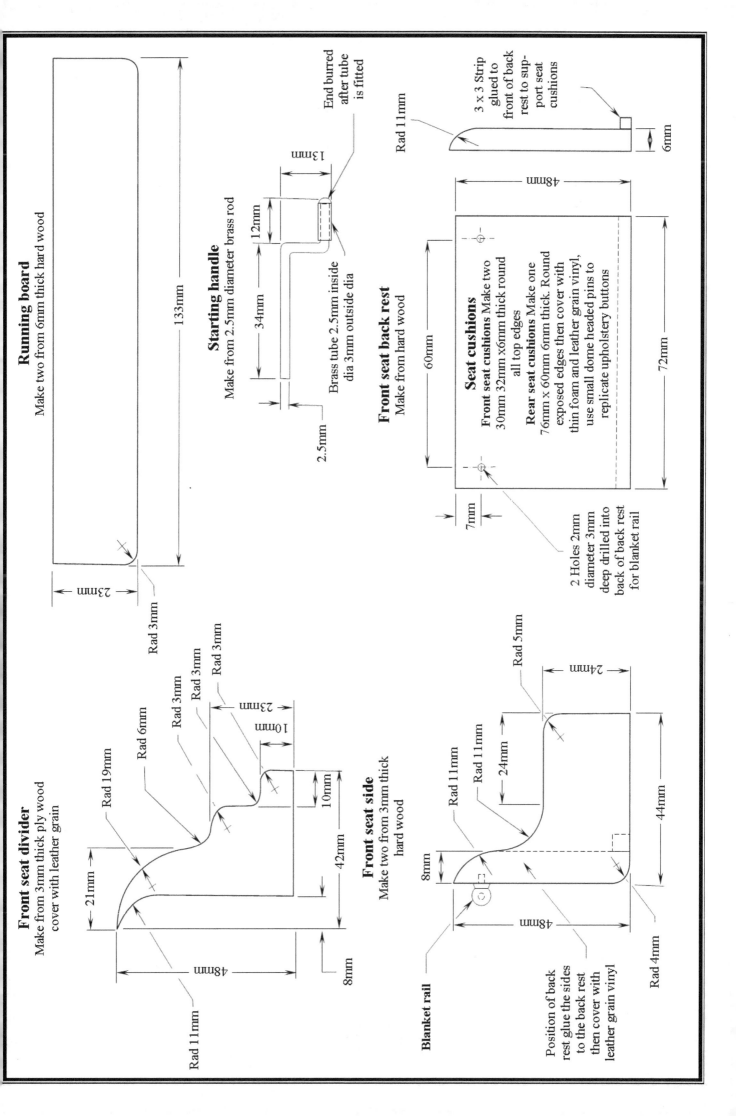

Rear body side panel
Make two, one of each hand from 11mm thick hard wood

Note: After the rear body side panel has been shaped cut out the door with a fine blade then thin the door thickness to 7mm chamfer all edges and then glue the door back into position, remember to thin each door on inside faces only

Rear body side panel end view
showing nominal shaping of the side panel

Grid = 5mm x 5mm

7mm

109mm
92mm
77mm
50mm
47mm
44mm
8mm
Rad 72mm
Rad 64mm
Hole 2mm diameter 3mm deep
16mm
8mm
38mm
46mm
77mm
Rad 14mm
Rad 2mm
8mm
39mm
Rad 43mm
Rad 64mm
Rad 43mm
Rad 2mm
15mm
Position of rear seat plinth
111mm
24mm
Rad 2mm
Rad 43mm
Rad 64mm
42mm
80mm
6mm

Back panel
80mm long x 88mm high 11mm thick shape to suit contour of side panel

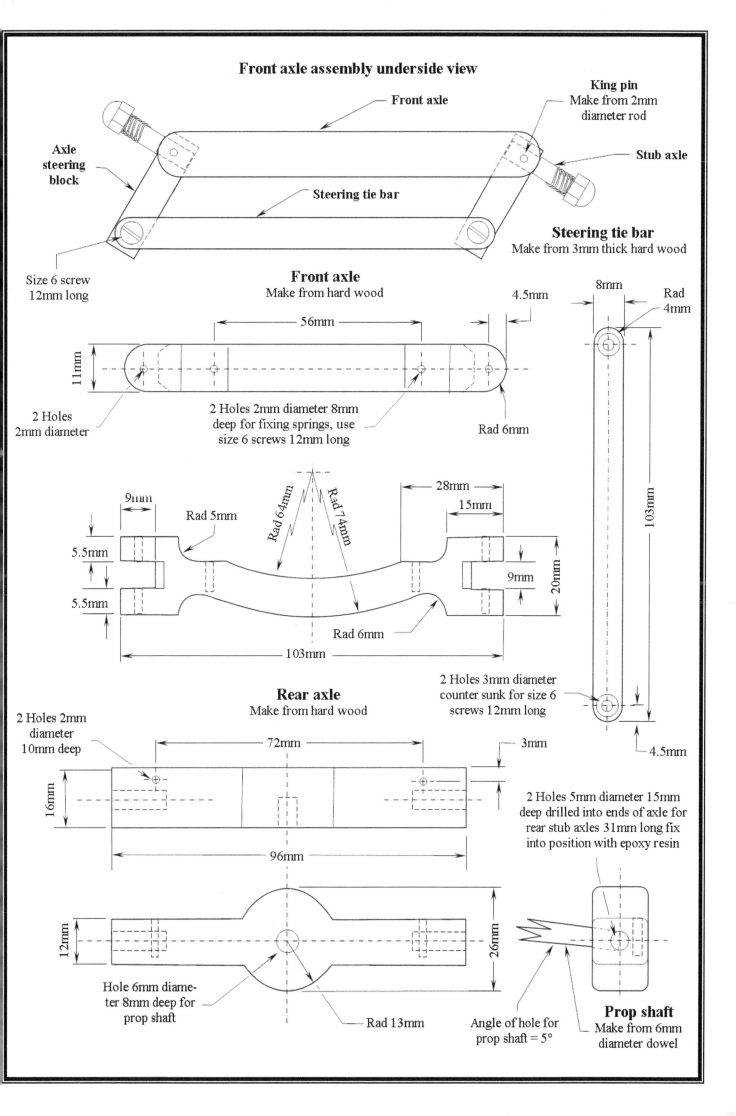

Front stub axle

Hole 2mm diameter
4.75mm
28mm
4.75mm

Axle steering block
Make two from hard wood

34mm
Hole 5mm diameter
9mm
4.5mm

Pilot hole 2mm diameter 8mm deep
Hole 2mm diameter
9mm
4mm
4.5mm

Rear brake drum
Make two 3mm thick

22mm
Hole 5mm diameter

Front spring brass plate
Make 4 from 0.6mm (.025") thick brass

28mm
Rad 3.5mm
Hole 2.5mm diameter
6 Holes 1mm diameter 6 equal pitches
3mm
4mm
Rad 81mm
Rad 88mm

Figure of eight front and rear spring hangers
Make 8 from 0.6mm (.025") thick brass

Rad 14mm
20mm
Rad 14mm
2 Holes 2.5mm diameter
3.5mm
8mm

Running board support
Make 2 dimension L 50mm and 2 dimension L 45mm from 6mm thick hard wood

17mm
29mm
3mm
9mm
9mm
Dimension L
Rad 6mm

Front cross member
Make from 6mm hard wood

50mm
16mm
9mm
Hole 2.5mm diameter for starting handle
8mm

Rear spring front hanger
Make 4 from 3mm thick hard wood

Hole 2.5 mm diameter
26mm
33mm
12mm
5mm
4mm
12.5mm
Rad 4mm

Second cross member 57mm x 16mm x 6mm thick
Third cross member 61mm x 16mm x 6mm thick
Rear cross member 64mm x 9mm x 6mm thick

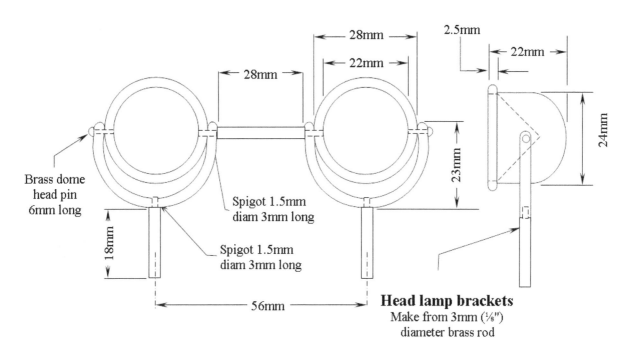

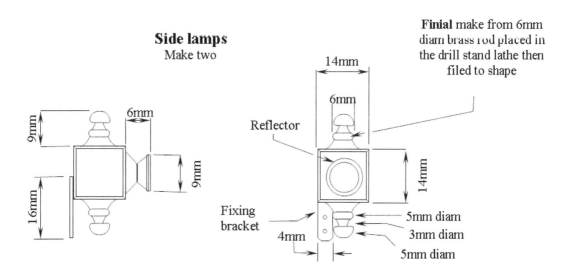

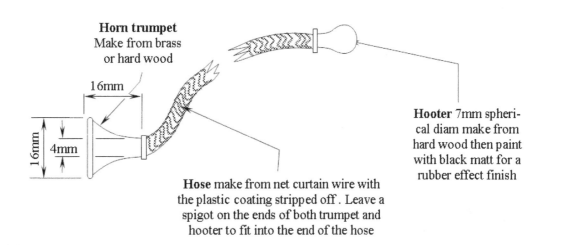

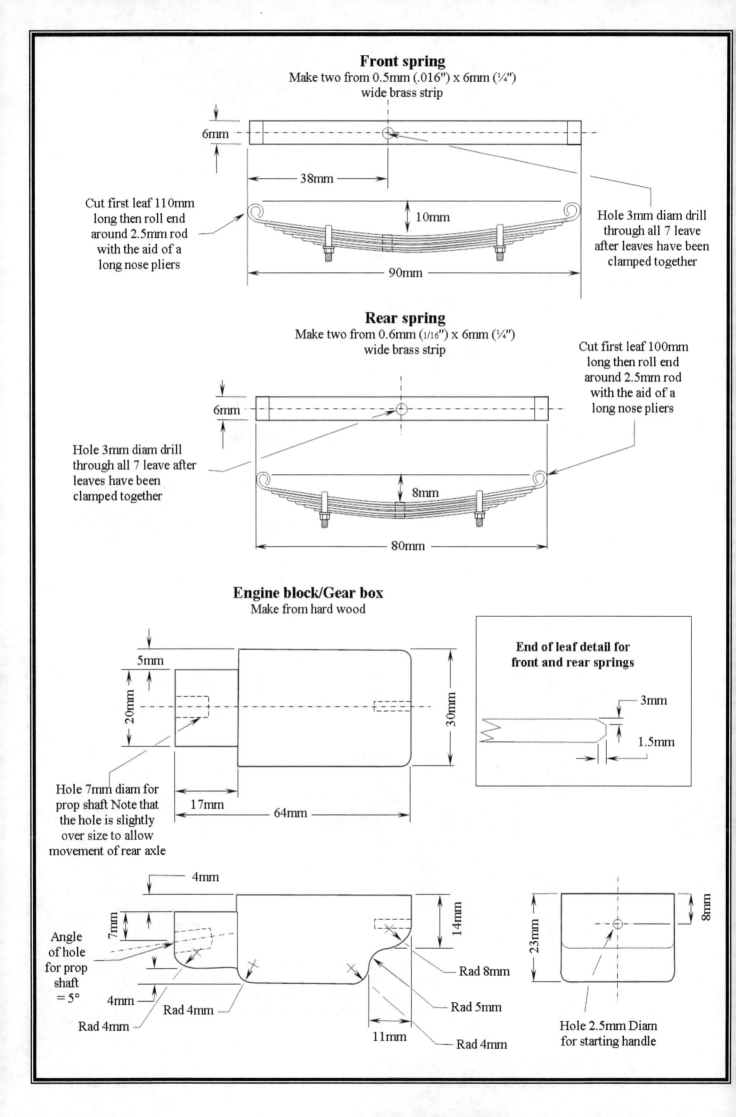

Blanket rail
Fitted to rear of drivers seat

Dimensions as door Knobs hole only drilled half way through

2.5mm Diam brass rod

60mm

1.5mm Diam spigot 2.5mm long

Clocks/Dials
Make three from 6mm diam brass rod

8mm, 5.5mm, 1.5mm, 4mm, 4.5mm

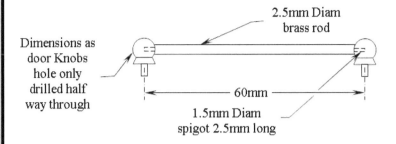
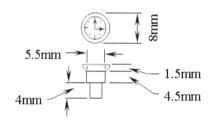

Wing mirror

- 8mm Diam
- 6mm Diam
- 3mm Diam
- 10mm Diam brass rod
- 2mm Diam brass rod

10mm, 8mm, 9mm, 6mm, 5mm, 7mm

Radiator cap
Make from 6mm diam brass rod wings make from 0.5mm thick brass

6mm, 3mm, 16mm, 4mm

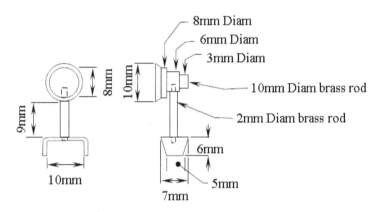
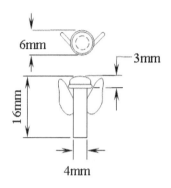

Hand brake/Gear lever
Make two one dimension L 45mm the other dimension L 35mm from 1.5mm thick brass

Hole 1mm Diam

4mm, 2.5mm

Make a hack saw cut at this point then file to shape

Dimension L

Gear lever quadrant
Make from 0.5mm thick brass

8mm, 5mm, 11mm

Hole 1.5mm

Rivet gear and brake lever into position with brass dome head pins

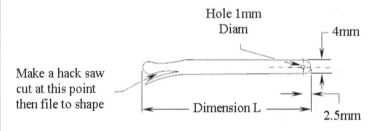
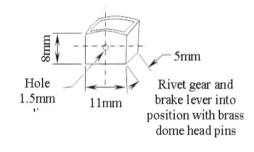

Hand grip scroll
Make two from 1.5mm diameter brass wire

8mm, 22mm

2 Holes 1mm diam flatten ends drill the holes then bend to shape fix into position with 6mm dome head pins

Door knob
Make two

3mm diam, 3mm diam, 2mm diam, 6mm, 3mm, 7mm, 7mm, 2mm

Brass ring Make from 1.5mm diam brass wire

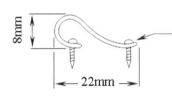
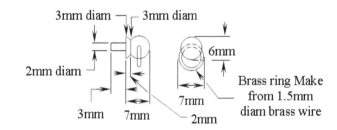

Wind screen restraining bar
Make two from 1.5mm diam brass rod

Flatten end of rod then drill the 1.5mm diam and file to shape

6mm, 100mm

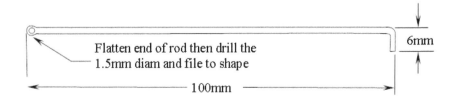

Toy and Model Projects

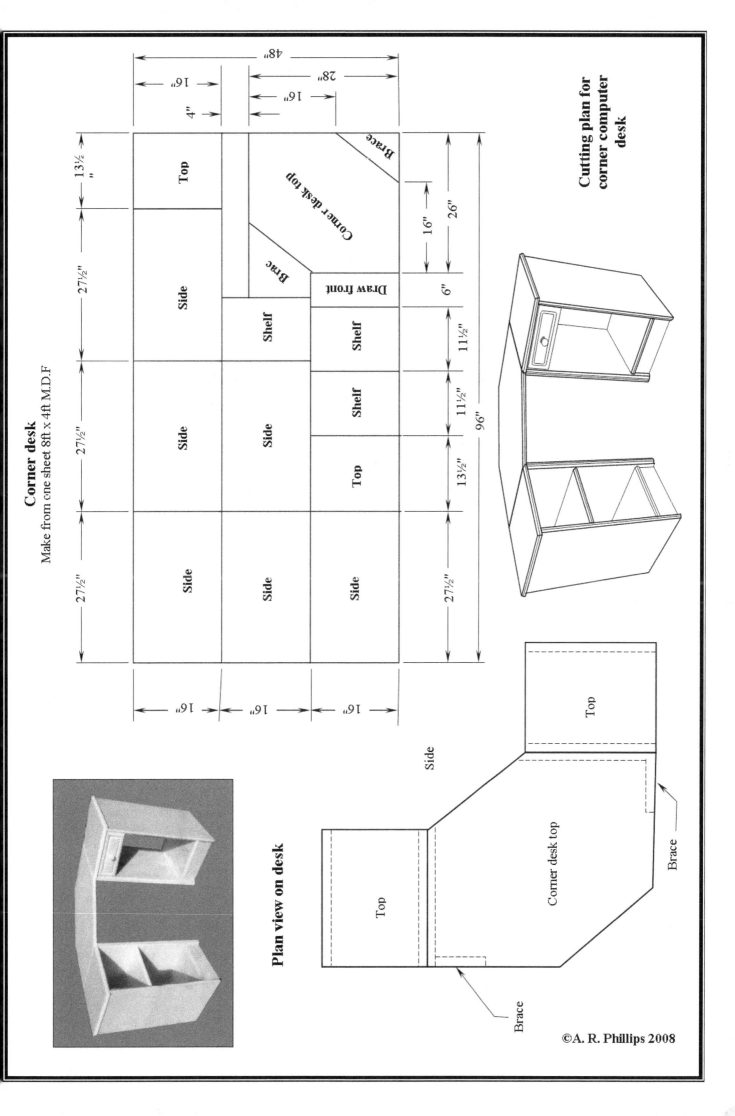

Display Cabinet

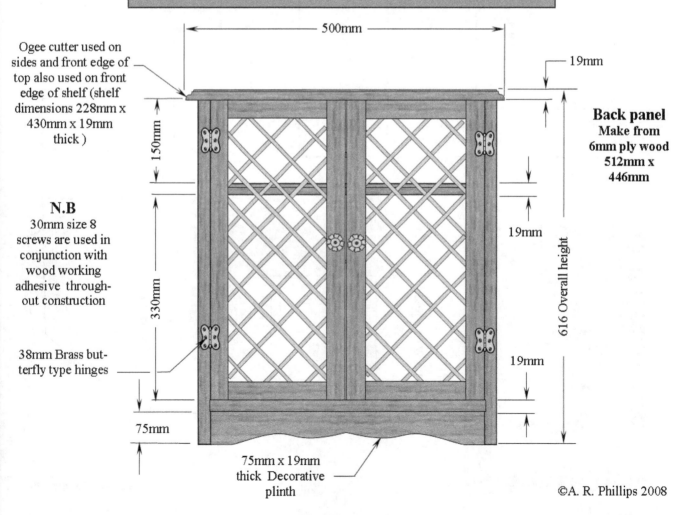

Ogee cutter used on sides and front edge of top also used on front edge of shelf (shelf dimensions 228mm x 430mm x 19mm thick)

500mm

19mm

Back panel Make from 6mm ply wood 512mm x 446mm

150mm

19mm

N.B 30mm size 8 screws are used in conjunction with wood working adhesive throughout construction

330mm

616 Overall height

19mm

38mm Brass butterfly type hinges

75mm

75mm x 19mm thick Decorative plinth

©A. R. Phillips 2008

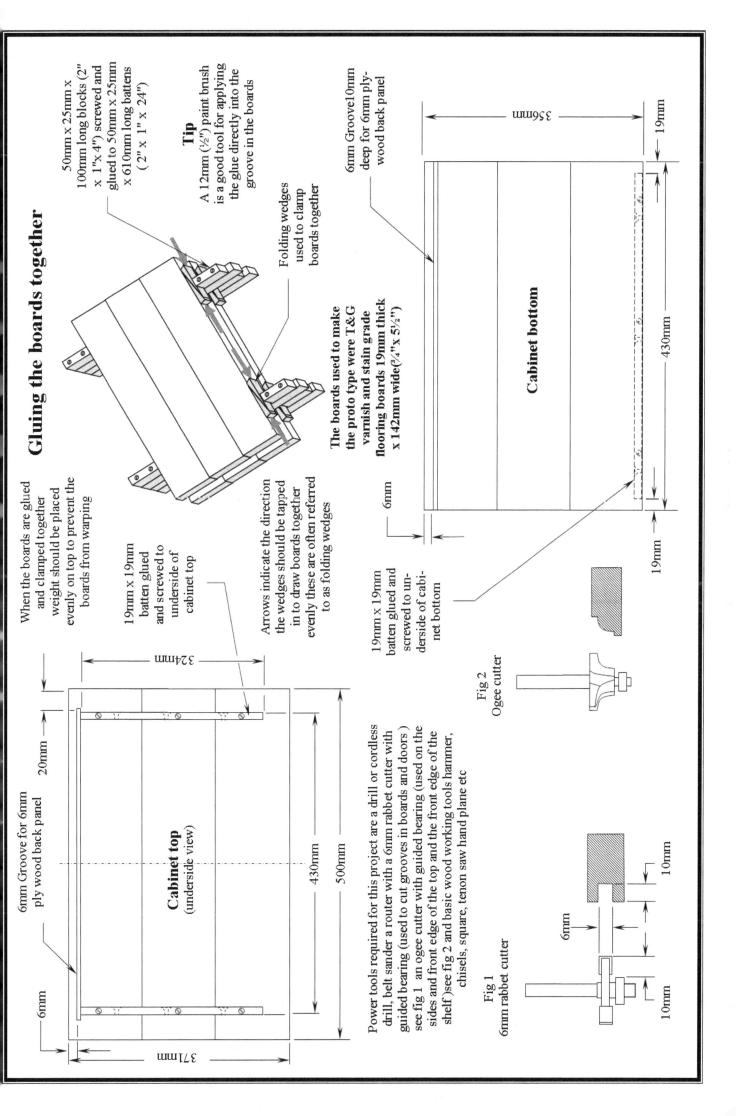

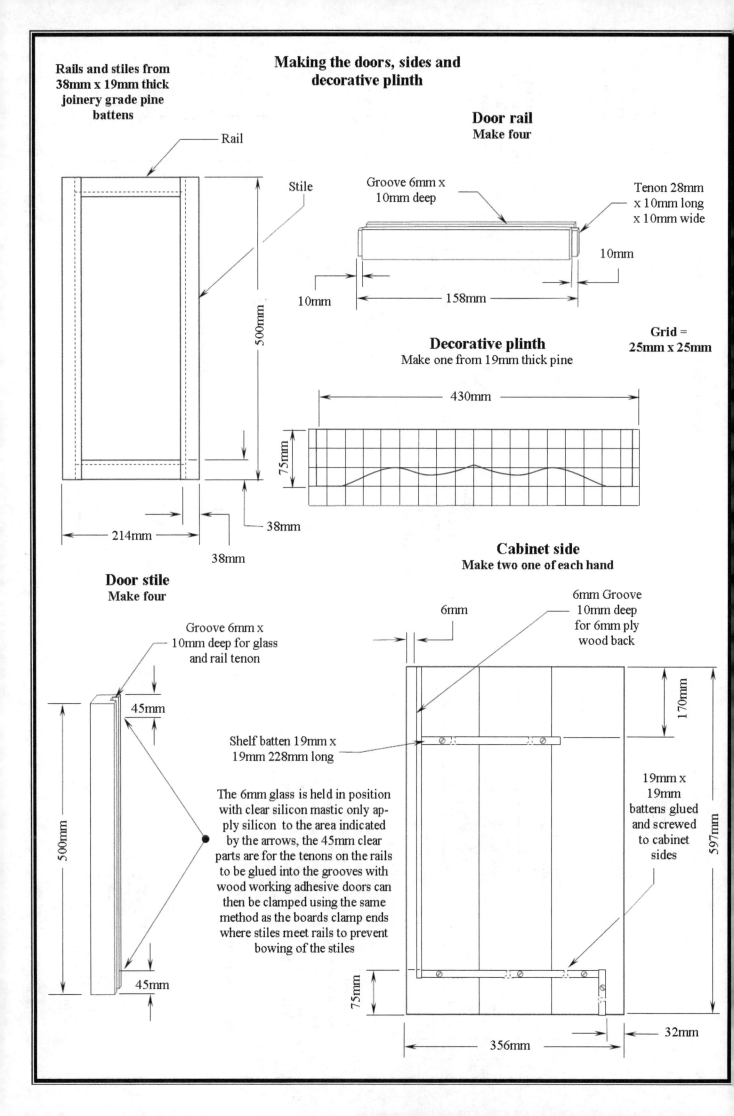

Tile top coffee table plan
533mm (21") x 533mm (21") x 406mm (16") high

The proto type was made from oak. Then 100mm x 100mm x 9mm thick tiles were fitted diagonally. Eighteen are required six of which will need to be cut in half diagonally

Side view of coffee table

Plan view of coffee table showing tiles fitted diagonally

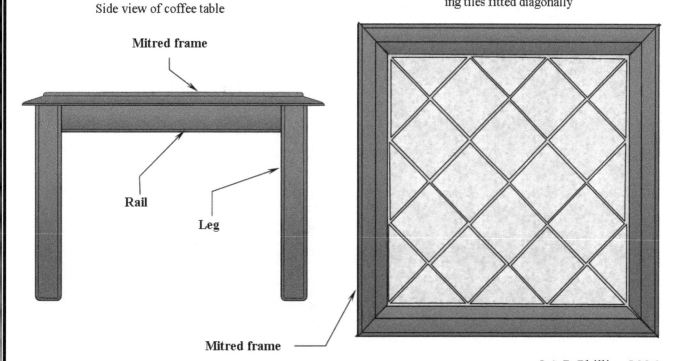

©A.R Phillips 2006

Table saw set up for forming the moulding on the mitred frame

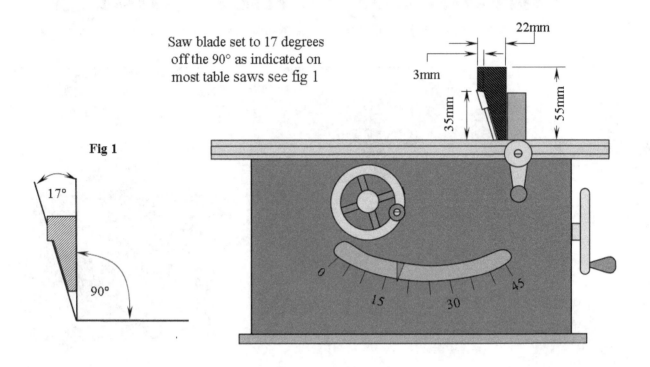

Simple jig for more accurate mitre joints
Ill fitting mitre joints can be rectified with this simple jig

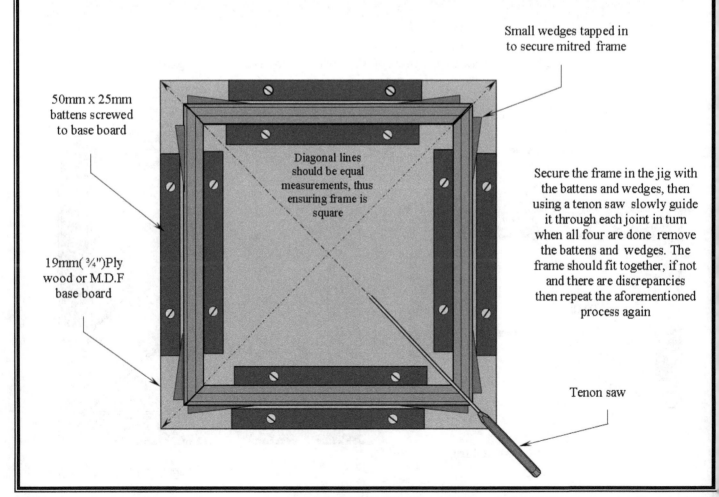

Underside view of assembled table

Rail

Ply wood
427mm x 427mm x 9mm thick, Fixed to corner braces with size 8 screws 30mm long. P.V A the top of the ply before fixing the tiles

Mitred frame

Leg

16mm x 16mm Strips glued and pinned to inside face of rail

Corner brace
Glued and screwed to rail with size 6 screws 50mm long

Leg
Make four

Mortise 13mm x 30mm x 25mm deep

30mm, 10mm, 50mm, 10mm, 381mm, 10mm, 50mm, 10mm

Mortise 13mm x 30mm x 25 mm deep

30mm

Diagram of counter bored hole

8mm, 18mm, 4.5mm

Three counter bored holes, counter bored holes 8mm diameter 18mm deep, through holes 4.5mm diameter to fix mitred frame to rail with size 6 screws 50mm long

Rail
Make four

10mm, 30mm, 50mm, 10mm, 22mm

13mm, 70mm, 70mm

25mm, 460mm, 25mm

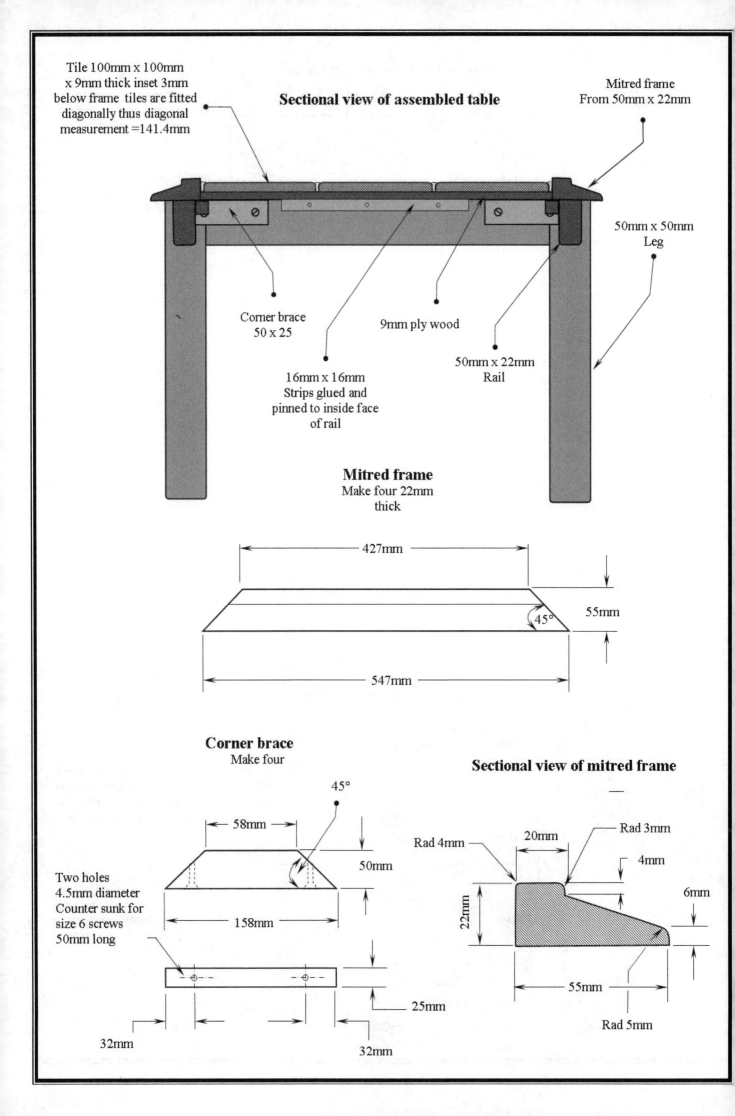

PINE BATHROOM CABINET PLAN
346mm high x 324mm wide x 114mm deep

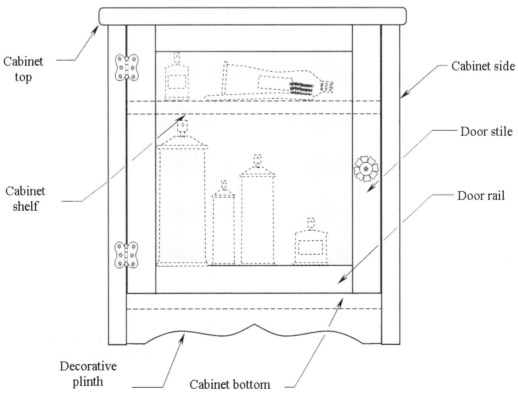

Cabinet top

Cabinet shelf

Cabinet side

Door stile

Door rail

Decorative plinth

Cabinet bottom

Making the cabinet door

Rail
Make two 19mm thick

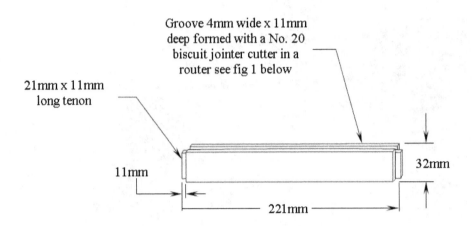

Groove 4mm wide x 11mm deep formed with a No. 20 biscuit jointer cutter in a router see fig 1 below

21mm x 11mm long tenon

11mm   221mm   32mm

Stile
Make two 19mm thick

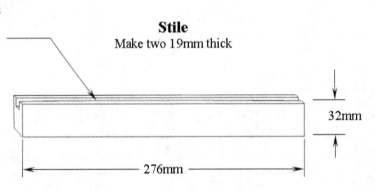

Groove 4mm wide x 11mm deep formed with a No. 20 biscuit jointer cutter in a router see fig 1 below

276mm   32mm

Fig 1
No. 20 biscuit jointer cutter, width of cut 4mm depth of cut 11mm this size cutter is ideal for 3mm thick mirror

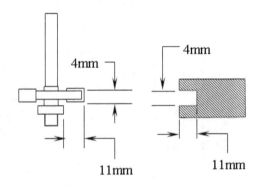

Mirror dimensions =
234mm x 216 Glue rail and stiles together with mirror fitted then mask off mirror and stain varnish or paint
30mm Decorative butterfly type hinges were used on the proto type then a 20mm diameter brass door knob was fitted a magnetic type door catch was used to keep the door closed

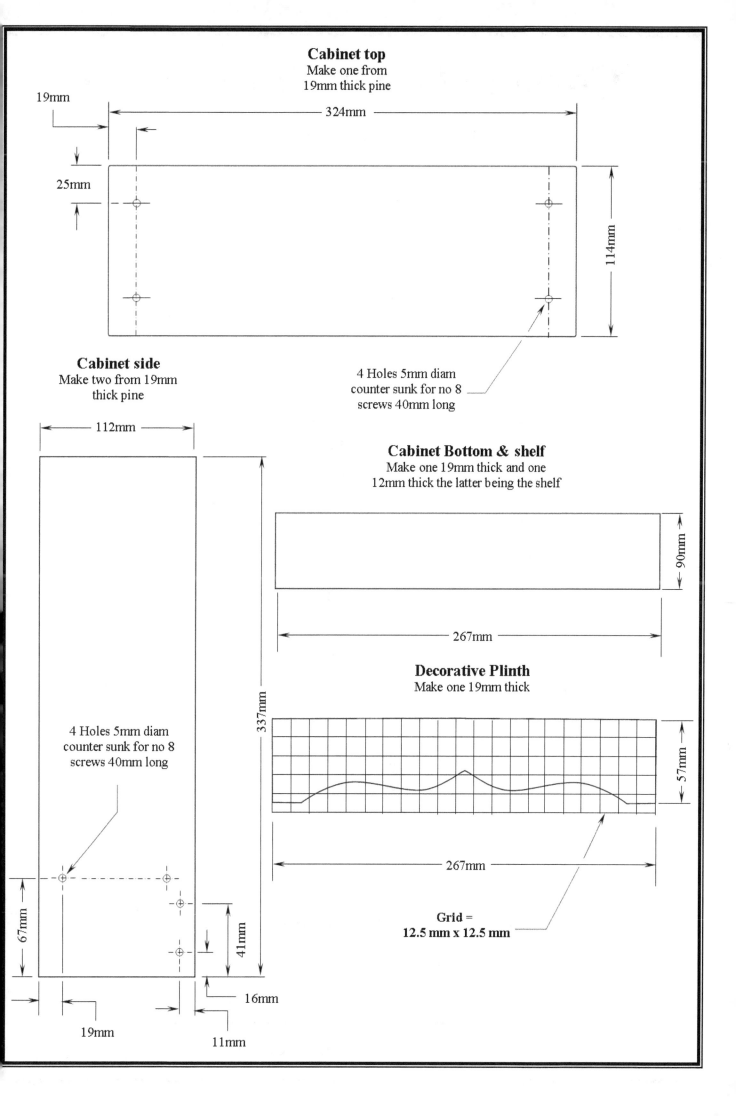

Corner shelf with suspended platform plan

Photography by Marina Garner

©A. R. Phillips 2008

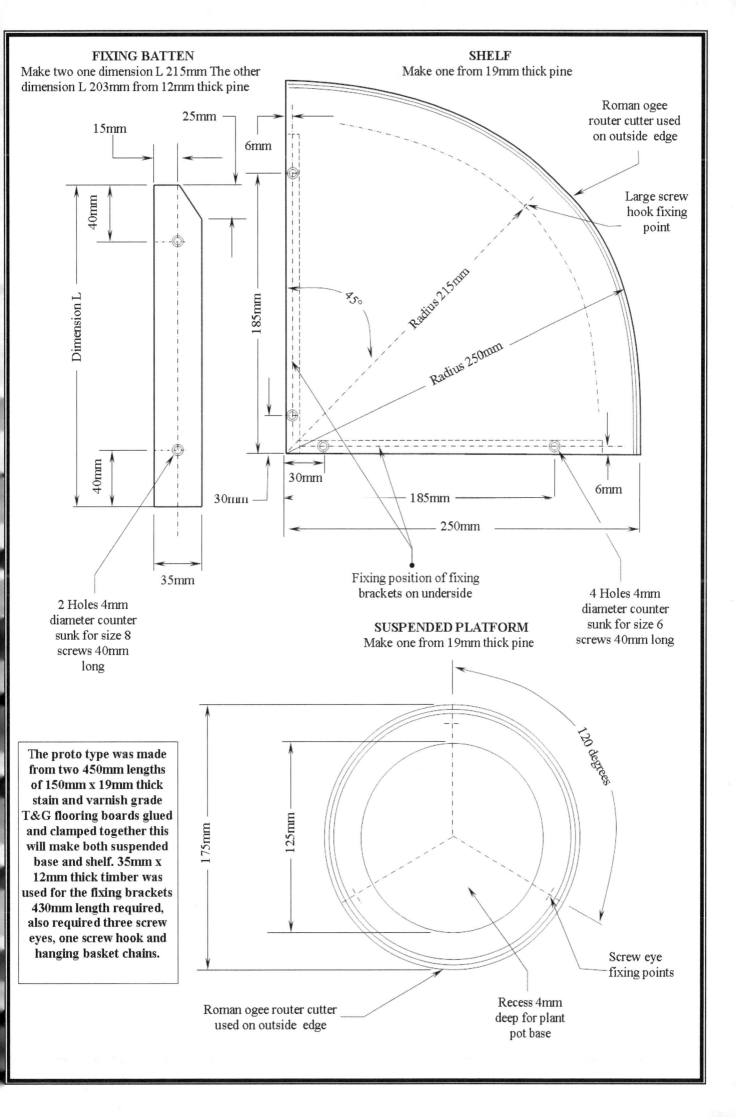

Corner shelf with suspended platform

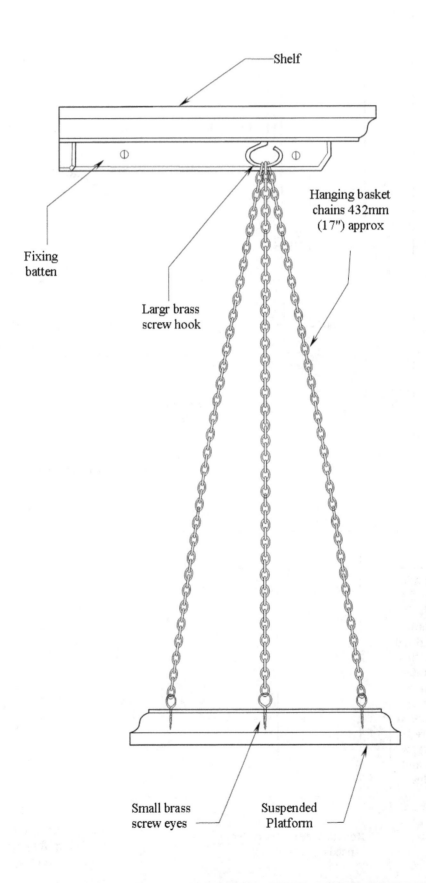

Children's Bed Projects

Princess bed plan

The whole bed was made using one sheet MDF two 6ft lengths of 2 x 1 batten and a 2ft length of 2 x 2 timber, Includes plan for cutting sheet and profiles drawn on grids

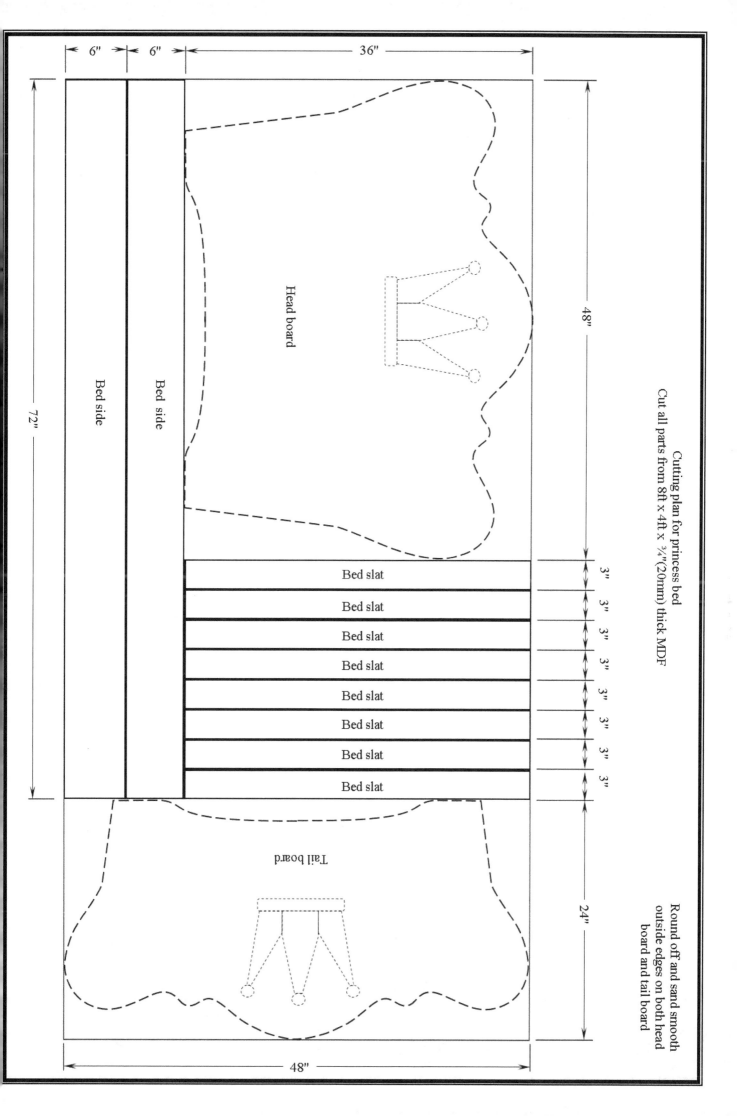

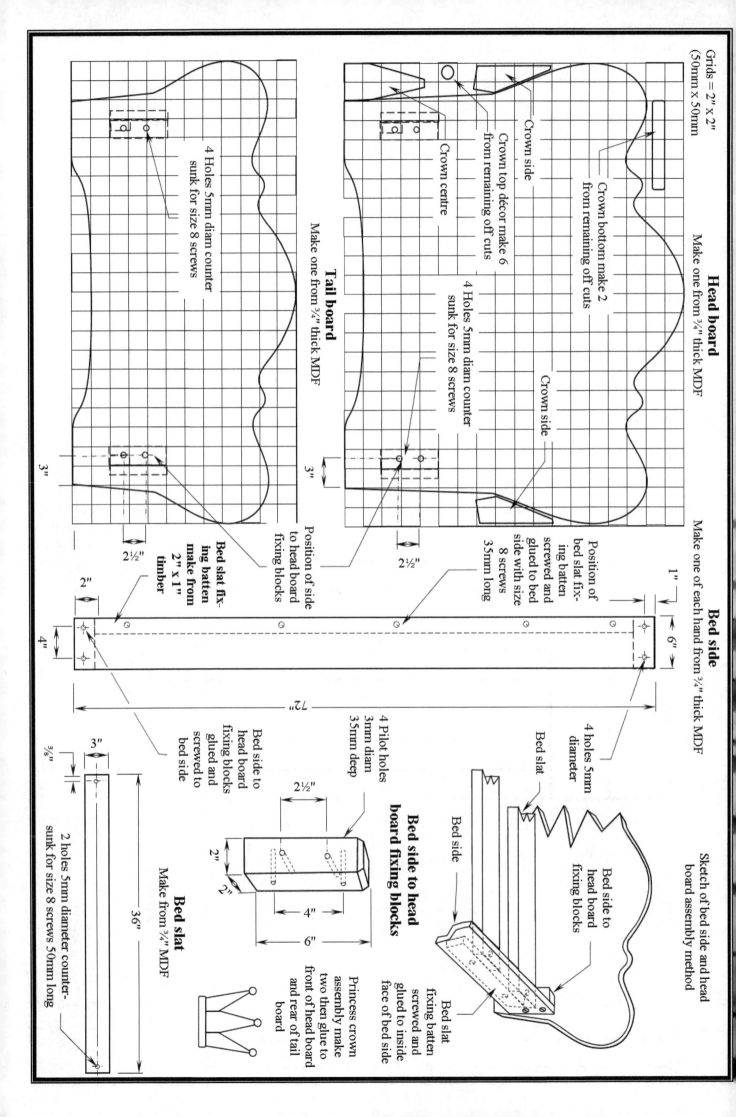

Race car bed plan

This race car bed was made using two full sheets 1/2" (12mm) thick MDF

Side view

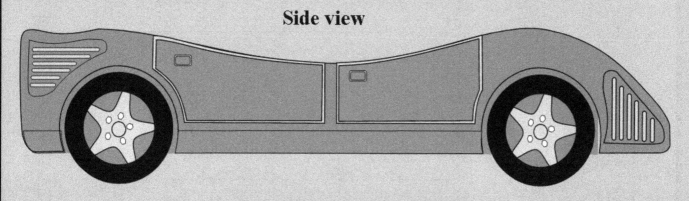

Front view

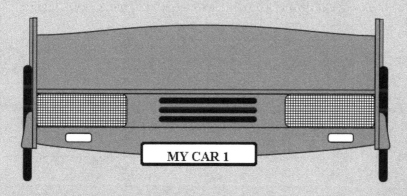

MY CAR 1

Assembly diagram
(Not to scale)

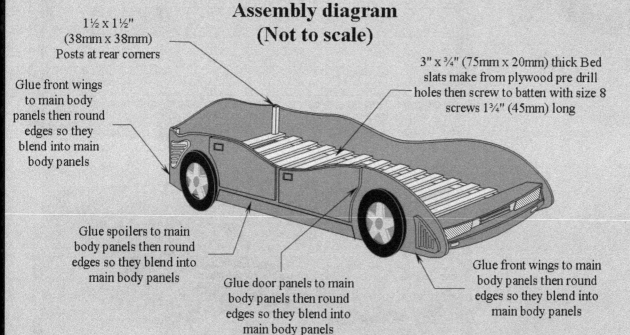

1½ x 1½" (38mm x 38mm) Posts at rear corners

Glue front wings to main body panels then round edges so they blend into main body panels

3" x ¾" (75mm x 20mm) thick Bed slats make from plywood pre drill holes then screw to batten with size 8 screws 1¾" (45mm) long

Glue spoilers to main body panels then round edges so they blend into main body panels

Glue door panels to main body panels then round edges so they blend into main body panels

Glue front wings to main body panels then round edges so they blend into main body panels

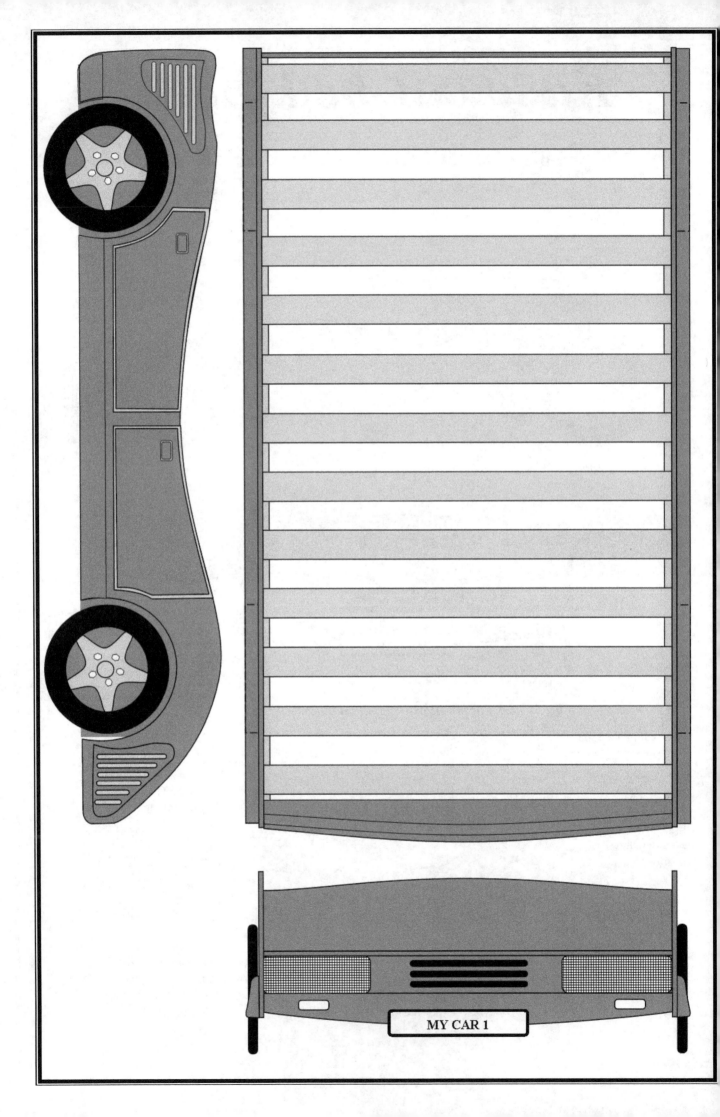

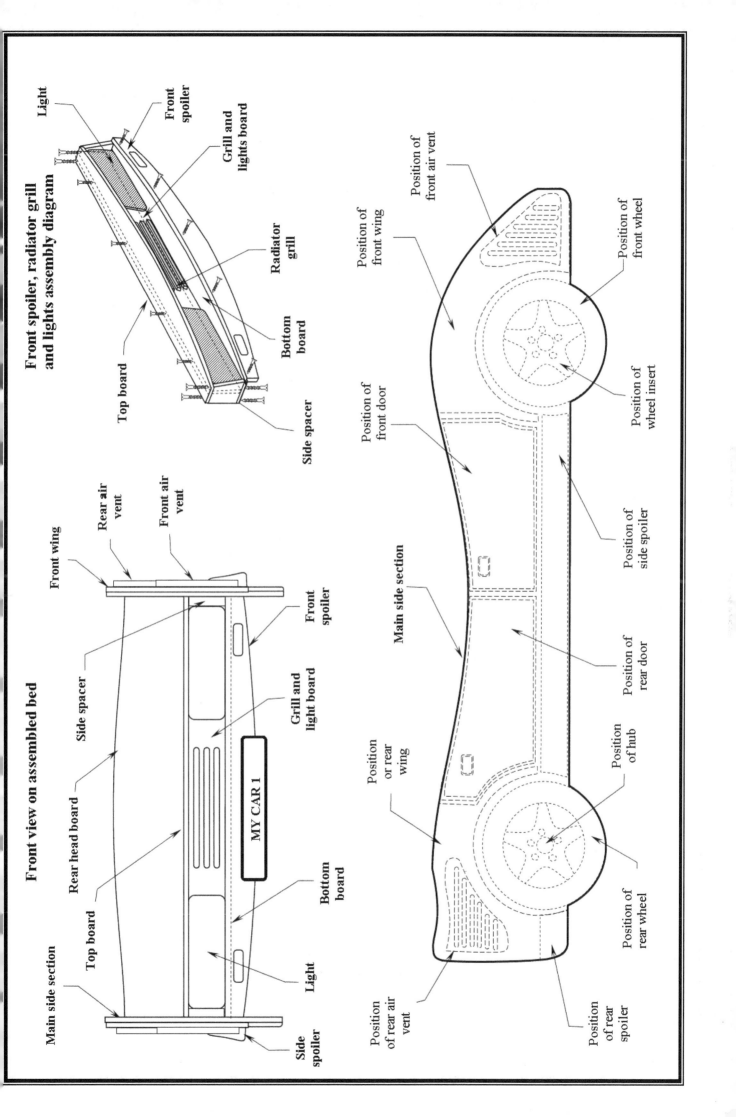

GRID = (2" X 2")
50mm x 50mm

All parts to be made from 12mm (½") MDF unless stated otherwise

Rear air vent

Front door

Rear door

Recess 3mm(⅛") deep on all four doors

Rear wing

Main side section

Main side section

Number plate

50mm x 25mm (2" x 1") Batten screwed and glued to inside face of main side section to fix mattress slats

Front air vent. Air vent louvers are made from semi circular pieces of dowel cut to the appropriate lengths

Rear wing

Rear door

Front door

50mm x 50mm (2" x 1") Batten screwed and glued to inside face of main side section to fix rear head board

Mattress slats
Make 13 from plywood
1067mm x 75mm x 19mm thick
(42" x 3" x ¾")

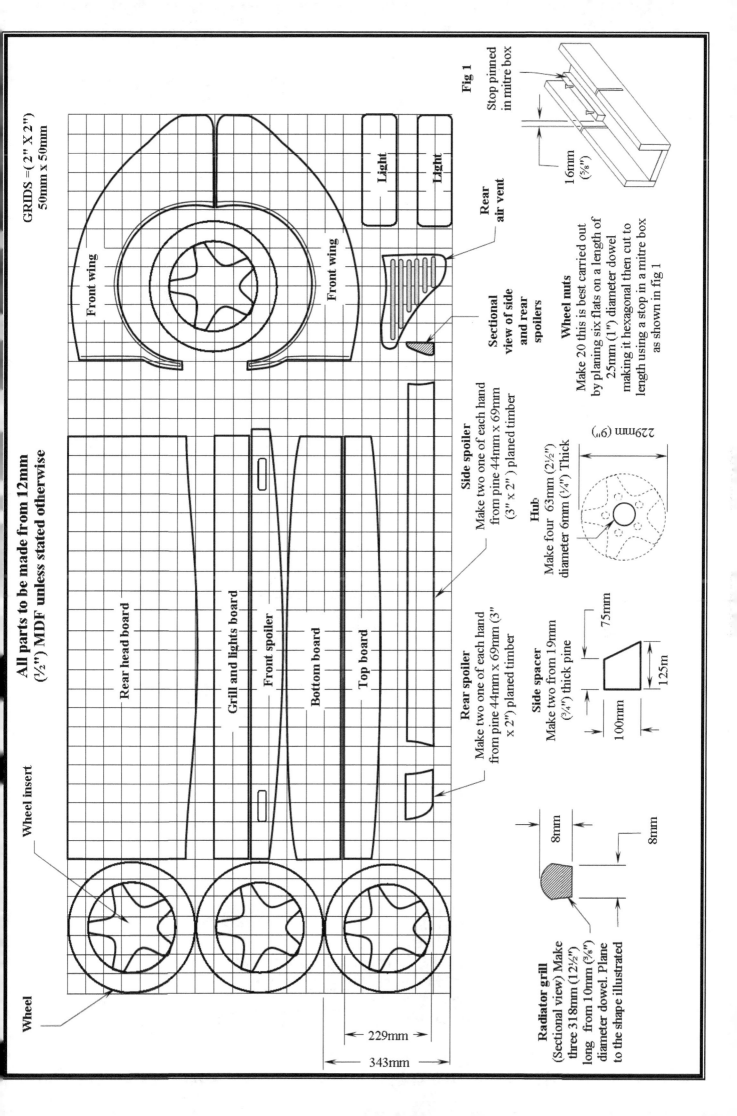

Tank engine bed plan

This tank engine bed was made using two 8ft x 4ft x ½" thick sheets of MDF and made to suit a 3ft x 6ft mattress

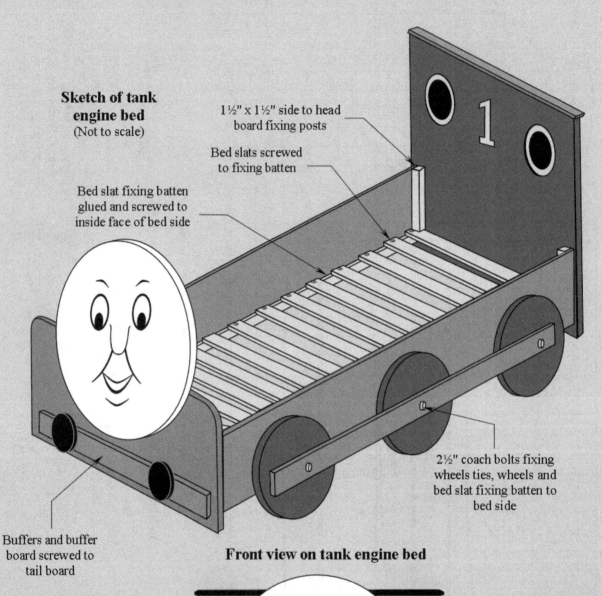

Sketch of tank engine bed
(Not to scale)

1½" x 1½" side to head board fixing posts

Bed slats screwed to fixing batten

Bed slat fixing batten glued and screwed to inside face of bed side

2½" coach bolts fixing wheels ties, wheels and bed slat fixing batten to bed side

Buffers and buffer board screwed to tail board

Front view on tank engine bed

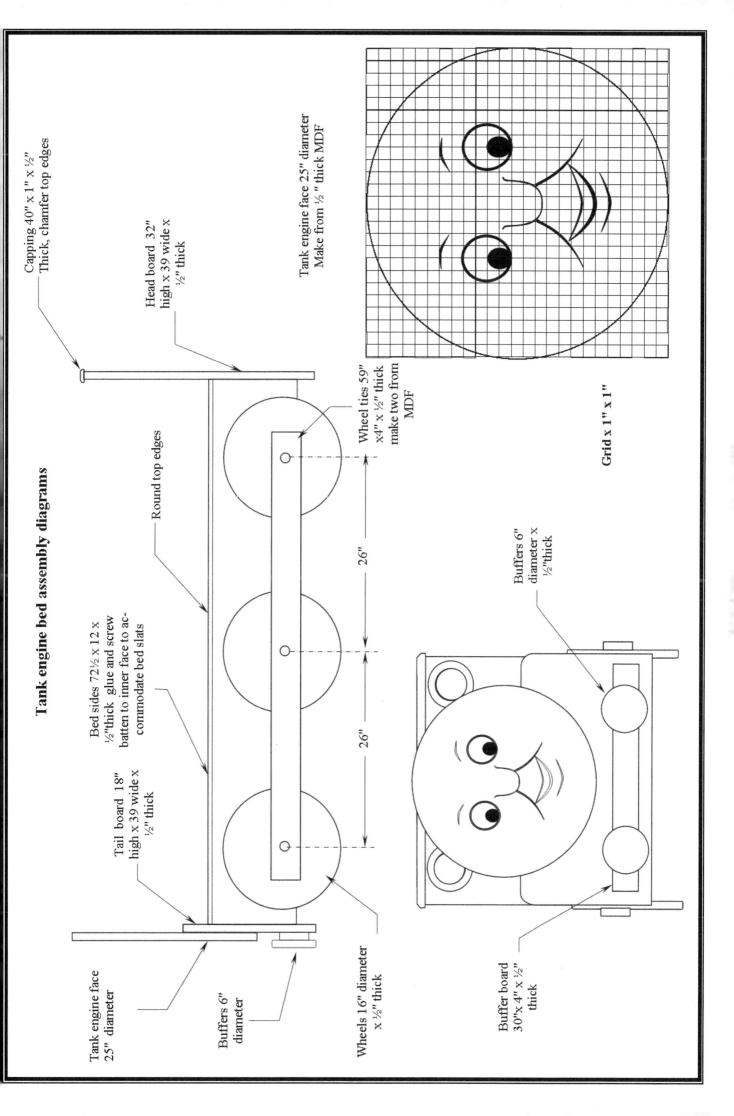

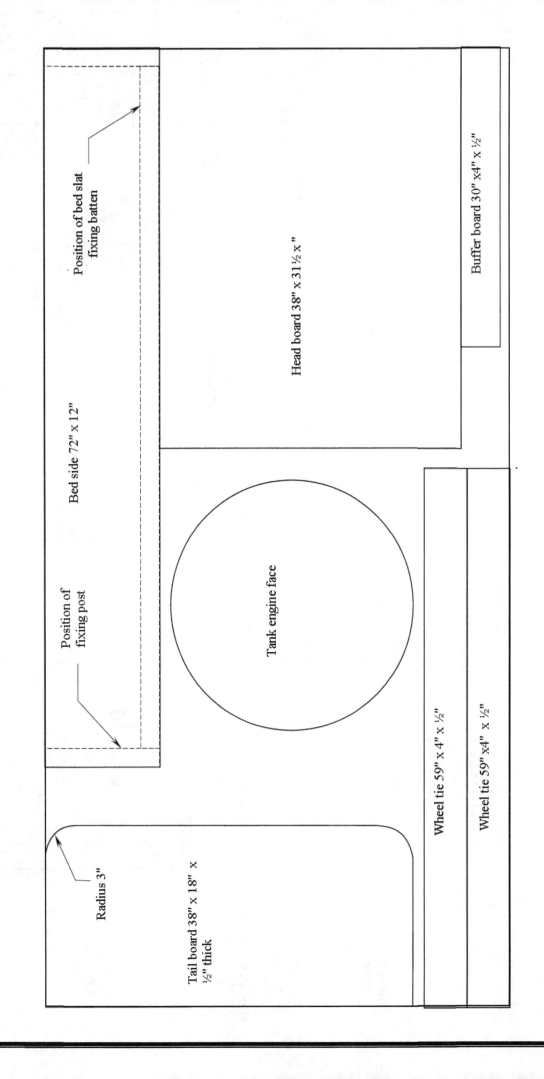

Tank engine bed parts layout 8ft x 4ft sheet MDF ½" thick

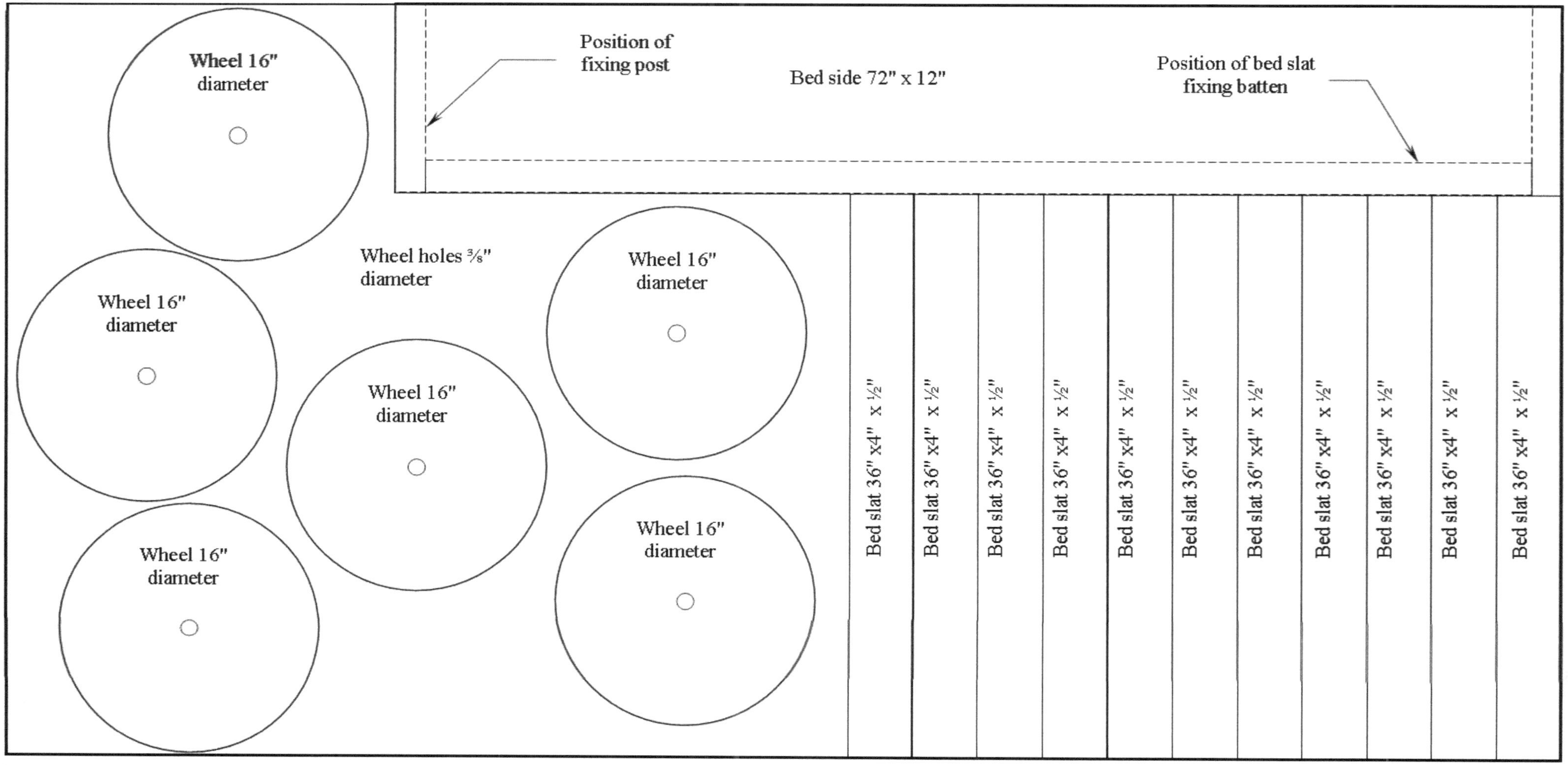

Bed side 72" x 12"

Position of bed slat fixing batten

Position of fixing post

Bed slat 36" x 4" x ½" (×11)

Wheel 16" diameter (×6)

Wheel holes ⅜" diameter

CPSIA information can be obtained
at www.ICGtesting.com
Printed in the USA
LVHW100346181220
674500LV00017B/246